ROUTLEDGE LIBRARY EDITIONS:
THE ENGLISH LANGUAGE

Volume 17

COCKNEY PAST AND PRESENT

COCKNEY PAST AND PRESENT

A Short History of the Dialect of London

WILLIAM MATTHEWS

LONDON AND NEW YORK

First published in 1938

This edition first published in 2015
by Routledge
2 Park Square, Milton Park, Abingdon, Oxon OX14 4RN

and by Routledge
711 Third Avenue, New York, NY 10017

Routledge is an imprint of the Taylor & Francis Group, an informa business

British Library Cataloguing in Publication Data
A catalogue record for this book is available from the British Library

ISBN: 978-1-138-92111-5 (Set)
ISBN: 978-1-315-68654-7 (Set) (ebk)
ISBN: 978-1-138-91593-0 (Volume 17) (hbk)
ISBN: 978-1-138-91596-1 (Volume 17) (pbk)
ISBN: 978-1-315-68992-0 (Volume 17) (ebk)

Publisher's Note
The publisher has gone to great lengths to ensure the quality of this reprint but points out that some imperfections in the original copies may be apparent.

Disclaimer
The publisher has made every effort to trace copyright holders and would welcome correspondence from those they have been unable to trace.

COCKNEY
PAST AND PRESENT

A Short History of the Dialect of London

By

WILLIAM MATTHEWS, M.A., Ph.D.

LONDON

GEORGE ROUTLEDGE & SONS, LTD.

BROADWAY HOUSE: 68–74 CARTER LANE, E.C.

First published 1938

Printed in Great Britain by Butler & Tanner Ltd., Frome and London

CONTENTS

Of all those historic dialects which still distinguish, to a greater or less degree, the speech of most Englishmen, none is of such interest as Cockney, that noble blend of East Mercian, Kentish, and East Anglian, which, written by Chaucer, printed by Caxton, spoken by Spencer and Milton, and surviving in the mouths of Sam Weller and Mrs. Gamp, has, in a modified form and with an artificial pronunciation, given us the literary English of the present day.

PROFESSOR ERNEST WEEKLEY.

The Cockney mode of speech, with its unpleasant twang, is a modern corruption without legitimate credentials, and is unworthy of being the speech of any person in the capital city of the Empire.

Report of the Conference on the Teaching of English in London Elementary Schools, 1909.

The average Cockney is not articulate. He is often witty; he is sometimes eloquent; he has a notable gift of phrase-making and nick-naming. Every day he is enriching the English tongue with new forms of speech, new clichés, new slang, new catchwords. The new thing and the new word to describe the new thing are never very far apart in London. But the spirit, the soul, of the Londoner is usually dumb.

EDWIN PUGH in *Harry the Cockney*, 1902.

PREFACE

OF all the non-standard forms of English, Cockney is the most generally despised and downtrodden. The languidness of the Oxford accent and the mint-new precision of the B.B.C.'s young men draw more abuse than they warrant; but they are more often admired. Regional dialects provide targets for music-hall artists and journalists, but most of us accord to them the reverence due to a presumed antiquity, and accept the catchwords concerning their peculiar virtues. Who has not at some time praised the delightful burr, the rich brogue or the downright vigour of some dialect which he found difficulty even in understanding? We may venture to express a dislike for the dialect of some of the larger towns, Glasgow or Bradford for instance, but we would as soon keep our hats on in church as to speak slightingly of the county dialects. And as for the dialect speakers, they are intoxicated with their own counties and their own music. We mere Londoners, who humbly suffer the gibes of even Glaswegians at our dialect, are always impressed by the self-regard of the many societies of ——shire men who gather year by year to hymn in reassumed dialects the praise of reassumed beverages. We may wonder why their gatherings are held in London —*dulcior dissipere in loco!*—but we are profoundly impressed.

There is no Society of Cockneys. Not even in the outposts of Empire do Londoners meet together to renew formally the delights of four-ale and spring onions or to admire the speech of Bethnal Green and Peckham Rye. So far from priding themselves upon their dialect, most Londoners are acutely conscious that it is pitch. Cockney is the characteristic speech of "the greatest city of the greatest empire that the world has known". But Cockney is such a pariah that not even the philologists have a good word for it. They deny it the status of a dialect and describe it as a vulgar speech based upon error and misunderstanding. No bones would have been broken had harsh words been all. But the disrepute of Cockney has been so repellent to scholars that no serious attempt has ever been made to study the vulgar speech of London either historically or in its existing form. The county dialects commanded the time and money of the English Dialect Society for a generation and inspired one of the greatest of all works on language, Wright's *English Dialect Dictionary*. The dialects of Pewsey and Windhill—how many people have ever heard of them?—have been the subjects of two brilliant books. But Cockney, the characteristic speech of a city of six, or is it seven million people, has been ignored. Even in Wright's dictionary it is represented only by an occasional note. A few continental students have refused to be put off by the lowness of Cockney, but even they have sheltered under the umbrella of literature. They have given us studies of the Cockney dialect according to Dickens, according to Thackeray, according to *Punch* and even according to Shaw. But it has occurred to nobody to give us a study of the dialect according to Mr. 'Enery 'Awkins of New Cut.

"Nobody loves a fairy when she's forty," runs the old song. People have always been willing to praise the Cockney of the old days, but ever since pundits first began to discuss the dialect they have abused it in its existing form. I had always been a little puzzled why Cockney should have been singled out for such contempt, until I found in Walker's *Pronouncing Dictionary*, 1791, what appears to be the true explanation. Cockneys, says Walker, "have the disadvantage of being more disgraced by their peculiarities than any other people. The grand difference between the metropolis and the provinces is that people of education in London are generally free from the vices of the vulgar; but the best-educated people in the provinces, if constantly resident there, are sure to be tinctured with the dialect of the country in which they live. Hence it is that the vulgar pronunciation of London, though not half so erroneous as that of Scotland, Ireland, or any of the provinces, is, to a person of correct taste, a thousand times more offensive and disgusting." When we reckon with the glamour which the pastoral tradition has given to the country dialects, Walker's explanation enables us to understand why the language of a remote village claims the attention of scholars, while the language of London is neglected or abused.

For my own part, I have no great objection to Cockney being described as vulgar or even to its being denied officially the status of a dialect, although I should like to enter a formal protest against a recent dictum that it cannot be a dialect because it has not a characteristic pronunciation and because its vocabulary is principally thieves' slang. I think I could guarantee to pick out a Londoner in heaven or hell, and the cant which forms a small proportion of Cockney slang is common to many of the county dialects themselves. The neglect of Cockney is more serious than the vilification of it, however. For, as the characteristic speech of the capital of England, it has been by far the most important of all non-standard forms of English for its influence upon accepted speech ever since accepted speech emerged. It is impossible to write a satisfactory history of standard English without understanding the history of Cockney.

The Cockney dialect is being gradually suppressed. Its natural vigour is so great that it refuses to die with decent celerity. But the feeling of inferiority induced by the attacks of business men and school-teachers makes the Cockney ashamed of his dialect. He may not give it up immediately: natural independence will make the Cockney child throw off the schoolmaster's yoke as soon as he gets outside the class-room. But the time soon comes when he is forced to submit, when he finds that business advancement and social respectability are incompatible with a Cockney accent. He waters down his speech until it approximates to the ideal of the schoolmaster. He is seldom wholly successful: I have heard Cockney nuances in the senior common-rooms of University colleges. But hundreds of thousands of Londoners who, but for the attacks upon Cockney, would have been using the colourful speech of the capital, now use that thin gruel of a language, Modified Standard.

Cockney is being done to death by snobbery, supported by arguments drawn from shoddy æsthetics, utilitarianism and false history. Such factors are not new in linguistic history: very readable studies might be written on the influence of prudery and dogmatic ignorance on the English language. The chief difference is that the educational system has provided an army for the attack. The gibes of critics in the eighteenth and early nineteenth centuries had little effect: when they were taken up by thousands of school teachers they became steamrollers. But while acknowledging the antiquity of such attacks and their naturalness to pedagogues, we may venture to doubt their wisdom. Year in and year out the Cockney dialect has enriched Standard English, not with the frozen words of scholarship and science, but with words rich in personality, words informed by mockery, optimism, cynicism, humour. To suppress the Cockney dialect, the most creative form of English, will not necessarily stop the creation of such words altogether, but it will certainly reduce the supply. The language of a costermonger compels attention, but has anybody ever been titillated by the language of a London clerk?

Schoolmasters cannot ignore Cockney, and few of them would dare to praise it. Many doubt the wisdom of suppressing it, however, and they believe they can resolve their dilemma by advocating a double standard. I know teachers who tell their pupils that it is their own concern how they speak among themselves, but for their own good they should also be able to speak standard English. This attitude, which has recently been adopted by the B.B.C. too, seems to me to add insult to injury. Is Cockney a poor relation to be kept in the back room when there are visitors? And is it imagined that Cockneys will be satisfied to use among themselves a dialect which is not good enough for conversation with educated people?

The present book is an attempt to remedy some of the injuries of Cockney by tracing, so far as the available material will permit, the growth of the vulgar speech of London from the sixteenth century until the present day. I dare not hope that I shall succeed in checking the vilification of the dialect: I cannot imagine anybody restraining the thousands of provincial teachers who daily lay down the laws of correct speech to Cockney children. And I have no desire to inaugurate a Society for the Preservation of Cockney: we have more than enough of such mausoleums already. I shall feel amply satisfied if I merely succeed in correcting some popular errors concerning the dialect and in persuading English philologists that æsthetic and moral dislike of vulgar forms of speech are inadequate reasons for leaving them to be dealt with by foreigners.

To the many Cockneys who consciously or unconsciously have assisted me with this book, I tender my sincere gratitude. Few of them will read this book, but will those few accept on behalf of all my thanks for the enjoyment I have had in hearing them talk and in listening to their reminiscences? To two people I owe a particular debt. To my mother I am indebted for many details drawn from her extensive repertoire of music-hall songs and children's chants and from her intimate knowledge of the dialect as it was spoken about forty years ago.

To Mr. Eric Partridge I am grateful for several valuable suggestions and for the loan of proof sheets of the additional material for the new edition of his dictionary of slang. My indebtedness to this great work is obvious in my discussion of present-day Cockney slang.

COCKNEY PAST AND PRESENT

CHAPTER I

THE SIXTEENTH AND SEVENTEENTH CENTURIES

THE material for the study of Cockney in the sixteenth and seventeenth centuries is far from being what one would wish. Despite the prejudices of reviewers and literary men, the best observations come from solemn people. Those flashes of insight which one may always rely upon a reviewer to discover in another novelist are as often the erratic light of the *ignis fatuus* as a *lumen siccum*. One would like to have a solemn, painstaking phonetic treatise on the London speech of this period. But, although studies of English pronunciation were written from the middle of the sixteenth century, they were concerned solely with accepted speech, and it was not until the eighteenth century that the phoneticians began to consider Cockney. In default of the comments of authorities, we have to fall back on the Cockney dialogue in Elizabethan and Jacobean plays and on documents written in a colloquial style by Londoners of the time. In basing our discussion upon dramatic dialogue, we run the danger of being deceived by the usual vices (from the objective point of view) of literary work, convention, fantasy, burlesque, and reminiscence of other literary works, and in using documents written by Cockneys we are hampered by the fact that a pen gives whoever holds it a sense of style and, therefore, modifies his native colloquialism.

There is no lack of plays dealing with London life in the Elizabethan and Jacobean drama, although they do not begin to appear until Shakespeare's time. Before then dramatists were too concerned with imitating Plautus or Terence or too fascinated by the splendid perversions of Italy and the scenical struttings of Tamerlanes and Tamerchams to have any inclination towards the more sober attractions of English homes and English beauty. But with the development of the chronicle play writers came to realise that there was drama in English stories and traditions, and that a character with an English name might be as effective on the stage as one whose name ended in *o*. Some writers, notably Heywood and Middleton, became primarily dramatists of English life. Some, like Jonson, turned aside now and then from their survey of foreign fields to regard the English scene, and others compromised, with a fine indifference to probability, by planting Dogberries in Messina or Bottoms in fairyland.

It was but natural that London and Londoners should receive most attention in this appeal to local interest. The apprentices and merchants who, despite the opposition of the City, filled the theatres liked to be flattered as well as thrilled, and how frequently the players flattered them may be gathered from the complaint of the Citizen in *The Knight of the Burning Pestle*:

> "If you were not resolved to play the Jacks, what need you study for new subjects, purposely to abuse your betters? why could you not be contented, as well as others, with 'The Legend of Whittington', or 'The Life and Death of Sir Thomas Gresham, with the building of the Royal Exchange', or 'The Story of Queen Eleanor, with the rearing of London Bridge upon Woolsacks'?"

So often did the dramatists turn to London life for their themes that, as Professor Schelling points out, "the City was celebrated on the stage almost ward for ward and street for street, in plays such as *A Chaste Maid in Cheapside*, *The Cripple of Fenchurch Street*, *The Boss of Billingsgate*, *The Lovers of Ludgate*, *The Devil of Dowgate* and *The Black Dog of Newgate*, nor were the neighbouring precincts of Westminster, Croydon, Mortlake and Hogsdon forgotten". Many of the plays, of course, were the outcome of the City's dislike for the stage and are satirical. It will be remembered that the retort to the Citizen's demand for a play in honour of the City was, "Why, what do you say to 'The Life and Death of Fat Drake, or the Repairing of Fleet-privies'?" and that *The Knight of the Burning Pestle* itself is a gibe, if a kindly one, at the egotism and intellectual failings of the City.

The characterisation of London life did not proceed far enough, fortunately, to result in an absolute convention of "The Eternal Cockney" kind. This absence of a London convention has the regrettable effect, from our point of view, that very few plays give the slightest hint at the characteristics of Cockney speech. How inseparable the stage dialect is from the puppet character may be judged from the dialect characters of the Elizabethan stage itself. There were only four types, the Irish, the Welsh, the Southerner and the Northerner, and not only did they speak conventional dialects and do the same conventional things, but they actually used the same phrases and the same jokes. Just as a modern music-hall audience would feel cheated if a stage Cockney did not say "Gaw Blimey", so the Elizabethan audiences insisted upon an Irishman saying "fait and trote" and upon a Welshman making an uproarious confusion between "big" and "pig". It is therefore in the characters who are nearest to being types, the citizen made bumptious by prosperity, the illogical and doting citizeness, and the ignorant but officious constable, that we find most of our material for this essay. There is practically none in the realistic work of such writers as Heywood and Middleton.

Shakespeare's treatment of the Cockney is best shown in the character of Mistress Quickly, a supreme portrayal of a character which has since become one of the puppets in the dramatist's cupboard, the Cockney charwoman. Although she is given but few Cockney pronunciations, her outbursts diverge from the laws of polite speech in a way that tallies with that of the other London characters, although more naturally:

> "I am undone by his going; I warrant you he's an infinitive thing upon my score. Good Master Fang, hold him sure: good Master Snare, let him not 'scape. A' comes continuantly to Pie-corner—saving your manhoods—to buy a saddle; and he is indited to dinner at the Lubber's-head in Lumbert street, to Master Smooth's the silkman: I pray ye, since my exion is entered and my case so openly known to the world, let him be brought in to his answer. A hundred mark is a long one for a

poor lone woman to bear: and I have borne, and borne, and borne; and have been fubbed off, and fubbed off, and fubbed off, from this day to that day, that it is a shame to be thought on. There is no honesty in such dealing; unless a woman should be made an ass and a beast, to bear every knave's wrong. Yonder he comes; and that arrant malmsey-nose knave, Bardolph, with him. Do your offices, do your offices: Master Fang and Master Snare, do me, do me, do me your offices." (*Henry IV*, Part II, II. i.)

The comic constables, Dogberry and Verges, Elbow and Froth, come much nearer to being conventional Cockneys. They may have a temporary habitation in Messina or Vienna, but they speak "auspiciously" like London citizens. It is not improbable indeed that on Shakespeare's stage the majority of his low-life characters were played as Cockneys. Juliet's nurse has a number of tricks of speech in common with Mistress Quickly, the commoners who open in *Julius Cæsar* pun and equivocate like the plebeians in London plays, the gravediggers in *Hamlet* have the Cockney's perilous fondness for Latin tags, and the mechanics in *Midsummer Night's Dream* often remind one of Dogberry and Verges.

Beaumont and Fletcher's *The Knight of the Burning Pestle* is the most careful study of Cockney speech to be found in the drama of the period. Ralph, the romance-stricken apprentice, is so besotted with the jargon of *Palmerin* and other romances that he speaks no tongue known to mortal man, but George the grocer and Nell his wife are Cockney treasures. It is difficult to illustrate their colloquial style in a single quotation, as most of their speeches illustrate single characteristics, but the following passage is more representative than most. It is prompted by Merrythought's refusal to take back his wife:

> *Wife.* He's not in earnest, I hope, George, is he?
> *Citizen.* What if he be, sweetheart?
> *Wife.* Marry, if he be, George, I'll make bold to tell him he's an ingrant old man to use his bed-fellow so scurvily.
> *Citizen.* What! how does he use her, honey?
> *Wife.* Marry, come up, sir saucebox! I think you'll take his part, will you not? Lord, how hot you are grown! you are a fine man, an you had a fine dog; it becomes you sweetly!
> *Citizen.* Nay, prithee, Nell, chide not; for, as I am an honest man and a true Christian grocer, I do not like his doings.
> *Wife.* I cry you mercy, then, George! you know we are all frail and full of infirmities. (III. v.)

Dekker's *The Shoemaker's Holiday*, although one of the pleasantest comedies of London life, is not quite so rich in Cockney language. It is true that Simon Eyre, the shoemaker who became Lord Mayor of London, has an unorthodox way of speaking, but it cannot safely be regarded as representative of Cockney. Simon is drawn as a compliment to the City, and he has a "brave" way of speaking, pouring out words with a fine flourish:

> "Where be these boys, these girls, these drabs, these scoundrels? They wallow in the fat brewis of my bounty, and lick up the crumbs of my table, yet will not rise to see my walks cleansed. Come out you powder-beef queans! What, Nan! What, Madge Mumble-Crust! Come out, you fat midriff-swagbelly whores, and sweep me these kennels that the noisome stench offend not the noses of my neighbours. What, Firk, I say: what, Hodge! Open my shop-windows! What, Firk, I say!"

One may have found an occasional Londoner who spoke

like this, but such a Rabelaisian delight in an undammed spate of words cannot represent the habit of Cockneys as a whole. We may suspect that the directness of Simon's abuse and his habit of decorating a spade was common among the lower classes, but we doubt whether they did it with his fine inventiveness. Simon Eyre, like Falstaff, was an original. The Shoemaker's journeymen do not speak differently from the ordinary run of characters and they are not intended to represent anything but the Cockney sense of fun. But Margery, Simon's wife, is more genuinely a product of observation of the speech of London. Many of her speeches and mannerisms strike a familiar chord, as in this passage:

> "Well, Hans and Roger, you see, God hath blest your master, and, perdy, if ever he comes to be Master Sheriff of London—as we are all mortal—you shall see, I will have some odd thing or other in a corner for you: I will not be your back-friend: but let that pass. Hans, pray thee, tie my shoe." (III. iv.)

Ben Jonson often turned to London life for his satirical humour, and it is doubtful whether Londoners have ever been better portrayed in literature than in *Every Man in His Humour*, *The Alchemist* and *Bartholomew Fair*. But although Jonson was given to exploiting his special knowledge and observation, he does seem to have been very interested in Cockney speech. *The Alchemist* has characters which might have been convincingly drawn as Cockneys, Doll Common and Abel Drugger for example, but Jonson did not seize the opportunity and they speak in the ordinary idiom. *Bartholomew Fair* is a brilliant skit upon low-life in

London, the Jacobean equivalent of Pierce Egan's *Real Life in London*, but even its reputation as a mine of contemporary slang is hardly unwarranted. This play of the Puritans and the "Bartholomew birds" might have been rich in Cockney had the early dramatists been provided with Cockney characteristics of the Sam Weller kind, for when such conventions were at hand Jonson made abundant use of them, as with the Irish character, Captain Whit. The cheapjacks, horse-doctors and bawds of the fair may have been given Cockney pronunciations by the actors, but apart from the horse-terms used by Knockem there is not much in the play of interest to the student of vulgar speech. The chief exception is Dame Ursula the pig-woman's talent for abuse, that "Bartholomew wit" which was the equivalent of our "Billingsgate":

> "Do you sneer, you dog's head, you trendle-tail! You look as you were begotten a top of a cart in harvest time, when the whelp was hot and eager. Go snuff after your brother's bitch, Mistress Commodity; that's the livery you wear, 'twill be out at the elbows shortly. It's time you went to't for the t'other remnant."

Jonson's best efforts in Cockney characterisation from the linguistic point of view, are Oliver Cob the water-bearer and his wife Tib, in *Every Man in His Humour*. Cob in particular is interesting for his emphasis of certain mannerisms used occasionally by other Cockney characters. In the following passage we have a fairly typical specimen of his dialect:

> "Nay, soft and fair; I have eggs on the spit; I cannot go yet, sir. Now am I, for some five and fifty reasons, hammering,

hammering revenge; oh for three or four gallons of vinegar, to sharpen my wits! Revenge, vinegar revenge, vinegar and mustard revenge. Nay, an he had not lyen in my house, 'twould never have grieved me; but being my guest, one that, Ile be sworn, my wife has lent him her smock off her back, while his one shirt has been at washing; pawned her neckerchers for clean bands for him; sold almost all my platters to buy him tobacco; and he to turn monster of ingratitude and strike his lawful host! Well, I hope to raise up an host of fury for't; here comes Justice Clement." (III. vi.)

The plays of Thomas Heywood are mostly set in London and have citizens for characters. But apart from a slight inclination towards sententiousness and proverb-mongering among the citizens held up for admiration, his plays contribute little to our knowledge of Cockney. Even where one might have expected some burlesque of Cockney mannerisms, in the speeches of the comic servants for example, the idiom is that of the clown, the professional corrupter of words. Thus Fiddle, the clownish servant in *The Fair Maid of the Exchange*, is blood-brother to Shakespeare's Feste:

"God give you the time of the day. Pardon gallants, I was so neere the middle that I knew not which hand to take. . . . And yet because I will be sure to give you a true salutation, *Cripple*, *quomodo vales?* Good morrow, *Cripple*, good e'ne, good Master *Barnard*, Master *Bowdler*, *Bonos noches*, as they say, good night; and thus you have heard my manner of salutation."

And as for Middleton's many London plays, the only one that yields anything of value for us is *The Roaring Girl*, in which Gallipot the apothecary, a meek and doting Sunday-citizen married to a far from meek wife, occasionally employs the Cockney terms of endearment already made familiar to us in *The Knight of the Burning Pestle*.

Finally, some information may be obtained from that delightful play, *Eastward Hoe*, by Jonson, Chapman, and Marston. Although this comedy of London citizens and the pride that goes before a fall disappoints us in our Cockney expectations, the play is valuable for two nicely contrasted linguistic types, Touchstone the honest goldsmith and Quicksilver his raffish apprentice. Quicksilver in particular is a good study of the prodigal apprentice, catching at the fashions of the coxcombs in dress, behaviour and speech:

> "'Sfoot, man, I am a gentleman, and may swear by my pedigree. God's my life, sirrah Golding, wilt be ruled by a fool? turn good fellow, turn swaggering gallant; and *let the welkin roar, and Erebus also.* Look not westward to the fall of don Phoebus; but to the east, *Eastward hoe.*
>
> '*Where radiant beams of lusty Sol appear,*
> *And bright Eous makes the welkin clear.*'
>
> We are both gentlemen, and therefore should be no coxcombs: Let's be no longer fools to this flat-cap, Touchstone, eastward bully! this sattin belly, and canvas back'd Touchstone—'Slife, man, his father was a maltman, and his mother sold gingerbread in Christ-church." (I. i.)

It is surprising that in the wealth of Elizabethan drama we should find only this small change. Some people have been led to think that because the dramatists used no definite Cockney dialect, it follows that there could have been no such dialect in the sixteenth and seventeenth centuries. If Cockneys used such a distinctive pronunciation and idiom as they do now, it is argued, the playwrights would surely have seized upon it. The argument is not convincing, however. It ignores the fact, so evident in the Cockney music-hall songs of Marie Lloyd, Albert Chevalier and others, that details are usually left to the actual performers. Literary dialects are at most symbolistic, and in plays and songs the writers are content to leave pronunciation to the actors and performers. Until the eighteenth century plays were written almost solely for performance, and unless they had a fully developed convention to hand, authors were content with giving hints about dialect.

In the plays we have discussed the most remarkable omission is a formal Cockney pronunciation. Other marks of vulgar speech are not lacking. Cockney mannerisms and idiom are consistently used, both for realistic and for comic effect, and most of the dramatists sufficiently indicate the grammatical solecisms of the ordinary Londoners. Even pronunciation is not entirely neglected. Pronunciations which, as we shall see later, were characteristic of vulgar London speech are sprinkled in the dialogue of Cockney characters. Apart from the frequent reduction of unaccented words—*i' the purse*, *a' God's name*, *we ha' done*, or *God b' wi' you*—we find such phonetic spellings as *fegares* (figaries), *ance'try* (ancestry), *moe* (more), *Isbel* (Jezebel), "the *Lubbers*-head in *Lumbert* street", *exion* (action), *Wheeson week*, *pulsidge* (pulses), *debuty*, *Peesel* (Pistol), *atomy* (anatomy), *desartless*, *fartuous* (virtuous), *vagrom* (vagrant), *chrisom* child, *aligant* (elegant), *continuantly*, *vigitant*, *suffigance*, *neck-kerchers*. Pronunciation is the only element in a dialect which involves no departure from the script in performance, and that the occasional vulgar pronunciations used by the dramatists were hints to the actors seems fairly clear. It is certain beyond doubt that some pronunciations were far more common among the poorer classes of London than among good speakers, and as such pronunciations always raise a laugh in the theatre, the actors of Shakespeare's time must have been very different from the rest of their kind if they failed to gather so easy a harvest.

For the details of early Cockney which are lacking in the plays we have not far to look. They are abundant in the writings of Londoners themselves.

The most informative, as well as the most entertaining of these writings is the diary of Henry Machyn, kept in the years 1550–63. Machyn, citizen and merchant-tailor of London, was a maker and furnisher of funeral cloths and trappings, one of those middle-class Londoners who were the butts of the wits. But Machyn was no figure of fun. His diary reveals a most engaging gusto and curiosity. The great enthusiasm he displays for the elaborate funerals of the time is apt to pall, but it is akin to the enthusiasm of Simon Eyre, Touchstone, John of Newbury, and other craftsmen in Elizabethen and Jacobean literature. The diary does not discuss his own labours, but for the productions of his trade he had a relish which Dekker loved to portray as the spirit of middle-class life in Elizabethan England:

> Work apace, work apace,
> Honest labour makes a merry face.

Above all other things, Machyn loved pageants and merry-makings. He could find solid satisfaction in an elaborate cortège, but he delighted most to record the great dinners of the merchant companies, the May-games in the London streets, the masques produced by the city companies and the inns of court, and the goings-on in his own parish:

> "The xix day of Aprell was a wager shott in Fynsbere feld of the parryche of the Trenete the lytyll of vj men agaynst vj men and one parte had xv for iij and lost the game: and after shott and lost a-nodur game.
>
> "The sam [day] owre master parsun and entryd in-to helle and ther ded [died] at the barle breyke with alle the wyffe of the sam parryche, and ever was master parsun in the fyre [fire], ser Thomas Chambur; and after they whent and dronke at Hogston vij[s] in bred and bere, butt ij quarttes of claret, alle, and after they cam to the Swane in Wyttyngtun college to on master Fulmer a vetelar, ther they mad good chere, and payd for yt." (p. 132.)

These entries catch the same spirit as *The Shoemaker's Holiday*, and in the following passage, with its personal reference and its satisfaction in good eating, there is something of the Falstaffian gusto which still fills that nonpareil of the London music-halls, Harry Champion:

> The xxx day of July (1557) master Dave Gyttons, master Meynard and master Draper, and master Smyth, master Coldwelle and master Asse and Gybes and master Packyngtun and monser the Machyn de Henry, and mony mo, ded ett alff a busshell of owsturs in Anckur lane at master Smyth and master Gytton's seller apone hoghedes, and candyll lyght, and onyons and red alle [ale] and clarett alle, and muskadylle and malmesey alle, fre cope, at viij in the mornyng.

The spelling of these entries, it will have been observed, is in the style of that "auricular orthography" which Lord Chesterfield bantered in ladies of the eighteenth century. Such spellings are invaluable as evidence of the writer's pronunciation. In these two entries there are several phonetic spellings which reflect Cockney variants, *anodur*, *vetelar*, *mo* "more", *monser*, *alff*, etc. The whole diary is the best single guide to the vulgar pronunciation of London in the sixteenth century.

Among the most interesting of Machyn's spellings are those of place-names. So confirmed a sightseer was he that we are enlightened upon the Cockney pronunciation of many of the familiar streets and buildings of the City—*Gracyus* Street, *Crepullgate*, *Vestmynster*, *Smytfeld*, *Fanchyrche* Street, *Crussydfrers*, *Greyfreers*, *Belynggatt*, *Kyngsbynshe*, *Mynsyon lane*, *Garlykeheyffe*, *Hondyche*, *quenyffe* Stairs, *Kanwykstrett* (Candlewick Street), *Marshalsay*, *Powlles Cross*, *Radcliff*, *Gray-inn*, *Lynkolne-inn*, *Althergat* Street, *Lumbarstrett*, *Wostrett* (Wood Street), and the parishes of *sant Alberowgh* or *Albrowsse* (St. Ethelburga), *sant Towlys* (St. Olave), *sant Pulkers* (St. Sepulchre), and *sant Talphes* (St. Alphage). Some of the villages around London were called by the Cockneys, *Depforth*, *Honsley heth*, *Sordyche*, *Lussam* (Lewisham), *Bednoll Grene*, *Camurell*, *Barmsey* (Bermondsey), and *Darkyng*.

In idiom and grammar, too, Machyn's diary is faithful to the habits of Cockney speech. Such a passage as the following gives more detailed information upon such matters than most of the writings of the dramatists:

> The xxiij day of Desember was a proclamasyon thrugh London . . . that watt man somover thay be that doysse forsake testorns and do not take them for vjd a pesse for corne or vetelles or any odur thynges or ware, that they to be taken and browth a-for the mayre or shreyffe, baylle, justus a pesse, or constabulle or odur offesers. (p. 122.)
>
> The . . . day of Marche ther was never so low a nebe, that

> men myght stand in the mydes of Tames, and myght a' gone from the brygys to Belynggatt, for the tyd kept not ys course; the wyche was never sene a-fore that tyme. (p. 167.)

And as a last specimen of the style of the diary, we may quote a passage which amusingly reflects the Cockney's fondness for drawing the long bow:

> The xvj day of Aprell at viij of the cloke at nyght ther was a kyng cam from the dene of Rochester from super, and gohyng to ys logyng, and he had ij knyghtes that dyd wheyt on ym, and ther was shyche lythening and thunderyng, that yt thruw down on of ys knyghtes to the grond, and lykyd a bornyd the dodur [other], and on of servand was so freyd that ys here [hair] stod up, and yt wyll never come downe synes. (p. 231.)

Further information upon the pronunciation and grammar and some of the mannerisms of Cockneys may be obtained in abundance from London parish records. The churchwardens' accounts and vestry minutes of London parishes are particularly valuable in these matters. Some hundreds of volumes of these documents are among the treasures of the Guildhall Library, and it is upon some of these that we rely for our chief evidence upon the Cockney pronunciation and grammar of the sixteenth and seventeenth centuries.

Two churchwardens were appointed each year to be responsible for preparing the year's accounts and minutes. These wardens, the Dogberrys and Verges's of Shakespeare's London, were for the most part merchants and craftsmen. Sometimes they wrote their own accounts but, as reading and writing come by nature, some of them delegated the task to scriveners. The records are therefore nearly all anonymous, and we are justified only on probabilities in assuming that they reflect the vulgar speech of London. There can be little doubt that the writers lived in the City of London. The churchwardens resided in the parishes of which they were officers—they rarely failed to claim exemption when they moved—and there seems no reason why they should have employed any but their own clerks or local scriveners as amanuenses. A great number of people contributed to these volumes and since the majority of people living in London at any time are London-born, we may reasonably assume that when the entries diverge from accepted speech they reflect the linguistic habits of Londoners of the middle and lower-middle classes.

The contents of these parish documents are by no means so engaging as Machyn's diary. They deal principally with the upkeep of churches, the administration of church property, the collecting of rates and levies, and the relief of the poor—when it could not be avoided by driving them into other parishes. But the records are not always dull, and in the minutes we often catch the tone of the living voice. Like all who take minutes the churchwardens suffered from the verboseness of their colleagues, and now and again one finds that cryptic comment which convey a world of weariness, "There was much talk." Occasionally the idioms of the ordinary Londoner force their way through the formality considered proper for minutes:

> At the said Vestrie there was a requeaste made for the renewinge of a leasse of a howse at the bridge foote by Elizabeth Bullman widowe now Tennante thereof, vnto whome was answered by the said pishioners that betwene this and Christmas

nexte the said howse shalbe viewed by some of the said pishioners, And therevpon the said Elizabeth shall haue the same before anye other, gevinge as another will paie, and somethinge better chepe. (St. Bartholomew, 1574.)

Or, less frequently, one can catch the tone of the senior churchwarden as he explains himself to the vestry. Aggravation and annoyance clearly reveal themselves in such a passage as this:

I gaue them to vnderstand . . . y^{t} I was charged with many writings y^{t} should be in ye Chest wch I knew not whether they wer ther or no for I never ded see them, neyther ded I knowe whoe had ye kie of ye inner Chest. (St. Bartholomew, 1629.)

Perhaps men speak most naturally at meetings when they are annoyed. Certainly the most lively records in the vestry minutes are those in which the warden wrote while anger was still on him:

the said witton at Sondry Tymes hath much abvsed the pishe even to their faces making his Comparisons wth them and that as knaves he found them so knaves he would leave them and wth many other Lewd speeches wch the p̄ishioners have taken to hart. (St. Bartholomew, 1597.)

and:

I do disclame the same althought my name is used in the said bond it was with out my Consent and that the said William Bird in a publick place told me I was like a dog in a manger and he said that I would neither do good nor suffer others. (St. Peter Westcheap, 1649.)

Or sometimes the churchwarden will allow himself to comment. Such a passage is this from the minutes of St. Margaret Lothbury, with its amused innuendo:

att this vestry thare was moved by the Churchewarden (at the desier of the parsonn) that the enhabytors of this parishe should Come better, or to saie oftenar, to the Church on sondaies, and then the parsonn him selfe moved the saide parishonars in the same matter, at Large and showed thare smal aperance the sondaie before with such Lycke. . . . (1592.)

But as we have said the church records are chiefly of value for their lapses from normal grammar and their phonetic spellings. The following passages from the St. Bartholomew minutes, although they could not be called lively, have genuine interest, since they reflect many of the more sedate features of Cockney speech which the dramatists did not trouble to burlesque:

we shulld be carffull for the greyt playge and inffecyon dallye *growyth* in thys cyttyee and ys by greytt *necklygence* of our pyssheners that thooyes that *be* infectyyd *ys* not beytter seane vntoo *then* they ar, our streyts and kenylles *ys* not clensseyd nor well keypt as they *hawght* to bee. (1593.)

Att this vestrey it was *ffurder* menshoned whether the parishe would be pleased to *Accept of* m^r^ Gardener *for to bee* a Lecterrer in this Parishe every Wensday in the morninge through the yeare. And whether they would alow him *for* itt and so many as *was* there gaue there Consentte to Accepte *of* hime and to Alow him means and *to* this pourpose every man *seased* hime selfe. (1623.)

From the spellings of the churchwardens we may add to Machyn's evidence on the pronunciation of London place-names. Among the buildings, we find the Guildhall represented as *gulde hall* or *yeld halle*, the famous Saracen's Head tavern is called the *sarsyshed*, and the parish and street names include *St. Barthelemys*, *Thridnedlestreet*, *St. Buttolph*, *Bushops Gate*, *Cornewell* (Cornhill), *Cretched ffrers*, *St. Antholings*, *Groobstrete*, *Redriff lane* (Rotherhithe), *sente tanderes* (St. Andrew's), *Saint Katerns*, *Alhollowes barkin*. Of the renderings of villages around London, these are worthy of notice: *Hodgdon*, *muzel hill*, *Sutherock*, *wandsor*. The names of officials, merchants, and craftsmen were also pronounced differently from our manner, *shreyff* (sheriff), *Crowner* (coroner), *vargers*, *marchand-tayller*, *marser*, *hupholster* (upholsterer), *pulter* (poulterer), *Fyssmongers*, *carpenders*, *vitaler*, *Embrothers* or *broderers*, etc.

The abundance of these phonetic spellings in the churchwardens' records and in Machyn's diary makes it possible to analyse with some certainty the pronunciation of Cockneys in the sixteenth and seventeenth centuries. This aspect of our subject is dealt with in detail in a later chapter. Their pronunciation was very varied, many words being sounded in two or more ways by different speakers. Most of the variant pronunciations were by no means confined to Londoners or to the lower-classes. As Professor Wyld and other philologists have shown, good speakers did not employ an absolute standard of pronunciation until fairly recently. At this time they agreed with Cockneys in most of their variants.

Some pronunciations, however, were much more prevalent in London speech than in the accepted speech of the time. These variants may be claimed as the Cockneyisms of the sixteenth and seventeenth centuries.

The most prevalent Cockneyism was the use of short *e* in words which were more correctly pronounced with short *i*. Machyn and the churchwardens frequently use such spellings as: *consperacy*, *chelderyn*, *veseturs*, *kendred*, *weddowe*, *wretten*, *tell* (till), *ef* (if), etc. Such spellings are myriad, and although similar forms are not uncommon in the writings of good speakers they are not nearly so common as in London documents.

Instead of short *o*, Cockneys often used short *a*, as in *marow* (morrow), *caffen* (coffin), *falowing*, *maps* (mops), *Aspitall*, *bande* (bond), and the same variant was used before *r*, *Darking*, *sswarn* (sworn), *shartt* (short), etc. A vowel akin to that which we now employ in "far" often replaced the sound of *au* and *aw*, *dran* (drawn), *straberes* (strawberries), *warnut* (walnut), *dater* (daughter).

Instead of normal short *a*, the Cockneys of the sixteenth and seventeenth centuries frequently used a higher vowel, akin to the sound of short *e*, *stren* (Strand), *skevengers*, *Jenuarie*, *sattisfectory*, *texes*, *Perresh*, etc. Although similar spellings are occasionally used by good speakers they are far more frequent in London documents.

An abundance of spellings in these London records suggests that words normally spelt with *ol* were pronounced by Londoners with a diphthong similar to that which we now use in "howl". Among these spellings are: *Sowld*, *owlde*, *Rowle*, *towle* (toll), *towld* (told), *howlden*, etc. Other spellings indicate that sometimes they used instead a sound like that of short *o*, *bolles* (bowls), *solle* (soul), *colles* (coals), *poll* (pole), *wholl* (whole), etc. It is of interest that both these sounds, the diphthong and the short vowel, are used in present-day Cockney.

In a fair number of spellings, long *a* and *ai* are replaced by *i* or *y*: *chynes* (chains), *obtyninge*, *ordined*, *Byes* (bays), *Rile* (rail), *strynge*, *nighbower*, etc. On the face of it these spellings reflect a pronunciation which is regarded as the most characteristic of Cockney variants at the present time. Such spellings are rare in the writings of good speakers.

The London documents are also remarkable for the number of spellings in which normal *ou* or *ow* is represented by *u*; *shutt* (shout), *shruds* (shrouds), *fulle* (fowl), *Suthe* (South), *woodhusse* (woodhouse), *vtter* (outer), etc. This substitution seems to arise from a pronunciation similar to the sound of short *u* instead of the normal diphthong.

Initial unaccented syllables were frequently elided by Londoners, *raynyd* (arraigned), *salt* (assault), *countable* (accountable), *hedded* (beheaded), *stallyd* (installed), *pistles* (epistles), *paringe* (repairing), *vowson* (advowson). This process of aphesis has, of course, been common throughout the history of the language: the tennis term "vantage" is an example of its operation at the present time. But the process has always been commoner among the lower-classes than among good speakers.

Among the consonantal pronunciations characteristic of sixteenth- and seventeenth-century Cockney there are several that are familiar as the outstanding Cockneyisms in Victorian novels. Machyn and the churchwardens often interchanged *w* and *v*, *vomen*, *Vestmynster*, *Varren*, *vade* (Wade), *Villain* (William) and *welvet*, *woyce*, *wessells*, *woted*, *Westrey*, etc. They were also prone to drop initial *h* and to insert it elsewhere, as in *alffe* (half), *Amton* (Hampton), *olles* (holes), *Omsteade* (Holmstead), and *hoathe* (oath), *Hyslyngton*, *hanswered*, *hawght* (ought), *Harnold*, etc.

The additional of *t* after n, s, and f, and the addition of *d* after n, r, and l was quite common even among good speakers, but the number of such additions in the London documents far surpasses those in the writings of good speakers. Among them are *surgant*, *Rattclift*, *chefte* (chief), *sermonts*, *orfunt* (orphan) and *Nicholds*, *eindmate*, *gounds*, *kindsman*, etc.

The treatment of *th* by Machyn and the churchwardens strongly resembles the habits of present-day Cockneys. They sometimes replaced the two sounds of *th* by *f* or *v*, as in *frust* (thrust), *Frogmorton*, *Feverstone* (Featherstone), *tiues* (tithes) and *cloues* (clothes). More often they replaced them by *t* or *d*, *farding*, *anodur*, *togeder*, *Bednoll Grene*, *moder*, *der* (there), *doys* (those), *or Smytfeld*, *Elesabett*, etc. Often, too, they substituted *th* for normal *d*, *gunpowther*, *Sother* (solder), *Lathers* (ladders), etc.

The substitution of *sh* for normal *s* and of *s* for *sh* were also common in London, cf. *grandshyr*, *shepter*, *sherche*, *Russhall*, *shogers* (soldiers), *Lewish*; and *fysse* (fish), *fresse* (fresh), *marssys* (marshes), *parrysneres*, *Hogsfles*, etc.

The pronunciation of voiced consonants instead of the corresponding voiceless consonants and *per contra* of voiceless for voiced consonants was not uncommon even among good speakers. In particular, *p*, *t*, and *k* were often used where we should use *b*, *d*, and *g*, although *b*, *d*, and *g* were sometimes sounded where we pronounce *p*, *t*, and *k*. But some of these voicings and unvoicings were much more popular in London speech. The following spellings are but a small selection from the illustrative forms: *obbrobyus*, *babtyst*, *debytie* but also *Constaple*, *Apsent*; *marchand*, *hundyd*, *substitudes*, *carpindar* but also *salett* (salad), *ought* (owed), *dividentt*; *provete* (profit), *savelye*, *wives* (wife's), *elevant*, but also *festrye*, *roffer* (rover), *difident* (dividend), *scrifner*; *sagbottes* (sackbuts), *signesse*, but also *necklect*, *vacabond*.

These are the general variants which we are justified in claiming as Cockneyisms, but in reading through the London records one often comes across phonetic spellings which are unusual and which may very well have been features of the London dialect. Some of them are certainly given as London vulgarisms by later commentators. Thus Machyn often uses *a-for* instead of "before" and *the dodur* for "the other". The following spellings in his diary are also unusual, *yerle* (earl), *whatsomever*, *sertycatt* (certificate), *musyssoners*, *dolle* (deal), *gelevors* (gillyflowers), *sawgars* (soldiers), *aleblaster*, *mo* (more), *nodur* (neither), *fenerall* (funeral), *Goott Magott* (Gog Magog) and *strangwyllyon* (strangulation); and among the parish records there are these rare forms, *notamy* (anatomy), *strawing* (strewing), *corpuscis* (corpses), *Joyces* (joists), *Deboysnes* (debauchery), *mawned* (maimed), *Ianyver* (January), *somonsed* (summoned), *Chrisome* (christened).

A great many other variant pronunciations were commonly employed by Londoners of the time, although they cannot be claimed as Cockney characteristics either because the examples are few or because the same variants were just as common in the speech of the upper classes. These variants and their subsequent history are discussed in a following chapter. Unfortunately, no single quotation from either Machyn or the church records illustrates even a small proportion of these variants. But from the scattered phonetic spellings in the London documents we may suggest how an actor of Shakespeare's time would have interpreted the hints in a Cockney part. In the following passage from the Induction to *The Knight of the Burning Pestle*, I have substituted for the normal spelling phonetic spellings taken from London documents of about the same period:

> I pree you, youth, lat 'im ha' a shute o' reperell. I'll be swarn, gantlemen, my husban tills you true; 'a woll ect you sometimes at our 'usse, thet all the nighbours cry ut on 'im: 'a woll fatch you op a ceraging pert so in the garret, thet we aire all as fairt, I varrant you, thet we quake agen; we'll fair our cheldering vith 'im; ef they be naver so onruly, do but cry 'Rafe comes, Rafe comes!' to thim, an' they'll be as quiet as lambs. Ole op thy 'ead Rafe, shuwe the gantlemen wot thou canst do; spake a huffin' pert; I varrant you the gantlemen vill except of it.

CHAPTER II

THE EIGHTEENTH AND NINETEENTH CENTURIES

SO far in this preliminary sketch of the history of Cockney we have had no authoritative comment upon which to rely. The scholars who wrote upon English speech in the sixteenth and seventeenth centuries were concerned mainly with formulating rules for correct speech, and apart from the permitted exceptions to their rules they rarely discussed variant pronunciations. It was not until the eighteenth century, when the standard of correctness had been fairly well settled, in theory if not always in practice, that orthoepists and grammarians began to discover the interest of non-standard forms of speech. In consequence, we have had to wait until the middle of the eighteenth century for any valuable comment upon the characteristics of the vulgar speech of London.

Before the scholars began to turn their attention to vulgar English, a few literary men had been attracted by the county dialects. The dialect poetry of John Byrom and Tim Bobbin and *The Exmoor Courtship* are among the first proofs of the new interest in the vernacular speech of England. It is not surprising, therefore, that the earliest signs of interest in Cockney speech are the weirdly spelled letters which appear in some eighteenth-century novels. These letters burlesque an orthographical style with which we are familiar from the churchwardens' records and Machyn's diary, and although the letters are not to be regarded as serious linguistic studies, they contrive to reflect some of the pronunciations which we know were prevalent in Cockney speech in the two preceding centuries.

The earliest letter of this type which I have found is the epistle which Jonathan Wild, the Cockney hero of Fielding's novel, indicted to the adorable Miss Tishy. The ordinary speech of Jonathan is impeccable, even exalted. Although the author adhered faithfully to the history of his hero, he claimed the freedom to embellish his diction with some flourishes of his own eloquence. But in this letter the author takes away his purple cloak and reveals a style which might have been worthy of censure in a low and scholastic creature, although we realise that it could have been no blemish in the sublime greatness of Jonathan Wild:

Most Deivine and Adwhorable Creeture,

I doubt not but those IIs, briter than the son, which have kindled such a flam in my hart, have likewise the faculty of seeing it. It would be the hiest preasumption to imagin you *eggnorant* of my loav. No, madam, I sollemly *purtest*, that of all the butys in the unaversal glob, there is non kapable of *hateracting* my IIs like you. Corts and pallaces would be to me deserts without your kumpany, and with it a wilderness would hav more charms than *haven* itself. For I hop you will beleve me when I sware every place in the *univarse* is a *haven* with you. I am konvinced you must be *sinsibel* of my violent passion for you, which, if I endevored to hid it, would be as impossible as for you, or the son, to hide your buty's. I assure you I have not slept a wink since I had the hapness of seeing you last; therefore hop you will, out of Kumpassion, let me have the honour of seeing you this afternune; for I am with the greatest adwhoration,

Most deivine creeture,
Iour most passonate *amirer*,
Adwhorer and slave,
JONATHAN WYLD.

Similar letters appear occasionally in Smollett's novels. In *Roderick Random*, he reproduces a letter from Clarinda, a well-to-do London lady, to Mr. Jackson, which is a stronger caricature of Cockney orthography and pronunciation than Jonathan Wild's:

Deer *Kreeter*,

As you are the *animable hopjack* of my contemplayshins, your *aydear* is infernally skimming before my keymerycal fansee, when Murphy sends his *puppies* to the *heys* of slipping mortals; and when Febus shines from his *merrydying* throne; whereupon, I shall *canseeif* old whorie time has lost his pinners, as also *Cubit* his *harrows*, until thou enjoy sweet *purpose* in the *loaksheek harm's* of thy faithfool to *commend*,

Clayrennder,

Wingar-yeard, Droory Lane, January 12th.

And in *Peregrine Pickle*, there is the following choice epistle from Deborah Hornbeck, the merchant's wife, to Peregrine:

Coind Sur,

Heaving the playsure of meating with you at the *ospital* of anvilheads, I take this *lubbertea* of *latin* you know, that I *lotch* at the *hottail de May cong dangle rouy Doghouseten*, with two *postis* at the gait, naytheir of um vory hole, *ware* I shall be at the *windore*, if in kais you will be so good as to pass that way at sicks a cloak in the *heavening*, when Mr. Hornbeck goes to the *Calfhay de Contea*. Prey for the *loaf* of Geesus keep this from the nolegs of my *hussban*, ells he will make me leed a hell upon urth. Being all from, deer Sir,

Your most *umbell servan wile*,
Deborah Hornbeck.

These three letters show a progressive familiarity with those pronunciations which were employed by Machyn and the churchwardens of the sixteenth and seventeenth centuries and which later became the hall-marks of Cockney speech in novels and plays. It would appear that about this time, either because of developments in Cockney or standard speech which made the vulgar characteristics more obvious, or because the dialects, regional and social, were becoming subjects of interest, the Cockney dialect and the Cockney character were beginning to take a definite place in literature. It is an interesting feature of subsequent literature that the Cockney becomes more popular as he becomes more definitely a dialect character. Probably the development of the absolute standard of English in the eighteenth century was a contributory factor, for the growth of the language has done much to determine the tendencies of literature.

The dramatists of the Restoration had had little interest in this kind of vulgarity, for the movement towards standard English gained strength only with the domination of the middle class, which began late in the seventeenth century. The endless maids and servants of Restoration plays, who at other times might have been portrayed as Cockneys, are treated by Congreve and his rivals as parallel characters to their Millamants and Valentines. They may seem a little more mercenary, but that comes from their pandering to the tastes they share. Certainly they are not distinguished in speech. The maids may occasionally use a mincing vulgarism like "O Jiminy" but they are usually as fluent and often as witty as their mistresses and the gentlemen who visit them. Even such a character as Mrs. Amlet, that trollopy vendor of knick-knacks to the ladies, is free from Cockney traits.

The Cockney returns to the stage as he had left it. The best of the Elizabethan stage-Cockneys were the product of the conflict between the City and the stage. When the Cockney reappears, in the farces of the eighteenth century, he is still an Aunt Sally. Bickerstaffe's farce, *The Hypocrite*, 1768, founded upon Colley Cibber's play, *The Non-Juror*, 1718, was the outcome of the religous attacks upon the stage which had been opened by Jeremy Collier. The play amusingly burlesques the hypocritical zeal of the London Nonconformists, among them Maw-worm, the pious shopkeeper. Maw-worm, who maintains that he did nothing *clandecently* and compliments a fellow-worshipper for being a *malefactor* to all goodness, is a traditional figure. In his combination of hypocrisy with linguistic vulgarity he joins the attributes of Jonson's Puritans and Shakespeare's constables. But Maw-worm's vulgarity is much more developed than that of the Elizabethans, particularly in grammar:

> "I believe, doctor, you never know'd as how I was instigated one of the stewards of the reforming society. I convicted a man of five oaths, as last Thursday was se'nnight, at the Pewter Platter in the Borough; and another of three, while he was playing trap-ball in St. George's Fields. . . . And yet, if you would hear how the neighbours reviles my wife, saying, as how she sets no store by me, because we have words now and then, but, as I says, if such was the case, would ever she have cut me down that there time as I was melancholy, and she found me hanging behind the door? I don't believe there's a wife in the parish would have done so by her husband."

Such burlesques, in which the writers satirise their characters for vulgarity of mind as well as vulgarity of speech, have an importance which transcends the mere record of Cockney attributes. They have helped to foster the opinion that Cockney is a mean and vulgar speech which must be avoided by all who pretend to respectability.

Samuel Foote, the actor and dramatist, was one of the first writers to formalise the Cockney, and the lasting popularity of some of his farces may have helped to stimulate the vogue which Cockney enjoyed a little later. Like many other writers of farces, Foote was partial to dialect characters; Irishmen, Scotchmen, and West-Country men frequently appear in his plays. In other plays he burlesques the City merchants, poking fun at their self-importance and their offences against the English tongue. Their dialect is not always fully developed into that type of Cockney which one associates with Sam Weller, for they speak partly like Elizabethan stage-Cockneys and partly like the Cockneys of nineteenth-century novels. In *Taste*, 1752, the representatives of London are the alderman Pentweazel and his wife. They are not unlike the Citizen and his wife in *The Knight of the Burning Pestle*, with whom they share many traits of character and speech. Their tendency to malapropism is familiar—"I was always employed in painting your Lanskips, playing upon the Haspicols, making Paste or something or other." But their other vulgarisms—"I have heard, good Sir, that every Body has a more betterer and more worserer Side of the Face than the other", "them pretty Paintings", and such pronunciations as *ingenus* and *perdigious*—belong to a later school of Cockney characters. Ephraim Suds, the City soap-boiler in *The Orators*, 1762, commits some similar errors—"It is the onliest way to rise in the world", "all them kind of things", "I want to be made an orator on", etc.—although otherwise he, too, resembles the Elizabethan Cockneys. He has a familiar fondness for wise saws, "Soft, soft and fair; we must walk before we can run—I think I have had a pretty foundation—The Mansion-house was not built in a day"; he has Mistress Quickly's liking for "says"—"for, says Alice, says she"—he is liable to drag in Latin tags as in "Well, 'tis but seeing, says she, so wolens nolens, she would have me come hither," and, like the Citizen and his wife, he is given to tutoyage, "thee must learn", "dost not see", "I tell thee what", etc.

None of these personages is completely represented as a dialect type, but their vulgarisms indicate that the Cockney was about to join the small group of dialect characters. Foote appears to have been the first writer to effect the introduction. In *The Mayor of Garratt*, 1764, he drew a complete Cockney, Jerry Sneak, the City penmaker. A good specimen of this dialect occurs in the scene where Jerry, backed by his friend Bruin, makes the grand stand against his wife's domineering:

Mrs. Sneak. Where is the puppy?
Sneak. Yes, yes; she is axing for me.
Mrs. Sneak. So, sot! what, is this true that I hear?
Sneak. May be 'tis, may be 'tant, I don't choose to trust my affairs with a voman. Is that right, brother Bruin?
Bruin. Fine! Don't bate her an inch.
Sneak. Stand by me.

Mrs. Sneak. Hey-day! I am amazed! Why, what is the meaning of this?

Sneak. The meaning is plain, that I am grown a man, and vil do what I please, without being accountable to nobody.

Mrs. Sneak. Why, the fellow is surely bewitched!

Sneak. No, I am unwitched, and that you shall know to your cost, and since you provoke me, I will tell you a bit of my mind: what, I am the husband, I hope?

Bruin. That's right; at her again!

Sneak. Yes, and you shan't think to hector and domineer over me as you have done; for I'll go to the club when I please and stay out as late as I list, and row in a boat to Putney on Sundays, and wisit my friends at Vitsontide, and keep the key of the till, and help myself at table to what wittles I like, and I'll have a bit of the brown.

Although this henpecked citizen belongs to the tradition of burlesquing the merchants, and his favourite endearments, "lovy", "chicken", "chuck", "dove", smack more of Elizabethan than of Victorian Cockneys, his dialect begins a new literary practice. His pronunciations, particularly his interchange of *w* and *v*, establish him as the first of that great line of literary Cockneys in which Sam Weller, Mrs. Gamp, and Jeames Yellowplush are the outstanding figures.

Authoritative comments upon Cockney begin to appear about the same time. At first they are merely occasional remarks, condemning London pronunciations which diverged from the accepted rules. Thus, the schoolmaster, John Yeomans, in his little book *The Abecedarian*, 1759, makes this allusive rebuke: "A is rank'd the first letter in the order of every alphabet; but the citizens of *London* have injuriously converted its eligible pronunciation to that of *e*," a remark which patently refers to the frequent pronunciation of short *e* instead of short *a* which we discussed earlier. Eight years later, Granville Sharp in his *Short Treatise on the English Tongue*, 1767, has a slightly more detailed comment. "Mr. John Gignoux," he says, "in his 'Child's best instructor' . . . in his 'Table of Words written very different from their pronunciation' at page 82, has too much followed the common London pronunciation which, tho' perhaps in general the best, yet has some very exceptionable particularities, among which are *Potticary* for *Apothecary*; *Athist* for *Atheist*; *Awkurd* for *Awkward*; *Riccolas* for *Auricolas*; *Belcony* for *Balcony*; *Carrin* for *Carrion*; *Sirket* for *Circuit*; *Crowner* for *Coroner*; *Gorjus* for *Gorgeous*; *Hankerchur* for *Handkerchief*; *Iurn* for *Iron*; *Ilan* for *Island*; *Spanel* for *Spaniel*; *Stummuch* for *Stomach*; *Sound* for *Swoon*; *Thusty* for *Thirsty*; *Vawt* for *Vault*; *Venzun* for *Venison*; *Verdit* for *Verdict*." Sharp must have had some familiarity with Cockney errors, for before he engaged in his great work for the abolition of slavery, he had been a linendraper's apprentice in London and a freeman of the City. But, although the pronunciations he indicts were undoubtedly used in London (most of them are shown in the churchwardens' records) and some of them were even then vulgar, his list is aimed more against variations from the formal rules of correctness than against the habits of Cockney speech, and its chief interest is as evidence of the importance which the common London pronunciation was beginning to assume for the authorities. A third comment of the same type is a little more valuable, as its examples are familiar Elizabethan pronunciations which later sank into vulgarity. This comment occurs in Solomon Lowe's *The*

Critical Spelling Book, 1770, when the author discusses the standard of correct speech. "I have formed my rules", states Lowe, "upon what I conceive to be the most common way of pronouncing them among the better sort of people at London. Though even among them we find . . . corruptions which one may venture to declare inexcusable (ex. *bushop*, *kiver*, *scrouge*, *squench*, *squeege*, *yerb*, *yuern*)."

The earliest analysis of Cockney characteristics is to be found in the orthoepical works of James Elphinston (1721–1809). Elphinston was a Scot, who, after leaving the University of Edinburgh, acted as tutor to various noble Scottish families before he decided to join the procession across the Tweed. In 1753 he came to London and founded a school at Brompton. Through his pedagogic writings and some incredibly bad translations he became acquainted with some of the famous men of the time, although his pedantry and eccentricity, as well as his offences against the poetic Muse, made him something of a butt. His literary and pedagogical ventures undoubtedly justified the ridicule they received, but as an orthoepist Elphinston claims our attention. His chief scholastic activity was on the subjects of grammar and spelling reform, which he treated in *Principles of English Grammar Digested*, 1765, *Propriety Ascertained in her Picture*, 1787, and *Inglish Orthoggraphy epittomized*, 1790. In these works he commented incidentally upon various vulgarisms which he had noted in London, and one of his translations from Martial is rendered in such a way as to illustrate the Cockney speech of his time. The following is a specimen:

Ve have at length resoom'd our place,
And can, vith doo distinction, SET;
Nor ve, the great and wulgar met.
Ve dooly can behould the play,
Sence ve in no confusion LAY.
Of ruination vonc't afear'd
Veu ve vas NEITHER seen, OR hear'd;
Tell this day, wite as alablaster,
BEWRAYS me of myself no master.
ONE can't scarce recollect the tithe
Of all that hove th'equestr'an sigh:
Tis now some comfort, for to think
That we was ONLY on the brink.
A HUMBLE; no, AN HIGH delight
Pricks us for to assurt our right,
Cur'osity need never acs,
Nor need no wits be on the racks.
Childern can, as larn'd attest,
Of bond AND free, WHICH is the BEST.
Ef YOU but look AMONG mankind,
You'll see that THEY are not so blind,
As for to call them things in DOUBT,
Or on THOSE SORT of themes to spout.

Effusions of this kind certainly justified the satire which Burns and others directed against them. But this single translation has its own interest, even though I have not the heart to quote it in its entirety. The Cockneyisms which are illustrated in this poem and the others which are commented upon here and there in Elphinston's other works are valuable contributions to our knowledge of the dialect in the eighteenth century.

About the same time as Elphinston was writing his orthoepical treatises, novelists and dramatists were beginning to follow the lead given by Foote. In Dibdin's ballad-opera *The Waterman*, 1774, for example, we find another Cockney character, Tom Tug. Dibdin did not bother to represent all his Cockneyisms, but the few which he did set down in the script, *Miss Wileminy*, *sartain*, *us'd for to ply*, *Cupids and Wenisses*, *I makes*, show that Tom was intended to be played as a Cockney of the Sam Weller kind. This fact is worth the attention of some of our ballad-singers, for it seems to have been Dibdin's intention that Tom's fine song should be rendered in the style of Sam:

> And did you not hear of a jolly young waterman,
> Who at Blackfriars Bridge us'd for to ply?
> And he feather'd his oars with such skill and dexterity,
> Winning each heart and delighting each eye, etc.

In Fanny Burney's novel *Camilla*, too, we are introduced to another such Cockney, the Othello in a troupe of strolling players. This worthy, his hand upon his bosom, declared that he would "a round unwarnished tale deliwer". The Cockney was becoming one of the drawing-room amusements. The Cockney-barmaid imitations of some of our lady friends have an honourable ancestry.

The next serious discussion of Cockney is given in John Walker's *Pronouncing Dictionary*, 1791. Walker is an interesting figure in the social and literary life of the second half of the eighteenth century. He was at one time an actor in various touring companies and after playing minor parts in Garrick's company at Drury Lane finally succeeded Mossop in the group of players at the Crow Street Theatre, Dublin. In 1762 he returned to the London stage for a time, but finally gave up acting in 1768 in order to teach. His lectures on elocution met with considerable success, he even gave private lectures on the subject at the Universities. He was sufficient of a wit and scholar to enjoy the friendship of Johnson and Burke, and his writings on the English language, his Dictionary in particular, gained for him a considerable reputation.

It is in a prefatory section of his Dictionary, entitled "Rules to be observed by the Londoners", that we find his comments on Cockney. Unlike Elphinston's observations, these remarks are not given in a spirit of condemnation, but because his countrymen the Cockneys, "as they are the models of pronunciation to the distant provinces, ought to be the more scrupulously correct", a judicial attitude which gives the comments an added interest. Walker selects four pronunciations as the most characteristic of Cockney errors, the interchange of *w* and *v* in *weal* (veal), *winegar*, *vine* (wine), *vind*, etc., the loss and addition of initial *h*, *art* (heart), *harm* (arm), etc., the pronunciation of initial *wh* as *w*, *wet* (whet), *wile* (while), etc., and the introduction of a vowel before the plural of words ending in *-st*, post*e*s, fist*e*s, mist*e*s, etc. Many other Cockney pronunciations are noted in his general introduction to the Dictionary and under various words in the dictionary itself.

Practically all the Cockney pronunciations noted by Walker had been long established in London speech, and it was therefore fitting that although his condemnations were occasionally harsh, they were much more temperate than Elphinston's. After Walker had endeavoured to correct "some of the more glaring errors" of his fellow-citizens he maintained that "with all their faults, they are still upon the whole the best pronouncers of the English language; for though the pronunciation of London is certainly erroneous in many words, yet, upon being compared with that of any other place, it is undoubtedly the best; that is, not only the best by courtesy, and because it happens to be the pronunciation of the capital, but the best by a better title—that of being more generally received or, in other words, though the people of London are erroneous in the pronunciation of many words, the inhabitants of every other place are erroneous in many more". The strong tie between accepted and Cockney speech in the sixteenth and seventeenth centuries was still maintained, even though it was beginning to get worn.

The local patriotism which glimmers in Walker's comments burns brightly in Samuel Pegge's *Anecdotes of the English Language*, 1803. Pegge was a scholar and antiquary who seized upon the characteristics of vulgar London speech as a means of exhibiting his wide reading. Whereas most of the commentators on the dialect were vigorous in condemning its errors, and literary men took delight in burlesquing it, Pegge was concerned to defend the Cockney variations. He contrives to prove by a wealth of quotations that many of the so-called London vulgarisms had been used by the most eminent of writers, Chaucer, Shakespeare, Milton, Pope, Dryden, Prior, Addison, Swift, and even Dr. Johnson, and that others were the result of that principle of analogy which was always invoked by the pundits on English speech.

Pegge admits a number of "little peccadilloes" in Cockney pronunciation, most of which had already been described by Elphinston and Walker, *Villiam*, *westry*, *postés*, *ghostés*, *saacy*, *howsomdever*, *wonst*, *gownd*, etc.

But he had little difficulty in showing that most of the Cockney variations in verbal forms were due to the principle of analogy. The practice of using weak past tenses and past participles in strong verbs, *know'd*, *throw'd*, etc., were due to analogy with "sowed" and "mowed". The Cockneys were apt to confound the past participle with the preterite, *took* (taken), *rose* (risen), etc., but such forms might still be found in newspapers and they were used by Shakespeare, Swift, and Addison among other eminent writers. Even such Cockney preterites as *mought* (might), *fit* (fought) and *cotch* (caught) had respectable antecedents, and if the Cockneys erred in prefacing an infinitive by "for", they erred with Shakespeare. Many other grammatical solecisms of Cockney could be similarly justified, Pegge claimed. The possessive pronouns *ourn*, *yourn*, *hern*, and *hisn* were modelled on "mine" and "thine", and the reflexives *his-self* and *their-selves* were analogous to "thyself" and "myself". The substitution of *us* for "we" in *can us*, *shall us*, etc., may have been erroneous in the nineteenth century, but it was correct in the sixteenth and seventeenth, since many eminent writers used such forms. Even the double comparatives and superlatives of Cockney, *worser*, *more worser*, *most impudentest*, etc., might be found in the Bible and Shakespeare's plays. And the heinous Cockney practice of multiplying negatives was sanctioned by the usage of Chaucer, Ascham, Shakespeare, and Pope.

Had Pegge known of the churchwardens' records he would have been able to show that not only these grammatical errors but also the little peccadilloes of pronunciation had been used by Cockneys for nearly three hundred years at least. His recognition of the respectable ancestry of many Cockneyisms of the eighteenth and nineteenth centuries is, however, of considerable importance. He consciously shows the closeness of Cockney to early Accepted Speech and unconsciously reveals how wide the gap was becoming which separated Cockney from standard. Pegge deserves a place of honour in philological history, moreover, as one of the few linguists to break away from severe didacticism and as a man who contrived to treat language with humanity and humour.

An anonymous work on Cockney, *Errors of Pronunciation and Improper Expressions*, "used frequently and chiefly by the inhabitants of London", 1817, is not so enlightened. It records in the form of a dictionary a selection of pronunciations of the kind described by Pegge, Walker, and Elphinston, *harbour* (arbour), *viper* (wiper), *gownd* (gown), *persistes*, etc., and some of the grammatical solecisms defended by Pegge. The only aspect of Cockney upon which the work adds much to our knowledge is slang. Curiously enough, previous commentators had neglected the slang which was one of the most striking characteristics of the dialect. But the author of *Errors of Pronunciation* condemns with all the force at his command such "very low" expressions as *mulligrubs*, *muckenger*, and *inexpressibles*.

A second anonymous work published shortly afterwards, *Vulgarities of English Speech Corrected*, 1826, contains a chapter on Cockney errors, but as it merely reproduces examples of the vulgarisms in pronunciation and grammar, and some of the Cockney mannerisms described in the works we have already discussed, it does not warrant any extensive discussion.

This work appears to have been the last discussion of Cockney for some years. The lack of authoritative comment is compensated for, however, by an abundance of Cockney dialogue in literary works. By the beginning of the nineteenth century the Cockney had taken his place in literature as one of the chief dialect types. A good illustration of this fact is Maria Edgeworth's play *Love and Law*, 1817, where a London Cockney is contrasted with a group of Irish characters. Miss Bloomsbury, the uppish London servant, feels herself a cut above the Hibernians among whom she has to live:

> "Then, ma'am, I declare now, I've been forced to stuff my *hears* with cotton wool ever *sence* I *comed* to Ireland. But *this here* Honor M'Bride has a mighty pretty *vice*, if you dont take exceptions to a little nationality; *nor* is she *not* so smoke-dried: she's really a nice, tidy-looking like girl considering. I've taken tea with the family often, and they live quite snug for *Hirish*. I'll assure you, ma'am, quite *bettermost* people for Hibernians, as you always said, ma'am."

Hers is not a large part, but as this quotation suggests she contrives to commit most of the Cockney errors described by the critical works we have already discussed.

The Cockney character was soon to be followed by the novel of low London life, for although this literary genre did not flourish until the middle of the nineteenth century, its seed was Pierce Egan's *Real Life in London*, which began to appear in monthly parts in November 1821. Egan (1772–1849) was very well qualified to be the father of the London novel, for not only was he born and reared in London, but his reputation as a writer was first gained by his lively accounts of the sporting life of the capital. The best of this early work is *Boxiana*, 1818, a series of vividly written memoirs of famous pugilists. The work with which we are more concerned, *Real Life in London*, is wider in its interests, for it is inspired not only by Egan's familiarity with most aspects of London life, but also by Ned Ward's *London Spy* and by Grose's *Classical Dictionary of the Vulgar Tongue*, 1785. Like Ward's book, *Real Life in London* is a species of guide book to London scenes and London characters, with a strong predilection for the shadier scenes and the shadier characters, vivid journalistic work tinged with a scarcely appropriate moralising. And in its prepossession with the slang used by the various cliques it is strongly indebted to Grose's dictionary. The book is arranged in a series of alternate scenes of high life and low life in which the slang, colloquialisms, and jargon of each fraternity are displayed. So intent is Egan upon parading this vocabulary that the book appears at times to be a philological novel.

Cockney dialogue does not occupy so large a space in the book as one might expect, but Egan does deal with some aspects of Cockney which are ignored by other writers. His description of the Cockney and his language is itself of some interest, as it indicates the birth of the "Eternal Cockney"—"Cockney is universally known to be the contemptuous appellation given to an uneducated native of London, brought into life within the sound of Bow bell—pert and conceited, yet truly ignorant, they generally discover themselves by their mode of speech, notwithstanding they have frequent opportunities of hearing the best language. . . . You will hear these gentry frequently deliver themselves in something like the following manner:

> 'My eyes, Jim, vat slippy valking 'tis this here morning—I should ave fell'd right down if so be as how I adn't cotch'd ould of a postis—vere does you thinks I ave been? va all the va to Vapping Vall, an a top o Tower Hill—I seed a voman pillar'd—such scrouging and squeeging, and peltin vith heggs—ow funny!' "

Egan adds little to our knowledge of Cockney pronunciation and grammar, but he is certainly informative upon the less formal aspects of the dialect. Whenever Cockneys converse in his book they do so with the colouring of slang, clichés, and epithets which is still considered appropriate in the English of Stratford and Bow. A wholly modern note is struck in this pungent description of a Cockney lady: "She's a b——dy rum customer when she gets lushy", and apart from the archaic pronunciations the following might still be considered proper in the London markets:

> "Here's a bit of b——dy gammon—don't you see as how I am lost both my ass and his cargo, and if you von't leave me alone, and give me my bags again, I'll sarve you out—there now, that's all bl—st me! fair play's a jewel—let go my hair and don't kick up no rows about it—see vhat a mob you're a making here—can't you sell your mackerel ready sauced and let me go ater Neddy?"

The catch-phrase "fair play's a jewel" was apparently one of many tags used by the Cockneys of the time, as in a note upon it Egan says, "That's the time of day. That's your sort, that's the barber, keep moving, what am you arter, what am you up to, that's the Dandy, there never was such times, Go along Bob, &c., are expressions that are frequently made use of by the people of the Metropolis." The present-day Cockney is not less fond of such phrases now.

The strong traditionalism of Cockneys is also reflected in their habit of using songs as work chanties. It is still a practice in those factories where silence rules are not enforced for Cockney girls to use the popular songs of the day as chanties, sometimes sung solo, sometimes in chorus. Egan shows that the same practice was common in his time—"Particular trades have particular songs suitable to the employments in which they are engaged, which while at work the whole of the parties will join in. In Spitalfields, Bethnal Green, etc., principally inhabited by weavers, it is no uncommon thing to hear twenty or thirty girls singing, with their shuttles going—The Death of Barbary Allen, There was an Old Astrologer, Mary's Dream, or Death and the Lady." He also adds to our information on the London cries, particularly on the manner of their delivery. Prompted by the cry of a clothes-prop seller, "Buy a *Prap*, buy a *prap*!" he describes some of the strange pronunciations which were used by the hawkers:

> "The alteration of sound only arises from an habitual carelessness, with which many of what are termed the London Cries are given; a sort of tone or jargon which is acquired by continually calling the same thing and in which you will find he is not singular. The vendors of milk, for instance, seldom call the article they carry for sale, as it is generally sounded *mieu* or *mieu below*, though some have recently adopted the practice of crying *mieu above*. The chimney-sweeper, you will

find, instead of bawling *sweep*, frequently contracts it to *we-ep* or *e-ep*. The dustman, above curtailment, as if he felt his superiority to the flue faker, lengthens his sound to *dust-ho* or *dust-wo*. The cries of muffins in the streets it is difficult to understand, as they are in the habit of ringing a tinkling bell, the sound of which can scarcely be heard, and calling *mapping-ho*; and I remember one man from whom I could never make out more than *happy happy happy now*. There is a man who frequently passes through the Strand, wheeling a barrow before him, bawling as he moves along, in a deep and sonorous voice, *smoaking hot*, *piping hot*, *hot Chelsea buns*; and another, in the vicinity of Covent Garden, who attracts considerable notice by the cry of—*Come buy my live shrimps and periwinkles*, *buy my wink*, *wink*, *wink*. These, however, are exceptions to those previously mentioned, as they have good voices, and deliver themselves to some tune; but to the former may be added the itinerant collector of old clothes, who continually annoys you with—*Clow*, *clow sale*."

The passage might well be applied to the few remaining London cries, the shouts of newspaper-boys and old-clothes men, whose calls are symbolical rather than informative.

It is primarily for its vocabulary of slang, however, that Egan's book is of philological interest. Unfortunately, although the slang was definitely used in London it cannot be described as Cockney slang. The buckish heroes, Tom and Jerry, visit all the London haunts and their adventures enable Egan to make an exhaustive survey of the jargon and slang of most of the London cliques. For the most part, therefore, the slang is either technical or general, and although it is evident from *Real Life in London* that Cockney had achieved that slanginess which is now one of its chief traits, it would not be safe to rely on the book for an analysis of

Cockney slang. We may best represent this aspect of the book, therefore, by quoting the following narrative which was overheard by Tom and Jerry and which gives a good idea of the extent to which slang was used by the working classes at the beginning of last century:

> "I vas down at the Frying Pan in Brick Lane yesterday. Snivelling Bill and Carrotty Poll was there in rum order—you know Carrotty Poll?—So Poll (Good health to you) you know how gallows lushy she gets—vell, as I vas saying, she had had a good day vith her fish, and bang she comes back to Bill—you know she's rather nutty upon Bill, and according to my thinking they manages things pretty vell together, only you see as how she is too many for him: so, vhen she comes back b——t me if Bill vasn't a playing at skittles, and hadn't sold a dab all day; howsomdever he vas a vinning the lush, so you know Bill didn't care—but, my eyes! how she did blow him up vhen she com'd in and see'd him just a going to bowl and tip, she tipp'd him a volloper right across the snout vhat made the skittles dance again, and bang goes the bowl at her sconce instead of the skittles. It vas lucky for her it did not hit her, for if it had, I'll be d——d if ever she'd a cried Buy my live flounders any more—he vas at play vith Sam Stripe the tailor: so the flea-catcher he jumps in between 'em, and being a piece-botcher, he thought he could be a peace-maker, but it voudn't go, tho' he jump'd about like a parch'd pea in a frying-pan—Poll called him Stitch-louse, bid him pick up his needles and be off—Bill vanted to get at Poll, Poll vanted to get at Bill—and between them the poor Tailor got more Stripes to his jacket than there is colours in a harlequin's breeches at Bartlemy Fair—Here's good health to you—it was a bodkin to a but of brandy poor Snip didn't skip out of this 'ere vorld into that 'ere."

The adventures of Egan's heroes served as the basis for one of the most popular dramatic works of the first half of the century, W. T. Moncrieff's *Tom and Jerry*, 1826. This burlesque ballad-opera rivalled the success of *The Beggar's Opera*. It lacks the wit of Gay's work, but its variety and novelty justified the success which it enjoyed not only in London but in the provinces and America, too—it is said to have made £25,000 for the proprietors of the Adelphi Theatre. The opera contains much more Cockney dialogue than Egan's book, as characters who are merely described by Egan have speaking parts in the opera. These Cockneys use a lingo which is so replete with slang that it is almost incomprehensible. A typical passage is the dialogue between Mace, the publican, and Bob, the dustman, which follows upon the singing of "Nothing like Grog" at All Max tavern:

Bob. Now, landlord, arter that 'ere drap of max, suppose we haves a drain o' heavy wet, just by way of cooling our chaffers—mine's as dry as a chip—and, I say, do you hear, let's have a two-penny burster (loaf), half a quartern o' bees vax, a ha'porth o' ingens, and a dollop o' salt along vith it, vill you?

Mace. Bellay! a burster and bees vax—ingens and salt here. . . . Now then, here you are, Muster Grimmuzzle. (*Holding out his right hand for the money, and keeping the porter away with the other.*)

Bob. That's your sort, give us a hold on it. (*Takes Mace's empty hand.*) Vy, vhere?

Mace (*keeping the porter back*). Vy here.

Bob. Oh! you are afeard of the blunt, are you?

Mace. No, it an't that; only I'm no schollard, so I alvays takes the blunt vith von hand, and gives the pot vith t'other—It saves chalk, and prewents mistakes, you know.

Bob. You're a downey von—you'll not give a chance avay if you knows it.

Mace. Vy it 'ant times, Muster Grimmuzzle.

Bob. Now then for the stumpy. (*Searching about in his pockets for the money.*) My tanners are like young colts; I'm obliged to hunt 'em into a corner, afore I can get hold on 'em—there! hand us over three browns out o' that 'ere tizzy, and tip us the heavy.

The popularity of Moncrieff's and Egan's works did much to make the Cockney a favourite literary figure. The influence of their writings was soon observable in the work of Lytton, Ainsworth, Thackeray, Dickens, and others.

An interesting but neglected contemporary of the young Dickens was Renton Nicholson, whose *Cockney Adventures* appeared in 1837–8, a year after *Sketches by Boz*. Nicholson's work is coarser in grain than Dickens's, but it is racy and amusingly reflects the lighter side of Cockney life, the pleasure jaunts, parties, and love affairs. The formal aspects of his Cockney dialogue owe much to Egan, but he seems to have had a genuine command of Cockney idiom and slang. This is apparent in the story of the thimble-rigging at Epsom which Tom Gubbs's master recounts when the apprentice asks leave to go to the races:

"When I was about sixteen years of age, I was pertickerlerly fond of sporting and upon one occasion, asked leave of my master—the same as you have of me, Thomas,—to allow me to go to Epsom races. 'Wery well,' says my master, 'if yer likes to go, but mind as yer doesn't lose yer money.' We went in a *wan*. . . . We went in a wan cowered all over with bows, and I vos dressed as smart as a new pin: ve vere all wery merry, and as comfortable as ever ve could be, until Bill Smith, a young chap as vas along vith us, got drunk; and arter the first race was over, he would go and play at the thimble-rig, and he lost all his money, every farden; he hadn't got a mag left. So ven he com'd and told me on it, says I, 'Bill, vy you've been done.'—'That be d——d,' says he; 'I'll swear it,' says I; '*Walker*,' says he, but another of our party told him the same, and then he began to think as it vos true. 'Vell,' says he, 'if I've been nailed, I'll vallop the coves as did it, if you'll go along vith me.'

'Wery well,' says I, like a fool, and off I set with him arter the thimble and pea-table coves: ven ve com'd up vith 'em, they'd got a young countryman in tow, and he vas a vinning like fun; so he says to me on the sly, as he lifted up the thimble, while the man's head was turned away, says he, 'Do you see the pea?', says I 'I do'; 'Well,' says he, 'Go me halves in betting 'em two pound as it's under that one.' 'Wery well,' says I, and out I pulled a bran new golden guinea and puts it down by the side of this here young countryman's; up he takes the thimble, and the bird had flown; the pea vasn't there, though I'd seen it not a minute before. 'Vell,' I says to this young countryman, says I, 'D——d if ve arn't been done the same as this here young chap was,' pointing to Bill Smith, 'and I'm blowed if we wont wop these thieves, if you'll help us.' 'Certainly, I wool,' said the yokel, and I pulled off my coat and began to square away at the fellow with the table. All ov a sudden, I received a dreadful blow, behind my head. I fell down and then had a dozen kicks on my breech. Poor Bill Smith was knocked over me, and the countryman, in lifting me up, picked my pocket ov twelve shillings and sixpence."

Although he had little of Egan's or Moncrieff's familiarity with low-life, Mark Lemon (1809–70) was well acquainted with those Cockneys whose respectability debarred them from leading a real life in London. He utilised his experience in some of his plays, and although he does not add anything of value to our knowledge of London speech, his Cockney characters have some claim to our attention because of his friendship with Dickens and his editorship of *Punch*, in which the Cockney has always been as eternal as the other verities. Tom Chaff, the perky Cockney stable-boy in *My Sister Kate*, 1838, has some kinship with the younger

Weller, and in the following dialogue with Kate à propos of his master's courtship he yields us a good illustration of the milder form of Cockney used about the middle of last century:

Tom. I was always coming in for a bob or two. That love's expensive work—it cost me a matter of eighteen and sixpence, two years ago.

Kate. How, Mister Tom?

Tom. Why, I went to see a young 'oman as lived at a tallow-chandler's; and every time I took her out, it cost me something—she was so uncommon fond of sweetstuff and curds and whey.

Kate. And was that the reason you did not marry?

Tom. Not exactly: she'd a taste for the army; and used to go out with one of them long sticks of sealing wax—them life-guards.

Kate. Well, that was cruel.

Tom. Yes, considering how *sweet* I was upon her. It cut me up a good deal, I 'sure you: I went off my feed and got as lean and lanky as a two-year-old.

Kate. She must have had very little taste.

Tom. You think so? (*Aside.*) I've made her a little *on*easy I think. (*Aloud.*) Have you been long in service?

Kate. No; but I've had some good places. Is there any savings bank in this place?

Tom. Why?

Kate. Because I always put something by;—the want of a little money might some day lose me a husband.

Tom. Money's a great recommendation to a young woman. Many a poor girl dies *a* old maid, for the want of the browns.

The Cockney dialogue in Dickens's works is too familiar to need much discussion. Although there is no indication in any of the other works on Cockney that Sam Weller's favourite type of simile, "as the . . . said, when he . . ." was a habit of the Cockney or that Cockney women were so constantly lone and lorn as some of Dickens's ladies, the Cockney speech used in his novels exhibits exactly the same features as those discussed by the critics of Cockney and employed in other literary works. He does not appear to have made any special study of the dialect or to have tried to break from the well-established conventions. But his command of Cockney idiom was certain. Although it is supererogatory to quote from Dickens, it is *lèse majesté* not to do so. I, therefore, venture to reproduce a passage from *Sketches by Boz* which admirably illustrates the idiom and tempo of Cockney, that passage in which Ikey, the factotum in Solomon Jacobs's lock-up shop, recounts what Mr. Watkins Tottle was in for:

> "Vy, it's one of the rummiest rigs you ever heard on. He come in here last Vensday, which by the bye he's a going over the water to-night—hows'ever that's neither here nor there. You see I've been a going back'ards and for'ards about his business, and ha' managed to pick up some of his story from the servants and them; and so far as I can make it out it seems to be summat to this here effect. . . . This here young gen'lm'n's father—so I'm told, mind ye,—and the father o' the young voman, have always been on very bad, out-and-out, rig'lar knock-me-down sort o' terms; but somehow or another, when he was a wisitin' at some gentlefolk's house, as he knowed at college, he came into contract with the young lady. He seed her several times, and then he up and said he'd keep company with her, if so be as she vos agreeable. Vell, she vos as sweet upon him as he vos upon her, and so I s'pose they made it all right; for they got married 'bout six months arterwards, unbeknown, mind ye, to the two fathers —leastways so I'm told. When they heard on it—my eyes, there was such a combustion! Starvation vos the very least that vos to be done to 'em. The young gen'lm'n's father cut him off vith a bob, 'cos he'd cut himself off vith a wife; and the young lady's father he behaved even worser and more

unnat'ral, for he not only blowed her up dreadful, and swore he'd never see her again, but he employed a chap as I knows —and as you knows, Mr. Valker, a precious sight too well —to go about and buy up the bills and them things on which the young husband, thinking his governor 'ud come round agin, had raised the vind just to blow himself on vith for a time; besides vich, he made all the interest he could to set other people agin him. Consequence vos, that he paid as long as he could; but things he never expected to have to meet till he'd had time to turn himself round, come fast upon him, and he vos nabbed. He vos brought here, as I said afore, last Vensday, and I think there's about—ah, half-a-dozen detainers agin him down-stairs now. I have been," added Ikey, "in the purfession these fifteen year, and I never met vith such windictiveness afore!"

Although Thackeray was not so fond of vulgar dialogue as Dickens was, his burlesque, *The Yellowplush Papers*, is a rich fund of Cockney. The work reverts to the first form of literary Cockney; the unorthodox spelling and grammar of Jeames Yellowplush's articles and epistles are similar to and possibly inspired by the unorthodox epistles in the novels of Fielding and Smollett, as we may see from a typical passage:

"Skelton's *Anatomy* (or Skeleton's, which, I presume, is his real name) is a work which has long been wanted in the littery world. A reglar slap-up, no mistake, out-an'-out account of the manners and usitches of genteel society, will be appreciated in every famly from Buckly Square to Whitechapel Market. Ever since you sent me the volum, I have read it to the gals in our hall, who are quite delighted of it, and every day grows genteeler and genteeler. So is Jeames, coachman; so is Sam and George, and little Halfred, the sugar-loafed page;—all 'xcept old Huffy, the fat veezy porter, who sits all day in his hall-chair, and never reads a word of anythink but that ojus *Hage* newspaper. 'Huffy,' I often say to him, 'why continue to read that blaggered print? Want of decency, Huffy, becomes no man in our high situation; a genlman without morality is like a livry coat without a shoulder-knot.' But the old-fashioned beast reads on, and don't care for a syllable of what I say. As for the Sat'rist that's different: I read it myself reglar; for its of uncompromising Raddicle principils, and lashes the vices of the arristoxy. But again I am diverging from Skeleton."

The great value of *The Yellowplush Papers* for this essay lies in the very convincing phonetic spellings. Some of them have a measure of exaggeration due to burlesque, but not nearly so many as anyone who is not familiar with early manuscripts would think, and they are certainly too true to the habits of Machyn and the church-wardens, especially in the inverse spellings, to be entirely imaginative. We have the authority of other commentators that some Cockneys did spell in this way, and it is not unreasonable to suppose that Thackeray had contemporary models, even though he may have been inspired by.Smollett's *Humphrey Clinker*.

Most of Jeames's phonetic spellings reflect familiar Cockneyisms, the following being characteristic: *vinmill*, *wehicle*; *wack* (whack); *Halfred*, *usband*; *glars* (glass), *tawsing* (tossing); *sarvice*; *sirline*; *rowld*; *delooded*; *disperryted*; *instink*, *swinler*, *half-a-crownd*; *Chewsdy*; *uppards*; *nothink*; *perfession*; *dishcord*; *years* (ears); *ax* (ask), and *squeeging*. Other spellings suggest, however, that several pronunciations which are represented by only one or two examples in other works were much more widespread in London than might otherwise be thought, such pronunciations as *mouf* (mouth), *oaves* (oaths), *drenk* (drank), *ren* (ran), *gintleman*, *inymies*, *jallowsy*, *athlatic*, *seffral*, *enfy*, while other spellings indicate pronunciations that are not recorded in other contemporary notes on Cockney, *chawms* (charms), *millium*, etc. The epistolary style enabled Thackeray to break away in some directions from the convention for Cockney which had been established since the eighteenth century, and enabled him to reveal his own observation of London speech.

While Dickens and Thackeray were writing their early novels, Henry Mayhew was collecting the material for his great sociological work, *London Labour and the London Poor*, which was published in its complete form in 1861. This work is a sympathetic examination of the conditions of life and work of the London costermongers, beggars, vagrants, and criminals. Mayhew's method was to get Londoners to tell their own stories, and as he usually reproduces their own words, the four volumes of his work are an invaluable repository of Cockney as it was spoken in the first half of the nineteenth century. There is some variation in the pronunciations used by different speakers, but the rougher Cockneys do not differ greatly from one another. A typical specimen is the following:

> "I vos at von time a coster, riglarly brought up to the business, the times vas good then; but, lor, ve used to lush at such a rate! About ten year ago, I ses to meself, I say Bill, I'm blowed if this here game 'ill do any longer. I had a good moke and a tidyish box ov a cart; so vot does I do, but goes and sees von o' my old pals that gits into the coal-line somehow. He and I goes to the Bell and Siven Mackerels in the Mile End Road, and then he tells me all he knowed, and takes me along vith hisself, and from that time I sticks to the coals.
>
> "I niver cared much about the lush myself, and ven I got avay from the old uns, I didn't mind it no how; but Jack my pal vos a awful lushy cove, he couldn't do no good at nothink,

votsomever; he died they say of *lirium trumans* . . . vich I takes to be too much of Trueman and Hanbury's heavy; so I takes varnin by poor Jack and cuts the lush; but if you thinks as ve don't enjoy ourselves sometimes, I tells you, you don't know nothink about it, I'm gittin' on like a riglar house a fire." (Vol. II, p. 97.)

As this passage suggests, Mayhew adopts the conventions of Cockney pronunciation, and practically all the pronunciations he indicates are common in other works. The most valuable elements in his reports are the idioms and slang terms. The abundance of his dialogue, the variety of the speakers, all drawn from the lower ranks of Londoners, and his avoidance of literary effects make the book the most reliable evidence upon the slang and idiom of Cockney in the first half of the century. A larger vocabulary of slang words could be gathered from Pierce Egan's work and the slang dictionaries of the time, but these works cannot be relied upon as guides to the terms most popular among the ordinary working-men of London. But although Mayhew does not attempt to make his Cockney dialogue a philological parade, he does suggest that some Cockneys were over-fond of slang. Cockneys often employ slang as a form of wit, and one very interesting example of this is given by Mayhew in the form of the advertisement of a "springer-up" or slop-clothier. This advertisement is far richer in slang than the speech of the ordinary Cockneys who appear in Mayhew's book, but it gives a good idea of how far the Victorian Cockney could go:

Slap-up Tog and out-and-out Kicksies Builder.

Mr. —— nabs the chance of putting his customers awake, that he has just made his escape from Russia, not forgetting to clap his mawleys upon some of the right sort of Ducks, to make single and double backed Slops for gentlemen in Black, when on his return home he was stunned to find one of the top manufacturers of Manchester had cut his lucky and stepped off to the Swan Stream, leaving behind him a valuable stock of Moleskins, Cords, Velveteens, Plushes, Swandowns, &c., and I having some ready in my kick, grabbed the chance, and stepped home with my swag, and am now landed at my crib. I can turn out toggery of every description very slap-up, at the following low prices for

Ready Gilt—Tick being no go.

Upper Benjamins, built on a downy plan, a monarch to half a finuff. Slap up Velveteen Togs, lined with the same, 1 pound 1 quarter and a peg. Moleskin ditto, any colour, lined with the same, 1 couter. A pair of Kerseymere Kicksies any colour, built very slap up, with the artful dodge, a canary. Pair of stout Cord ditto, built in the 'Melton Mowbray' style, half a sov. Pair of very good broad Cloth ditto, made very saucy, 9 bob and a kick. Pair of long sleeve Moleskin, all colours, built hanky-spanky, with a double fakement down the side and artful buttons at bottom, half a monarch. Pair of stout ditto, built very serious, 9 times. Pair of out-and-out fancy sleeve Kicksies, cut to drop down on the trotters, 2 bulls. Waist Togs, cut long, with moleskin back and sleeves, 10 peg. Blue cloth ditto, cut slap, with pearl buttons, 14 peg. Mud Pipes, Knee Caps, and Trotter Cases, built very low.

"A decent allowance made to Seedy Swells, Tea Kettle Purgers, Head Robbers, and Flunkeys out of collar."

The novels of James Greenwood which appeared so frequently between 1865 and 1895 share much of the sincerity of Mayhew's work, and his sketches of London life and London scenes, although not so strictly sociological in purpose as Mayhew's study, are informed by direct observation more than was usual in novels of London life. The dialogue of Greenwood's Cockneys does not differ in essentials from the reports which appear in Mayhew's work. The interchange of *w* and *v*, which was the chief characteristic of Dickens's Cockneys, is used sparingly, but is not entirely dispensed with, so that such a passage as the following is in the direct line of the Cockney dialect which is represented by previous commentators. In this passage Bonsor, a London urchin whom the author had met at Epsom Downs, explains why the gamins of the London streets flocked to the racecourse:

> "Chance of picking up a job or so. That's what brings all us coves down here . . . there's the c'rect card coves—two bob a dozen at the Stand, and a werry tidy pull for coves with a bit of money to lay out; and then there's cigar-lights, and dolls to stick in the hats, and noses and hair, and clean yer boots, and all sorts of amoosing things for gents what wins. Then there's the brushing coves and them as fetches water, and them as looks arter the empty bottles and the bones. Lor'! I can't tell you half on 'em. Well, don't yer see, it's all spekerlation, and that's the beauty on it. You never know what's going to turn up one minit from another. Why, I knows a man who once had a pound given him for fetching a pail of water. . . . You might make a crown and you mightn't make enough to get a lift home in a wan." (*Journeys through London*, c. 1880.)

The humours of Cockney character and Cockney speech have always been grateful to *Punch*, and in no other source is it so easy to trace the changes in the dialect. The earliest Cockney dialogue in *Punch* is strictly in the style of Dickens and Thackeray. Thus, the two verse-letters which Mr. John Thomas of Belgravia sent to his cousin, Mr. Robert Snaffles, describing the Coronation of the Czar in 1856, which were published in October 1856, admirably burlesque the earliest form of literary Cockney:

"Well, fryda horgust twenty nine it was theer hopenin day
And if the Hentry into mosko were whats kawled a grand sooksay:
But ho! to tel you arf of wot I eard & thort & sor
Wood take me arf a wollum, wich peraps mite be a bor:
So though mi magnum bonum ave a kvorto at its tip,
Hile do as MISTUR ROGERS trewly ses the flees do—Skip!
Supphisit then to tell u the persesshink reeched a mile
And sumtimes made I cry Onkore, and sumtimes made I smile:
Fust cum a sqwod a Coarse sacks, with their trumpets & their drums,
A playink hof the Rooshin 'C the Konkrin ero cums':
Then on orses hand in youniforms, sum holdish and sum nu
A lot of Knobs or nobles, hall a ridink 2 & 2;
Nex road the warius races as the rooshin Zars ave wun,
Wich thanks to er Allize as yet the turkish izzent 1"; etc.

About twenty years later, *Punch* began to publish a series of Cockney letters which achieved considerable reputation, the rhyming letters written by 'Arry to his pal Charlie. The letters continued to be published for many years and 'Arry almost replaced Sam Weller as the archetypal Cockney. His language, although fundamentally of the traditional type, is interesting for the fact that the interchange of *w* and *v* is abandoned and that its vocabulary of slang has been strengthened by an accession of Americanisms. The following passage in which 'Arry describes his adventures on the Ice (23rd February, 1889) is a good specimen of his slangy Cockney dialect:

"We cannoned a pair of rare toffs, fur and feathers, mate, quite *ah lah Roose*!
We wos all in a pile in the hice, and the swell he let hout like the doose.
But his sable-trimmed pardner, a topper, with tootsies *so* tiny, dear boy,
Well I do not believe she arf minded, a spill is a thing gals enjoy.

'Old hup Miss,' I sez; 'no 'arm done: it's all right hup to now don'tcher know,'
And she tipped me a look from her lamps, as was sparklers and fair in a glow:
If she didn't admire me—well there, 'Arry don't want to gas, but 'Em Bates
Got the needle tremenjus, I tell yer, and threatened to take orf the skates.

I soon smoothed '*er* feathers down, Charlie. But, oh! the rum look and the smile
As that other one tipped me each time as we passed. She'd a heye for true style
She 'ad and no error. Lor' bless yer, the right sort, *they* knows the right sort,
And that's wy I 'old as Park-Skating's a proper Socierty Sport," etc.

A few years before *Punch* itself had made this type of Cockney *vieux jeu* by giving a specimen of the dialect which is essentially of the type now used by the portrayers of Cockney characters, in which *ow* is represented by *ah*, and long *a* by *i*. We leave the discussion of this, however, for the chapter on Modern Cockney.

The last of the orthoepists to describe a Cockney dialect which corresponds exactly with that represented by the scholars and novelists of the eighteenth and nineteenth centuries was Heinrich Baumann, whose *Londonismen*, a study of slang and vulgar speech, was published in 1887. Baumann was a graduate of the University of London and head master of the Anglo-German School in London. He claimed that the material for his book was collected by himself in the London streets:

Tell ye 'ow? Vy, in rum kens,
In flash cribs and slum dens,
I' the alleys and courts,
'Mong the doocedest sorts:

When jawin' with Jillie,
Or Mag and 'er Billie,
Ve shoved down in black,
Their iligant clack.

So from hartful young dodgers,
From vaxy old codgers,
From the blowens ve got
Soon to know vot is vot.

An examination of his book, however, suggests that this claim is not entirely justified. Much of the material was gathered from the slang dictionaries of Grose and others, or from the Cockney dialogue of Dickens, Mayhew, and Henry Sketchley, although he certainly collected a good deal of Cockney slang at first hand. But in pronunciation Baumann was content to describe the Cockney of literary convention. The vowels and diphthongs which we now regard as characteristic of Cockney were as common then as now, but Baumann does not mention them. His analysis of Cockney pronunciation and grammar differs hardly at all from that given by Elphinston, Walker, and Pegge. He regarded the interchange of *w* and *v* as still the chief Cockney characteristic, although Alexander Ellis declared about the same time that this pronunciation was unfamiliar to him in actual London speech. For these parts of his subject Baumann relied upon literary Cockney and not "the doocedest sorts".

The Cockney dialect described by Baumann had been a literary convention for over two hundred years. In that time it had scarcely changed. Its chief characteristics were the interchange of *w* and *v*, the omission of initial *h* and the insertion of *h* in words which normally begin with a vowel. In these and many of the minor characteristics the dialect had not changed from that employed by Machyn and the churchwardens in the sixteenth and seventeenth centuries. The only important development had been in slang. From the end of the eighteenth century slang came to be regarded as one of the chief characteristics of the dialect, and it was in this aspect of Cockney that novelists indulged their own observation. In pronunciation they were content to follow the convention.

The great difference between the pronunciations indicated by Dickens and modern novelists has given rise to an idea that Cockneys used to speak "good" English, vitiated only by a few comic mannerisms like *w* for *v* and *v* for *w*. On the other hand, the diphthongs and vowels which are now characteristic of Cockney are alleged to be recent barbarisms. Some German scholars have even formulated a great Cockney Sound-Shift which is supposed to have taken place about 1880! But, as we shall show later, there are strong reasons for believing that Dickens is not an infallible guide and that the Cockney Sound-Shift should be shifted.

CHAPTER III

PRESENT-DAY COCKNEY

THE existence of a Cockney dialect different from that represented in literary work since the eighteenth century broke in upon the literary consciousness about 1882. In a note to *Captain Brassbound's Conversion*, Bernard Shaw said he had taken the liberty of making a special example of Drinkwater's Cockney dialect—"for the benefit of the mass of readers outside London who still form their notions of Cockney dialect on Sam Weller". He adds a personal note on the subject:

> When I came to London in 1876, the Sam Weller dialect had passed away so completely that I should have given it up as a literary fiction if I had not discovered it surviving in a Middlesex village and heard of it from an Essex one. Some time in the eighties the late Andrew Tuer called attention in the Pall Mall Gazette to several peculiarities of modern Cockney, and to the obsolescence of the Dickens dialect that was still being copied from book to book by authors who never dreamt of using their ears, much less of training them to listen. Then came Mr. Anstey's Cockney dialogues in Punch, a great advance, and Mr. Chevalier's coster songs and patter. The Tompkins verses contributed by Mr. Barry Pain to the London Daily Chronicle also did something to bring the literary convention for Cockney English up to date. But Tompkins sometimes perpetrated horrible solecisms. He would pronounce face as fice, accurately enough, but he would rhyme it quite impossibly to nice, which Tompkins would have pronounced as nawce: for example, Mawl Enn Rowd for Mile End Road.

> This aw for i, which I have made Drinkwater use, is the latest stage of the old diphthongal oi, which Mr. Chevalier still uses.

This judgment, as we shall see, is somewhat exaggerated. But it is certainly true that the vowels and diphthongs which we now consider characteristic of Cockney find little or no representation in literary Cockney before Tuer began his Cockney imitations.

Tuer was not the first writer to comment upon these new sounds, however. In *Punch's Almanac* for 1882, under du Maurier's drawing "The Steam Launch in Venice", there appears the following passage of Cockney dialogue:

> *'Andsome 'Arriet.* Ow my, if it 'yn't that bloomin' old Temple Bar, as they did aw'y with out o' Fleet Street!
>
> *Mr. Belleville (referring to Guide-book).* No, it 'yn't. It's the fymous Bridge o' SIGHS, as Byron went and stood on: 'im as wrote OUR BOYS, yer know.
>
> *'Andsome 'Arriet.* Well, I NEVER. It 'yn't much of a SIZE any'ow.
>
> *Mr. Belleville.* 'Ear, 'ear! Fustryte.

And on the 4th December in the same year, the Reverend A. J. D. D'Orsey, who was professor of Public Reading at King's College in the University of London, wrote to the School Board for London the following description of the speech of London children:

> Such words as *paper*, *shape*, *train*, are pronounced *piper*, *shipe*, *trine*,—the very first letter of the alphabet being thus wrongly taught. *Cab* is *keb*, *bank* is *benk*, *strand* is *strend*; *light* is almost *loyt*; the short *i* is made *ee*, e.g. "second edeeshon"; *no* is *now*; *mountain* is *meowntain*; *stupid* is *stoopid*, and many more. The final consonants are so feebly uttered that it is sometimes impossible to tell whether the pupil says *life*, or *like*,

or *light*. "H" is constantly transposed. "G" is dropped in such words as *coming*, *going*, etc., or is turned into *k* in *nothink*. Most pupils cannot trill the *r*, burring it in the throat, or making it a *w*, *dwink* for *drink*. In many cases *r* appears improperly at the ends of words, thus *Maida-hill* as *Myder-eel*, *Maria Ann* as *Maria ran*.

Although these quotations contain references to some pronunciations with which we are familiar in the earlier type of Cockney, they are principally concerned with those diphthongs and vowels which are now considered characteristic of vulgar London speech. They are, therefore, our first authoritative evidence upon the existence of the present-day Cockney dialect.

As Shaw indicates, the first writer to make any extensive use of the new dialect was Andrew W. Tuer, who was responsible for *The Kaukneigh Awlminek*, edited by "'Enery 'Arris" and published by Field and Tuer in 1883. In this work the chief characteristic of the older type of Cockney is formally buried: "in regard to the use of the letter V for W, 'Bevare of the viddy, Samivel my boy, bevare of the viddy,' Mr. Samuel Weller was exceptional in his pronunciation". This, the predominant feature of literary Cockney in the nineteenth century, is replaced by a group of new sounds, as in this passage:

There's a lot uv well dressed yeng fellers 'oo rides regler by 'bus to en' from the City wich I can't sem'ow quite myke out. They awlwiz try for a seat by the driver, 'oo appears to be their deerist friend, en' they 'ev a noddin' acquynetince with 'moust every 'bus driver they meets. They talks bettin' en' blahsphemy about 'arf en' arf, en' moustly speaks in a unedookyted sort uv a manner; en' (enlike en' me, they leaves out their *g*'s et the end uv words wich ought t' 'ev 'em, ez

> *bettin'*, *smowkin'*—they all smowke—*gemblin'*, *swearin'* en' sitchlike) . . . them eyen't soadern milk yeng men: them's beer en' skittles yeng men.

And in his *Thenks Awfly*, 1890, this type of dialect is slightly developed in an attempt to make the phonetic representation more exact.

The new sounds represented by the Tuer's phonetic spellings are the following—the examples being taken from both the works mentioned:

> *Long a pronounced long i:* myke, engyged, relytions, eyen't, acquynetince.
>
> *Long i pronounced ah or oi:* tahm, quaht, nahn, mah, bah; or noight, loike, moine, foine, toime.
>
> *Long o pronounced ow:* owm (home), Jowve, now (no), sowp, down't, bouth, stoun.
>
> *Ow pronounced ah or aow:* flahs (flowers), paounds, naow, abaout, craown.
>
> *Short u pronounced like short e:* entil, ether, kentry, seppers, inselt, etc.

These spellings cannot be regarded as exact phonetic representations (and Alexander J. Ellis said he did not recognise the last of them as a Cockneyism at all), but they are sufficiently like some dominant sounds used in present-day Cockney to show that the present-day dialect was fully developed about 1880. Many of the other pronunciations represented by Tuer as features of this dialect are by no means new, however, as we may see from such typical spellings as: *towld*, *ould*; *ketchin'*, *bellence*; *lawst*, *tauss*, *dawg*; *amooz*, *moosic*; *fust*, *wuss*; *ivvery*, *ginerly*; *parding*, *a-settin'*; *'eard*, *'orses*; *wot*, *wite*; *drawring*, *jawrache*; *winder*, *yeller*; etc.

Before leaving Tuer, we may draw upon another of

his works, the interesting little booklet, *Old London Street Cries*, 1885, for a description of the pronunciation of the names of the stations on that recent London acquisition, the Inner Circle Railway. It is significant that the new Cockney pronunciation was associated with railway porters, since the older type of Cockney had for so long been associated with cabbies. Only one of the station-names, Tuer alleges, was pronounced in the normal fashion, the names being sounded as follows: *Emma Smith*, *South Kenzint'un*, *Glawster Rowd* (*owd* as in "loud"), *I street Kenzint'un*, *Nottin' Ill Gite*, *Queen's Rowd Bizewater*, *Pride Street Peddinten*, *Edge-wer Rowd* (by common consent the Cockney refrains from saying Hedge-wer), *Biker Street*, *Portland Rowd*, *Gower Street* (the only one usually pronounced as other people do), *King's Krauss* (often abbreviated to *ng's Krauss*), *Ferrinden Street*, *Oldersgit Street*, *Mawgit Street*, *Bishergit*, *Ol'git*, *Mark Line*, *Monneym'nt*, *Kennun Street*, *Menshun Ouse*, *Bleckfriars*, *Tempull* (pull-pull-Tempull), *Chairin' Krauss*, *Wes'minster* (one sometimes hears *Wesminister*), *S'n Jimes-iz Pawk*, *Victaw-ia*, *Slown Square* (*own* as in "town").

Anstey's Cockney dialogues were not so strongly phonetic in the new style as Tuer's. He inclined to avoid the new vowels and diphthongs as well as the Dickensian *w*'s and *v*'s. But in the sketch "In an Omnibus", which was published in a volume of reprints from *Punch* called *Voces Populi*, 1890, he gives a passage of Cockney repartee which is quite modern:

> *The Conductor.* Benk, benk! (*he means "Bank"*) 'oborn benk! 'Igher up there, Bill, can't you?

A Dingy Man Smoking, in a Van. Want to block up the ole o' the road, eh? That's right!

The Conductor (roused to personality). Go 'ome, Dirty Dick! syme old soign, I see,—"Monkey an' Poipe!" (*To Coachman of smart brougham which is pressing rather closely behind.*) I say, old man, don't you race after my bus like this—you'll only tire your 'orse.

[*The Coachman affects not to have heard.*]

The Conductor (addressing the brougham horse whose head is almost through the door of the omnibus). 'Ere, '*ang* it all!—step insoide, if yer want to!

[*Brougham falls to rear—triumph of Conductor as scene closes.*]

Albert Chevalier made his reputation with the coster songs he began to sing in the early 'nineties. The published versions of these songs do not usually reflect the new Cockney sounds in detail. But Chevalier ventured a fairly detailed phonetic representation of Coster dialect in his sketch, *The God and the Star.* After his tour in America, he was approached by Ellen Terry to give a performance on behalf of the Society for the Prevention of Cruelty to Children. Chevalier thereupon suggested that he and Ellen Terry should do a Cockney *Romeo and Juliet.* The suggestion did not bear fruit, but its outcome was this duologue between the costermonger 'Enery 'Awkins and the actress Nell Perry. The first speech of 'Enery shows the kind of Cockney dialect which Chevalier employed:

"Lor lumme! Wot a lot of toffs there is abaht! One o' them fancy dress balls at the Garding last night. Ain't the boys been a chivvyin' some on 'em! Them as can't git cabs to take 'em 'ome! I've just left King Charles an' Oliver Cromwell 'avin' a cup o' thick an' a doorstep at the corfee stall. King Charles was off 'is peck but 'adn't 'e got a thirst on 'im! Lor! couldn't he shift the corfee! 'Ere! this won't do. I can't afford ter do the eavy an' lounge abaht!—my time's valuable. If I buys cheap an' sells dear, I'm a-goin' to take the doner to the theatre to-night to see Nell Perry act—an' she can act! Lor! when I see 'er play Desdemoner, I wanted to git dahn an' prop Otheller, an' I would too if Lizer 'adn't clawed 'old of me. Lizer finks I'm stuck on Nell Perry, but as I sez, I admires 'er as a hartist, but it don't foller 'cos I blews a bob for a front seat in the Gawds of a Saturday night as I'm goin' to hoffer 'er marriage. Nell Perry's ore right in 'er business, varry good; but for Eppin' or 'Ampstead, or for a 'op rahnd in front of a barril orgin, give me Lizer."

Two stages may be observed in Barry Pain's Cockney. His earliest work either shuns the interchange of *w* and *v* and ignores the new Cockney sounds, or it makes a moderate use of the Dickensian features. Thus in his early book *De Omnibus Rebus*, 1888, he gives the following specimen of Cockney:

"Werry sorry to hinterrup' you, mum," says the conductor, looking in, "but didn't you say 'Wigo Street' 'cos we passed that hever so long ago? . . . your conwersation were that hinter*est*ing, I never thought about the street a-flyin' past—I'm werry sorry I'm sure, mum." (p. 174.)

although in an earlier conversation in the same book (p. 9) between two old Cockneys of nearly eighty there is no example of the interchange of *w* and *v*, and even the old man of eighty-four who breaks in on their conversation fails to use that old Cockneyism. On the other hand, in the Tompkins verses in *The Daily Chronicle*, Barry Pain adopted the type of Cockney first used by Tuer, and later even developed it. Thus in *De Omnibus*, 1901, he made a valiant attempt to grapple with the difficulties of representing modern Cockney. The conductor's opening complaint about females is typical:

"I don't unnerstand femiles.

"The other dye I 'appened ter pick up a extry 'alf-thick-un throo puttin' money on my opinyun of the Gran' Neshnal. Well, nar, the fancy tikin' me, I drops in on a plice as were a cut above whart I patterinizes as a yooshal thing. As I sye, I were a-goin' ter enjy myself, so I orders my steak, cut thick, underdone, and a bit o' fat to it, an' my pint o' Burton sime as if I'd bin the Lord Meer 'isself. Then I tikes a look rarnd. Theer were two femiles, as 'ed jest done. They were settin' doin' nutthink. Theer were a witer oppersite ter them, close enough ter 'ave bit 'em, and 'e weren't doin' nutthink neither. Pressintly a gint calls 'im an' orf 'e goes. The momint 'e stawts ter wite on summun else they both of 'em 'ollers art 'Witer' as if they 'adn't a second ter speer. Pressently 'e comes. One of 'em says, 'Give me the bill, witer.' 'E pulls 'is shoulders up ter wheer an Hinglishman would wear 'is 'at, and begins ter mike art theer bill.

" 'Tew breads an' tew butters,' 'e says.

" 'Nutthink o' the sort,' says the femile. 'It's tew butters an' one bread.' 'E orlters it an' 'ands 'er the bill.

" 'Oh, you silly man,' she syes. 'I wants tew bills. My lyedy-friend 'ere pyes fur 'er own.' "

Shaw's own attempt to transfer Cockney to paper was as detailed as it could be without the use of a phonetic alphabet. He made a few blunders in his transcription, one at least being due to an imperfect understanding of the phonetic symbols used by Sweet, but as the following specimen of Drinkwater's dialect in *Captain Brassbound's Conversion*, 1899, shows, Shaw was on the whole a careful and original observer:

Bless yr awt, y' cawnt be a pawrit naradys. Waw the aw seas is wuss pleest nor Piccadilly Suckus. If aw was to do orn thet there Hetlentic Hawcean the things aw did as a bwoy in the Worterleoo Rowd, awd ev maw air cat afore aw could turn maw ed. Pawrit be blaowed!—awskink yr pawdn, gavner. Nah, jest to shaow you ah little thet there striteforard man y' mide mention on knaowed wot e was atorkin abaht: oo would you spowse was the marster to wich kepn Brarsbahnd served apprentice, as yr mawt sy? . . . Gawdn, gavner, Gawdn o Kawtoom—stetcher stends in Trifawlgr Square to this dy.

The authors mentioned by Shaw were by no means the only pioneers of the modern literary Cockney. Some writers, like George R. Sims, continued to use the old convention for a time, even though they were very familiar with the dialect actually spoken by Londoners. But most authors whose work involved using Cockney dialogue adopted the new manner, Somerset Maugham in *Liza of Lambeth*, 1897, Pett Ridge in *Mord Em'ly*, Richard Whiteing in *No. 5 John Street*, Edwin W. Pugh in *A Street in Suburbia* and many later novels and sketches, Clarence Rook in *The Hooligan Nights*, A. Neil Lyons in *Hookey* and later stories. Since that time the Cockney convention settled in the 'eighties has remained unchanged.

Edwin W. Pugh, whose work has been sadly neglected in the few discussions of Cockney speech, reveals an intimate knowledge of the dialect, particularly of its vocabulary and idiom. He does not attempt to give a complete representation of Cockney pronunciation, but his acquaintance with the subtleties of Cockney speech, the differences of idiom and slang as between Cockney and Cockney, is the outcome of a sympathetic understanding of Londoners themselves. His first book, *A Street in Suburbia*, 1895, which deals with incidents in the ordinary life of the inhabitants of Marsh Street, is a remarkable study of Cockney life, free from the excessive humour and sensationalism of many other writers.

This intimacy is admirably reflected in the speech which old Sheckles made at the marriage-feast of Jack Cotter and Maria Canlan, a speech which in its mixture of pedantry, sentimentality, and affection represents justly those Cockney characteristics which were overdrawn or idealised in the Coster ditties of the music-halls:

> "I ain't much of a speaker," said Sheckles, when everyone was quiet, "an' it ain't in me ter make a long fandangle. But I hev give away terday a m'iden to a man—which they're ole frien's both, though young otherwise or comparatively so—an' I've took on meself as a giver-away, the dooties o' thet parient who is, so ter speak, a time-expired man in the realms o' glory. . . . The poet sez, when somethin's whatsername we what d'yer call it mingle, an' I'm o' the syme opinion. There's a deal o' what I call mootual trust like abart a weddin'. The man 'e sez: "Ere's a woman as I ain't know'd long, but who I like instinctive. Fer all I know, she may turn art a reg'lar art an' art 'ot 'un, or a right-darn good 'un. Anyway, I'll tyke 'er an' make the best on 'er.' An' the woman she sez, 'I'm nuts on 'im.' Jest thet. But it means a lot. She don't weigh 'im up. Not she! She tykes 'im fer better or wuss, wi' the long odds on 'is bein' wuss. She's nuts on 'im —thet's ernough fer 'er. . . . I ain't a married man meself, through not never 'avin' bin pop'lar wi' the lydies, but I've often thort I'd like ter be one—thet's stri'ght. Don't laugh. P'r'aps you've felt a bit lonely yerself sometimes when you've bin settin' over yer fire, an' yer pipe wont drawr, an' yer back's cold. An' you've thort p'r'aps of other men wi' their wives an' children a' 'overin' round 'em. I know I hev. An' so I say: "Ere's luck an' health an' long life an' 'appiness ter the man an' woman as I've give away ter one another terday. May they always enj'y life, an' never 'ave no quarrels, trustin' in the good Lord, an' buckin' up fer theirselves when times is bad."
>
> Old Sheckles blew his nose and grinned vacuously.
>
> "Let 'er go," he said. And the toast was drunk with acclamation.

Clarence Rook's book, *The Hooligan Nights*, 1899, is of a very different kind. The author had been introduced by Mr. Grant Richards, the publisher, to a young thief, Alf of Lambeth, who had sent him a manuscript of confessions. Rook struck up a friendship with Alf and in this book he tried to set forth, as far as possible in Alf's own words, certain scenes from criminal life. Alf was a cheerful rascal who enjoyed his hand-to-mouth existence so much that when extracts from the book were published in *The Daily Chronicle* early in 1899, there was an outcry from its readers that the life of a criminal was being painted in alluring colours. The dialect of Alf is not a phonetic record, but his vocabulary is admirably represented. Alf used far too many canting terms, the technical language of thieves, to be regarded as a typical Cockney, but he used most of the normal slang, too. The following passage, in which Alf describes a fight he had with a labourer on Barnes Common, is free from cant and may stand as a good sample of "out-and-out" Cockney:

> I'd settled in me mind that I'd go a bit light for the first two or free rounds so's I could see what the lab'rer was made of wivout gettin' winded meself. But I soon found I'd got me work cut out if I wanted to stan' up 'gainst him for long. I was quicker'n what 'e was, but I was givin' 'im two stone an' more. After the first round it didn't look over an' above rosy for your 'umble. Still there wasn't nuffink broken, nor yet in the second round neiver.
>
> We 'adn't 'ardly got into the third round 'fore I see I'd got a reg'lar sneezer to 'andle. An' 'bout 'arf way froo I got a flattener on me razzo that pretty nigh laid me out, an' fore I knew anyfink more my right-eye went in for early closin'. 'Ealfy, wasn't it? Much as I could do to keep stannin' up that round.

> Well, I settled in me mind that round four was to be my look in if I wasn't to go under, so I went for the lab'rer wiv all me bloody might, an' got in free hot 'uns on 'is ribs that fair made 'is timbers crack, an' 'fore the round was finished I'd landed a couple of stingers on 'is dial that seprised 'im proper.
>
> The fifth round was 'ammer an' tongs again, an' the lab'rer got one of my teef to give notice, but I got one back on 'is jore, an' there was the lab'rer comin' at me wiv 'is tongue 'angin right out of 'is mouf. Well, I see me chance then, an' I give 'im a upper cut that made 'im fair bite into 'is tongue an' go down full length on the grass. The next round was the last, an' a little 'oliday it was wiv no error. 'E couldn't 'ardly put up 'is dukes be that time, an' I knocked 'im out first time I smacked 'im.

By the end of the nineteenth century the Cockney used by Dickens had passed into the limbo of outworn literary conventions, and a new convention for Cockney had been established. Thus in Pett Ridge's *Mord Em'ly*, 1898, the philological purpose which is evident in the work of Tuer, Shaw, and even Barry Pain has been modified for literary purposes, and the Cockney pronunciations, although of the new school, are symbolistic rather than exhaustive. This is evident in the dialogue between Mord Em'ly and Miss Gilliken à propos of Mr. Henry Barden:

> "He pelled on to me first," she said excusingly. "I'd seen him about once or twice before you went away, but he'd never spoke till Tuesday night. Up he comes and he ses, ''Ullo!' and I says, ''Ullo, your own self, and see how you like it.' "
>
> Mord Em'ly nodded her head in silent approval of this repartee.
>
> "And he ses, 'Where's that shortish gel,' he ses, 'with a round fice, and no colour to speak of, that used to be about with your set? Mother lives in Pandorer,' he says."
>
> "Meaning me?"

"So I says, 'What's it got to do with you?' and he says, 'Oh,' he says, 'I only ast.' And he goes off."

"What after that?" asked Mord Em'ly.

"Met him again to-night, and he comes up, and he says, 'There you are, then?' and I says, 'Well, what of it?' And he says, 'Seen anything of her?' And I says, 'Mind your own bis'ness.' And he says, 'Come for a strowl down the Walworth Road?' "

"Did he talk about me again?"

"He didn't talk much 'bout anything," said Miss Gilliken; "but all he did say was 'bout you, and——"

"'Ere's a 'orse down," interrupted Mord Em'ly. "Let's stop and watch."

A similar convention is observed in Richard Whiteing's *No. 5 John Street*, which made such a sensation when it was first published in 1899. Previously Whiteing had written books in the old style of Cockney. His early book, *Mr. Sprouts his Opinions*, 1867, was partly inspired by James Greenwood's work, particularly *Night in a Workhouse*, which had appeared in the previous year. The opinions are written by Mr. Sprouts in an orthographical style sanctioned by the epistles of Jeames Yellowplush, and the pronunciations thereby reflected are characteristically Dickensian, the chief features being the interchange of *w* and *v* and the loss and addition of *h*, with no hint of the diphthongs and vowels of the new literary Cockney. But in *No. 5 John Street* not only Whiteing's literary ability but his Cockney dialect, too, was transformed. Inspired by the work of Tuer, Pain, and Pett Ridge, he made the inhabitants of No. 5 speak the same dialect as Mord Em'ly and Miss Gilliken. A typical example is the passage in which Low Covey replies to enquiries about the inhabitants of No. 5:

> Who is the—the "old cure"?
> Blest if I know. They calls him Old '48. Sort o' Republican. No kings or queens. Billposter when he kin git it to do. But a Scholar though; I will say that. Always readin' and writin'. Preaches about it in Hy' Par'. Brings out a paper all by hisself, so I'm tould. Never done me no 'arm.
> And the tall man in black, who called him an old fool?
> Fellow-lodger. Foreigner. Mr. Izreel, or some name o' that sort. One of these 'ere Anarcheests—suthin abaout blowin' people inside out, I heerd say. Commune, if you know what that means: I don't.

These specimens of the new literary Cockney are sufficient for our purpose. Since the last decade of the nineteenth century the same convention has been observed by all writers. Some novelists, like Thomas Burke and Julian Franklyn, have genuine and intimate knowledge of the language of London. Others, and they are the majority, seem to know it only from books. A few writers attempt to show the most important sounds of the dialect and its characteristic vocabulary and idiom, others are satisfied with employing a few spellings like *piper* and *tahn*—or even *orl* and *wot* for "all" and "what"—and stock vulgarisms like "Gaw-blimey". The fact is that if a novelist attempted to reproduce Cockney as it is actually spoken few of his readers would understand it, the slang would necessitate extensive footnotes and the pronunciation would demand an interlinear gloss. This is evident from the brave attempt made by Mr. W. McEager, in an article in the *Contemporary Review*, 1922, to set down a specimen of Cockney:

> Vere was a bloke goin' dahn Tah'r Bridge Road, an' ve Decima Stree' click se' abaht 'im. Vey dropped 'im one, wen'

> froo 'is chain an' lockets, 'alf inched 'is splosh and lef' 'im barmy. Arter a bi' came along a parson, 'oo fought 'e was blindo an' steered righ' rahnd 'im. Arter annover li'l bi' one of ve club yobos came along, 'ad a dekko a' 'im an' said, "'Ere, I ain' goin' to be mixed up in a rough 'ahse, my name's drippin'!" so 'e 'opped it too. Bimeby came along a Jew boy, 'oo 'ad a peep a' 'im, an' felt real sorry for ve poor bloke. So 'e picked 'im aht of ve gu'er, fahnd 'is 'at and pu' it on 'is napper, an' took 'im to ve doss 'ahse, where 'e kipped 'imself. In ve morning, 'e said to ve boss, "Look 'ere, guvnor, this poor bloke ain' 'alf 'ad a kybosh, you look arter 'im an' I'll see you Sa'urday night." Nah ven, which of vose free blokes was a real Chrischen? . . . ve Jew boy? No' 'alf 'e weren't.

This story, a modern paraphrase of the parable of the good Samaritan, was told by the leader of a boys' club in Bermondsey. I am afraid it does not completely represent the Cockney pronunciation; no Cockney would think, for example, of pronouncing the *t* in "about", "thought", etc., or the *k* in "bloke" and "lockets", and a dyed-in-the-wool Cockney would probably replace the *p* in "napper" and "dripping" by the glottal stop. But the passage sufficiently indicates the dilemma of the novelist who would be realistic. The symbolistic treatment of Cockney is the only satisfactory method for the popular writer. Those readers who know the dialect will supply the deficiencies; the rest will be content in their ignorance.

The Cockney dialect at the present time is extremely varied, for many reasons. The London area is too large and the population too mixed for any uniform system of pronunciation to exist, and such social factors as education have produced many modifications of even the characteristic sounds. But broad Cockney, the speech of the slums and poorer districts, is as uniform as can be expected in a dialect. There are subtle differences in the speech of individuals, which correspond to the differences between village and village which exist in provincial dialects, but the different sounds belong to the same phoneme, or species. Many of these Cockney sounds, particularly the vowels and diphthongs, are due to the slackness of Cockney speech; Cockneys avoid movement of the lips and jaw as far as possible, preserving a roughly half-open position of the lips. This habit causes a slight but very noticeable nasalisation and leads to a slight rounding of vowel sounds which need a full opening of the lips for their correct articulation. As a further tendency of the dialect is to centralise back vowels and diphthongs, many sounds which are widely separated in standard speech become closer to one another in Cockney—this being the obvious cause of many confusions in the literary representations of Cockney, and the resultant acrimonious disputes between the observers of the dialect. The general effect of these tendencies is to make the dialect rather confused and flabby, an effect which is increased by the habit of many Londoners, particularly women, to drag out an accented syllable (e.g. whisk . . . ers, pota . . . to). The Cockney himself has no difficulty in understanding the dialect, of course, but to many outsiders it appears whining and flaccid. This judgment is probably true of the speech of many Cockney women, but other Cockneys, costermongers in particular, overcome the defect by a loud utterance which transforms the dialect into a speech which is vigorous and confident, although ugly and raucous. It is not insignificant that Cockneys are usually represented in literature and on the stage as either cheerful vulgarians or maudlin sentimentalists, a division which corresponds to the differences in speech.

In vowel sounds, the dominant feature of Cockney is its use of diphthongs in words which in standard English are pronounced with monophthongs, and its use of monophthongs where standard English employs diphthongs. Instead of standard [i:] in *me*, *see*, *tree*, *speak*, *seize*, etc., the Cockney employs a diphthong formed by a slight glide vowel, like the final vowel in "father", "extra", followed by a somewhat retracted form of the standard vowel: [məi], [səi], [trəi], [spəik], [səiz], etc. The vowel [u:] employed in standard English in such words as *too*, *do*, *boot*, *who*, *glue*, etc., is sometimes replaced by a diphthong, in which the first element is a similar glide and the second a slightly advanced form of the standard vowel, [təü], [dəü], [bəüt], [əü], [gləü]: at other times only the advanced vowel is used. For the standard diphthong [au] in *town*, *down*, *cloud*, *round*, *cow*, *sow*, *now*, a monophthong is employed in the broadest form of the dialect. This monophthong is a vowel between the standard *ah* and short *u*, long and slightly nasalised, the sound roughly represented in Cockney literature by *ar* or *ah*; but other Cockneys employ a diphthong, the second element being similar to the neutral vowel in "extr*a*", "fath*er*", viz. [tʌ:n] or [tʌən], [dʌ:n] or [dʌən], etc. It should perhaps be mentioned that the last two sounds represent different social dialects within the Cockney dialect. The monophthong is used only by the coarsest speakers and is often burlesqued by Cockneys who use the diphthong.

A few characteristic vowels and diphthongs agree with standard English, however, in being monophthongal or diphthongal. A raised vowel, practically the same as standard short *e*, often replaces the normal short *a*, [keb] *cab*, [ben] *ban*, [ev] *have*, [em] *ham*, etc., and a slightly raised and advanced form of standard *aw* replaces normal short *o* in such words as *off*, *cough*, *God*, *hospital*, *gone*, etc., [ɔ:f], [kɔ:f], [gɔ:d], [ɔ:spiʔu], [gɔ:n]. For the standard diphthong [ei] in *rain*, *pain*, *day*, *place*, *name*, *break*, *weigh*, etc., a central diphthong is employed in Cockney, the first element being approximately the standard sound of short *u* and the second a retracted form of short *i*, [rʌin], [pʌin], [dʌi], [plʌis], [nʌim], [brʌik], [wʌi]. This is the sound represented in literature in such spellings as *piper*, *tible*, etc., although the diphthong is considerably more raised and central than the standard long *i*. The standard sound of long *i* is replaced by a diphthong of the same type, but slightly raised and rounded. This is the sound represented by Tuer's and Anstey's spellings *soigne*, *foine*, *noight*, *toime*, etc., although those spellings considerably exaggerate the amount of rounding. Sometimes the sound is monophthongised, as represented in Tuer's spellings *tahm*, *quaht*, and Shaw's *aw* (high, I), *mawt* (might), etc. The standard diphthong, long *o*, is slightly unrounded and centralised, the first element approximating to short *u*, although rather higher and more retracted. This sound is represented very imperfectly by Tuer's spellings *down't*, *stoun*, *Jowve*, etc., the Cockney diphthong in such words being much higher than standard *ow*. The Cockney tendency to rounding gives the Cockney sound for long *ah* something of the quality of standard *aw*, although such literary spellings as *Kawtoom*, *awt* (heart), *Pawk*, greatly exaggerate the extent of the rounding. Similarly the tendency to centralisation makes the Cockney sound of short *u* more central than the standard sound. It is a vowel between the standard short *u* and the standard vowel in *bird*, *worse*, etc.

The chief consonantal feature of the dialect is the prevalence of the glottal stop, [ʔ], which is a complete break in the stream of sound caused by the closure of the epiglottis. In Cockney, the glottal stop replaces *t* and *k* between vowels, and there is a growing tendency for it to replace *p*. Thus instead of saying "What a lot of little bottles", or "hop up here", the thorough-going Cockney will say [wɔʔ ə lɔʔ ə liʔu bɔʔuz] or [ɔʔ ʌʔ iə]. As these phonetic representations suggest, he is also prone to vocalise *l* after vowels, replacing it by a form of [u], [teu] *tell*, [peu] *pal*, [sʌu] *sail*, *sale*, [tiu] *till*, etc. Shaw represents this sound by *ol*.

The voiced and voiceless forms of *th* are very frequently replaced by *v* and *f*, although this habit is not consistent among Cockneys, *free* (three), *first* (thirst), *fever* (feather), *farver* (father), etc., or even *vis* (this) *ver* (the). The *th* in *farthing* is usually replaced by *d*, and the same consonant is sometimes used in "this", "those", "these", and "further". Initial *t* sometimes takes on the value of [ts], particularly among women: [tsəi], *tea*, [tsəü] *two*, etc. The addition of *t* and *d* is quite common, particularly after *n*, *l*, and *r*, *sinst*, *wonst*, *ondly*, *gownd*, *schollard*, etc.

Finally, there is general agreement among Cockneys to neglect initial *h*, *'ard*, *'Enery*, *'igh*, *'ope*, etc. The aspiration of normally initial vowels, although it is commonly represented in literature in such spellings as *horfice*, *hice*, etc., is not a rule of Cockney and is, indeed, rather rare. I have heard the aspiration from some older Cockneys, particularly when they were trying to be dignified and correct, but I have not heard it from younger Cockneys, except accidentally. This was one of the points made by Tuer, who said it was a general rule among Cockneys to avoid the effort of pronouncing any kind of *h*.

These are the chief characteristics of Cockney pronunciation at the present time, from my experience of the dialect as it is spoken in the North of London. I have left the discussion of many minor features of the dialect for the moment, as they are connected with the discussion as to the continuity of Cockney, but the features I have described, together with certain grammatical forms and the large slang element in the dialect, are what strike people who are unfamiliar with the dialect. Most of the pronunciations are those which Tuer, Shaw, and Barry Pain tried to represent, and it is pretty certain that there have been few phonetic changes in the dialect since the end of last century.

CHAPTER IV

COCKNEY IN THE MUSIC-HALL

THE treatment of Cockney on the music-hall stage demands separate discussion. In the coster songs of the halls the Cockney expressed himself. Until quite recently a large proportion of the London music-hall artistes were themselves Cockneys. These songs have, moreover, a linguistic importance which is not shared by literary Cockney, for they have noticeably contributed to the Cockney dialect as it is spoken in the streets. Not only have they furnished catch-words and phrases by the hundred, but they have helped to popularise and diffuse the slang and clichés of the dialect even beyond Cockney.

The music-hall as we know it is a comparatively modern institution, dating from the middle of last century. The music-hall—the term "variety theatre" is a better description—brought together many forms of entertainment which had previously kept to separate paths. Distinguished singers like Sims Reeves were brought into the same bill with notorious comedians from the old song- and supper-rooms or with tumblers from the fairs. The kaleidoscopic mixture of entertainments did not mature until about 1850, but the Old Rotunda Assembly Rooms near Blackfriars Bridge and The Grapes in Southwark were pioneers of the variety programme, even though they cannot be called true music-halls. In the 'twenties and 'thirties of last century they were presenting varied entertainment. The Grapes actually later became The Surrey Music-Hall. Other assembly rooms were similarly transformed. One of the most popular of Victorian halls, the Middlesex Music-Hall (now The Winter Garden Theatre) derived its nickname "The Old Mo" from the name of the original rooms, The Great Mogul.

The first music-hall proper, The Canterbury Hall, later called The Canterbury Music-Hall, was built in 1848. The great popularity of this hall soon led to the building of new variety theatres, and ultimately to the boom of the 'sixties. The mere list of these new theatres is impressive testimony to the popularity of variety entertainment at the time: Frampton's 1858, Wilton's 1859, The Lord Raglan 1860, The Bedford, Camden Town 1861, Deacon's at Islington 1861, The Lansdowne (later Sam Collins's) 1862. Other halls followed so rapidly that in *The Music-Hall Critic* for 1870 over thirty London music-halls are listed.

This boom led to an unparalleled demand for entertainers. The singers and comedians of the old assembly rooms formed the core of the "profession" and they were augmented by converts from the legitimate stage, the concert hall, the opera, the ballet, the fair-ground, the public-houses. Still there was a shortage and every opportunity was given, through competitions and "extra turns", to draw upon the talent of Londoners. In this way the London music-hall became primarily an indigenous entertainment for Cockneys largely by Cockneys.

Of the old song- and supper-rooms we have few records. Perhaps it is as well. Colonel Newcome's disgust at the song which he had heard at one of these Caves of Harmony must have been well justified. Even when they had toned down their songs and patter for the more respectable music-halls the old singers were still obscene. The most famous legacy from these entertainments is the notorious but enduring *Samuel Hall*:

> My name it is Sam Hall, chimney sweep,
> My name it is Sam Hall.
> I robs both great and small,
> But they makes me pay for all,
> D——n their eyes, *etc. etc.*

begins the printed version, in which *etc.* represents an accumulation of oaths which obey no laws but metre and obscenity. This song, one of the favourite ditties at the Cyder Cellars, may not at first have been sung in Cockney dialect, for its exponent was an ex-compositor of Glasgow, W. G. Ross. But as it celebrates the last day of a London chimney sweep who died for the good of his country in the same way as his famous predecessor, Jonathan Wild, we may claim its lasting but dubious honours for London.

One of the chief singers at the Coal-Hole in the Strand —the original Cave of Harmony which shocked Colonel Newcome—was Charles Sloman. Sloman, a talented singer who appeared on more exalted stages than those of the taverns, made his first appearance at "The Vite Condick" in Clerkenwell. At the Coal-Hole and later in the music-halls he specialised in extemporising satirical verses, aimed mostly at his audience. He may also have sung Cockney ditties, for in Pierce Egan's *Real Life in London* he is credited with a Cockney song lamenting the "good old times":

> Ven I vent out to Hingy, if any von died,
> A good vooden coffin they used to prowide,
> But HIRON vons now keeps the poor vorms houtside
> O, the old times of Old England
> O dear, the good English old times.
>
> I valks up and down vith the tears in my hye;
> Vot they vonce call'd a vaggon is now called a fly;
> And the boys points their fingers, and calls I—a guy!
> O, the old times, *etc.*

The Eagle Saloon in Clerkenwell, the "Eagle" celebrated in "Pop Goes the Weasel", was a more decorous establishment. It was here that Robert Glindon (1799–1866), the buffo singer, used to oblige with his Cockney ditties, *Biddy the Basket Woman* and *The Literary Dustman*. The latter, which was first published in 1832, runs:

> Some folks may talk of sense, egad!
> Vot holds a lofty station;
> But, tho' a dustman, I have had
> A liberal *hedication*.
> And tho' I never vent to school,
> Like many of my betters,
> A turnpike man, vot varnt no fool,
> He larnt me all my letters.
>
> *Chorus.*
>
> They calls me Adam Bell, 'tis clear,
> As Adam vos the fust man,
> And by a co-in-side-ance queer,
> Vy, I'm the fust of Dustmen! *etc.*

One of the first costermonger songs belongs to this period, the burlesque *All Round My Hat*. The costermonger's patter which is interlarded in the song is sufficiently entertaining to justify quotation in full:

'Twas going of my rounds in the street I did meet her,
Oh, I thought she vas an hangel just come down from the sky.
(Spoken: *She'd a nice wegetable countenance,*
Turnip nose, Redish cheeks, and Carroty hair)
And I never heard a woice more louder and more sweeter,
Vhen she cried, buy my Primroses, my Primroses come buy.
(Spoken: *Here's your fine Colliflowers.*)

Chorus.

All round my hat, I vears a green villow,
All round my hat for a twelvemonth and a day,
If anyone should ax it, the reason vy I vears it,
Tell them that my true love is far, far away.

Oh my love she vas fair, and my love she vas kind, too,
And cruel vas the judge vot my love had to try.
(Spoken: *Here's your precious Turnips.*)
For thieving vas a thing she never vas inclined to,
But he sent my love across the seas, far, far away.
(Spoken: *Here's your hard-hearted Cabbages!*)

For seven long years my love and I are parted,
For seven long years, my love is bound to stay,
(Spoken: *'Tis a precious long time 'fore I does any trade to-day.*)
Bad luck to the chap vot'd ever be false hearted,
Oh, I'd love my love for ever, though she's far away.
(Spoken: *Here's your nice heads of Sallary!*)

There is some young men as is so precious deceitful,
A-coaxing of the young girls they wish to lead astray,
(Spoken: *Here's your fine valnuts, crack 'em and try 'em, a shillin' a hundred!*)
As soon as they deceive 'em, so cruel-ly they leave 'em,
And they never sighs nor sorrows, ven they're far avay.
(Spoken: *Do you vant any Hinguns to-day, Marm?*)

Oh, I bought my love a ring, on the werry day she started,
Vich I gave her as a token all to remember me,
(Spoken: *Bless her eyes!*)
And, vhen she does come back, oh, ve'll never more be parted
But ve'll marry, and be happy, oh, for ever and a day.
(Spoken: *Here's your fine spring Radishes.*)

Of the singers who graced both the Caves of Harmony and the new music-halls perhaps the most famous was

Sam Cowell. Cowell (1820–66) was an American who came to England when he was very young. His gift for comedy and his fine voice made him popular in many forms of entertainment, including opera. His greatest success was as a singer of ballads and burlesque songs, many of them Cockney burlesques. Perhaps his most popular songs were *Villikins and his Dinah*, *Billy Vite and Nelly Green*, and *The Ratcatcher's Daughter*. The first, through its revival by Muriel George and Ernest Butcher, is too well-known to need quotation, although it is perhaps necessary to remark that the idea that it was a sentimental ballad is a product of twentieth-century superiority; it was actually a burlesque on the sentimentality of some of the Catnach and Pitt ballads. We may, however, quote two verses from *The Ratcatcher's Daughter*, which Cowell had been singing in the 'forties at The Grecian Saloon in City Road:

Not long ago in Vestminstier,
There liv'd a rat-catcher's daughter,
But she didn't quite live in Vestminstier,
'Cause she liv'd t'other side of the vater;
Her father caught rats, and she sold sprats,
All round and about that quarter,
And the gentlefolks all took off their hats,
To the putty little rat-catcher's daughter.
Doodle dee! doodle dum! di dum doodle da!

She vore no 'at upon 'er 'ead,
No cap nor dandy bonnet,—
The 'air of 'er 'ead all 'ung down her back,
Like a bunch of carrots upon it;—
Ven she cried 'Sprats!' in Vestminstier,
She 'ad such a sweet loud woice, sir,
You could hear her all down Parliament Street,
As far as Charing-Cross, sir!
Doodle dee! *etc.*

The nature of the entertainments at the old song- and supper-rooms did not permit the artistes to go far in character singing. They were more like smoking-concerts than music-hall programmes. The singers did not attempt to make-up for their songs: they sang in their ordinary clothes and to indicate character merely changed their hats or at most raddled their noses for bibulous effects. This habit was preserved by most of the old singers who went over to the music-halls. But the theatrical nature of the new halls soon produced a new type of comedian, the character singer. These artistes made-up carefully for their songs and their characterisations were based upon first-hand observation, even if they exaggerated and idealised in the style of the halls.

The most celebrated of the early character singers was The Great Vance (1839–88). Alfred Peck Stephens, to give him his real name, was originally a solicitor's clerk, but finding the law less attractive than the stage, he managed to get employment as an actor of small parts. Like many other actors he soon succumbed to the popularity of the new music-halls, and in this form of entertainment he quickly gained the reputation of the best character comedian of the day. So popular was he that he formed his own variety company and toured the country. In these performances he sometimes acted twenty different characters in one night. Truly, Vance played many parts in his time, heavy swell, Parliamentary candidate, yokel, Irishman, racecourse tout, and a hundred others. Among them was the Cockney. In the character of a flash Cockney Vance sang one song which has endured longer than most music-hall ditties, *The Chickaleary Cove.*

Dressed in a shining beaver top-hat, with a yellow skirted-coat and light nankeen trousers, he was the quintessence of the dandy crook:

> I'm a Chickaleary Cove, with my one-two-three,
> Vitechapel was the willage I was born in,
> To catch me on the hop,
> Or on my tibby drop,
> You must vake up wery early in the mornin'.
> I've got a rorty gal, also a knowing pal,
> And merrily together we jog on,
> And a doesn't care a flatch,[1]
> So long as I've a tach,[2]
> Some pannum[3] in my Chest—and a tog on!

In many similar songs, *Costermonger Joe*, *K'rreck' Card*, *Going to the Derby* among the rest, Vance expressed not only the spirit of the Cockney, but also his pronunciation, slang, and idiom. And as he was singing such songs until he fell dead upon the stage in 1888, they form an important link between the Cockney burlesques of Sloman, Glindon, Cowell, and others and the songs of more familiar coster comedians like Albert Chevalier and Gus Elen.

The Cockney charwoman also made her bow upon the music-hall stage about this time. Henry Walker's ballad *Betsy Wareing*, "which goes out a chairing", admirably hymns a character who finds remarkable exponents to-day in Nellie Wallace and Lily Morris:

> I've had the Lumbager,
> Dyspepsy, and Ager,
> With Spiral complaints, and Neuralogy, too;
> Highstericks, and Swimmins;
> Delirious Trimmin's,
> Saint Vestris's Dance, and the Tictollyroo;

---

[1] Halfpenny. [2] Hat. [3] Food.

But not the whole bilin',
One's temper for spilin',
Warn't nuffin to this, which it's dreadful, oh! oh!
Drat these Roomaticks,
And plague them damp attics,
Which goes and ill uses a poor creeter so! *etc.*

Among The Great Vance's rivals in the 'sixties was J. A. Hardwick, whose numerous character-songs include several Cockney airs, such as *Cherry Ripe, and Lilly-Vite Muscles, O!* This song shares a characteristic of most of the songs of the Caves of Harmony, in that it was set to the tune of an old song, in this case "Bonny Bunch o' Roses, O!":

Oh, it's once I was as happy as the putty little flowers o' May,
Till love my buzzum wring-ed sore, and Coopid stole my heart away.
She vot I loved vas fairer far, than all the flowers vot blow-ow-ow,
She vos a dustman's darter, and she called out "Lilly-vite Muscles, O!"

I am a travelling fruit mer-chi-ant, and "Black-heart Cherries Ripe" I cries,
But she far more nor Kentish ones, and "Biggaroons", oh, did I prize,
She vos the apple o' my eye—like peach her cheek did glow-ow-ow,
And mellow as a Vinsor pear her woice, calling "Lilly-vite Muscles, O!"

I guved her change for sixpence once, and when I touched her tender hand,
I felt all over *magnified*, and like a fellow shocked did stand;
Her eyes they pierced me thro' and thro' like a *obelisk* I know-ow-ow,
And that's the time I wowed to live and die, for "Lilly-vite Muscles, O!"

George Sidney was one of the most prolific song-writers of this period. He wrote some hundreds of songs for most of the comedians. His work was of the most varied kind, ranging from sentimental ballads and "motto" songs to smutty songs for W. G. Ross of *Samuel Hall* fame. Sidney's Cockney ballads are mostly parodies like *The Ticket of Leave Man*, *Joe Spivins*, a parody on "Villikins and his Dinah", and *Bob Fells.* The last, a parody on

"Samuel Hall", is the most interesting as it tends to confirm our claim of the original as a Cockney ditty:

I'm honest vithout doubt,
Till found out, till found out,
I'm honest vithout doubt,
Till found out, till found out,
So if you feel's inclined,
A job for me you'll find,
My name in course you'll mind,
Bobby Fells.

Arthur Lloyd followed in the steps of Vance a few years later. His great success in character-songs came in the 'seventies. Like Vance he did not restrict himself to Cockney songs—he was, incidentally, a Scotchman—but like most of the comedians of the time, he played Cockney parts now and then. Lloyd, who wrote most of his own songs and some for other artistes, too, had comic talent of a literary as well as an acting kind. His songs are not so completely dependent upon the ability of the performer as most music-hall songs are. Their humour lies in quaintness of fancy, as may be seen from the first and last verses of *The Millingtary Band*, *c.* 1870:

I'm agoing to tell the Public of the way that I've been served,
And I also wish to ax 'em if they think it's been deserved,
'Ow a girl called Mary loved me, promised me 'er 'eart and 'and,
Then left me for a feller 'oom she thought was much more grand,
'Cos he played upon the cymbals in a Millingtary Band.

For a month I 'ad to leave 'er, hin the country I'd a job,
And little thought that hanyone my 'appiness would rob,
When I returned and 'eard the noos, Sir, I could scarcely stand,
She'd skedaddled with the cymbal man in the Millingtary Band:
He'd given 'er 'is 'eart and cymbals, in exchange for 'er 'eart and 'and.

The same humour is found in many of his other songs, such as the Cockney ditties *The Blighted Barber* and *The*

Shoreditch Toff, or the heavy-swell song, *The Bloated Aristocrat*.

This period also saw the rise to fame of two great comediennes, true predecessors of Marie Lloyd, Jennie Hill, "The Vital Spark", and Bessie Bellwood. Jennie, who began her career as a child singer in the 'sixties, was the daughter of a Marylebone cab-driver. She was not specifically a coster comedienne although, as she spoke Cockney herself, there was always a tendency for her impersonations to assume a Cockney quality. In this she resembled her spiritual descendant Marie Lloyd. But Jenny often sang slavey or 'Arriet songs, the most famous of them being *'Arry*. For this song, which was composed by E. V. Page in 1882, she assumed the raiment of a young Cockney dandy, a light billycock hat, a magenta skirt-coat with broad blue facings, and bell-bottomed trousers of the same colour enlivened by broad side-stripes of red. The whole ensemble was relieved by an enormous gold chain and albert. The song for which this garb was assumed is scarcely up to weight. Its literary quality was redeemed solely by the verve of the singer, that raucous impudence which endeared these comediennes to the Cockneys and men-about-town of Victoria's day:

Oh, 'Arry, what, 'Arry!
There you are then 'Arry!
I say, 'Arry,
By Jove! you are a don.
Oh, 'Arry! 'Arry!
There you are then 'Arry.
Where are you going on Sunday, 'Arry,
Now you've got 'em on.

Bessie Bellwood (1857–96), the daughter of a Bermondsey rabbit-puller, was of Irish extraction, but she too indulged in the same type of song as The Vital Spark. In fact, her most celebrated song, *What-Cheer 'Ria*, 1887, was of exactly the same kind as *'Arry*. The song is supposed to be sung by the boys in the music-hall gallery when 'Ria had dressed up in all her finery in order to sit at the chairman's table:

> What-cheer Ria! Ria's on the job,
> What-cheer Ria! did you speculate a bob?
> Oh Ria she's a toff and she looks immensikoff,
> And they all shouted "What-cheer Ria!"

One of the most popular comedians of the 'eighties was Teddy Mosedale, although he had been on the stage for nearly twenty years. He was not only a fine singer, but a remarkable dancer who specialised in step-dancing in a restricted space, his favourite area being a pocket-handkerchief. His repertoire included several coster and lower-class songs of the type made familiar by Albert Chevalier, *My Chestnut 'Orse*, *Sarah*, and *My Isabelle!* The choruses of the first and last of these, as recorded by the late Mr. Chance Newton, were:

> Like a hengine he could go,
> To 'Ackney, 'Ampstead Eaf, or Bow,
> I never shall survive the lorse
> Of poor old Jack, my Chestnut 'orse.

and:

> This was the toast that Joe would cry—
> "My charmin' belle, my scrumptious gel,"
> Oh! search the country thro' you shall,
> But yer won't find a gel like my Isabel.

These songs may not be literary gems but they certainly serve to show that Albert Chevalier was not the first of the coster comedians as is so commonly thought. We have already seen that coster songs were being sung as early as the 'thirties of last century, and Chance Newton's recollections of the halls do not suggest that there was any essential difference in the work of "Chivvy" either in language or in character. He instances J. W. Rowley as a good example of the portrayer of costers and illiterate workmen. "Over" Rowley had been singing idealised coster ballads like *Did You Ever Go to Hampstead in a Van?* for nearly twenty years before Chevalier took to the music-hall stage. Other artistes who specialised in Cockney songs contemporarily with Rowley were Walter Laburnam and Hyram Travers. According to Newton the latter was "absolutely the limit" in coster, hawker, and thieves' slang.

But if Chevalier was not the first of the coster comedians, he was one of the most artistic. This artistry may have come from his training on the legitimate stage—he made his debut with Sir Squire Bancroft. Certainly when he took to the halls in 1891 he was an immediate success. Few of his songs have any great literary merit, but his skill in presentation was incomparably superior to his literary talent. In whatever mood he assumed he idealised the coster, in the gay assertiveness of *Knocked 'em in the Old Kent Road*, the truculent gloom of *What's the Good of Anyfink—Why Nuffink!* the cheerful amorousness of *The Coster's Serenade*, the outrageous sentimentality of *Jeerusalem's Dead*:

> Yer won't see 'im pullin' the barrer no more,
> Wi' me an' the missis a-sellin' the coke.
> 'E died 's arfernoon at a quarter ter four,
> But I think that it's rougher on me than the moke.

The supreme gift of Chevalier, the ability to convey deep affection and pathos, was best expressed in *My Old Dutch*, perhaps the most celebrated of all the coster songs:

> I've got a pal,
> A reg'lar out an' outer.
> She's a dear good old gal,
> I'll tell yer all about 'er.
> It's many years since fust we met,
> 'Er 'air was then as black as jet.
> It's whiter now, but she don't fret,
> Not my old gal!
>
> *Chorus.*
>
> We've been together now for forty years,
> An' it don't seem a day too much,
> There ain't a lady livin' in the land,
> As I'd swop for my dear old Dutch.

Contemporary with Chevalier were several great comedians who specialised in the songs of the "pearlies", Alec Hurley, Paul Pelham, Fred Earle, Gus Elen. Alec Hurley, the husband of Marie Lloyd, was the perfect 'Arry to her 'Arriet. From 1890 until his death in 1913 he enjoyed great popularity in London as the singer of such songs as *The Sleepin' Beauty*, *The Coster's Banquet*, *The Coster's Sister*, and *Pretty Little Polly*. Other comedians, although not exclusively coster singers, occasionally trod the same ground. Thus Charles Coborn (b. 1852), the singer of *Two Lovely Black Eyes* and *The Man that Broke the Bank at Monte Carlo*, sang coster songs before Chevalier, songs like *The Nobby Coster Bloke* and *'E's all right when you know 'im, but you've got to know 'im fust*. Coborn is said to have given up these songs out of friendship for Chevalier.

The songs of Gus Elen, who still occasionally performs, were nearly all written by George Le Brunn, one of the most prolific and artistic song-writers of the music-hall stage. Gus Elen's success came at the same time as Chevalier's, early in the 'nineties. But the inspiration for his rendering of them goes back some twenty years, when he was singing songs in public-houses. Born in Pimlico in 1862, he expresses in every way, physically, sartorially, vocally, and linguistically, the coster of the last half of the nineteenth century. If he lacks the subtle artistry that characterised Albert Chevalier, his impersonations are much truer to life. Certainly his songs are more worthy of quotation. As Le Brunn, who wrote most of them, also composed songs for the other coster comedians of the time, a few examples of Gus Elen's successes will serve to represent the group.

Gus Elen's talent lies in realistic comedy, in expressing a sentiment or thought which is quite normal or serious in the character he portrays but which is highly amusing to others. An admirable vehicle for this talent was provided by Le Brunn in *The Golden Dustman*, 1897:

Me and old Bill Smiff's bin Dust 'oys,
  Allus work'd the same old rahnd;
Strange to say, we've struck a Klondyke,
  And we've shar'd the welf we've fahnd.
'Ow it 'appen'd, there's a miser,
  'Ud never let us shift 'is dust,
A Toosday night 'e died, and Wensday,
  Like two burglars in we bust;
Gets to work, and bless yer eyesight,
  Oh, such welf yer never saw,
Apeneys, fardens, Lor, in fousands!
  And to fink that last week I was poor!

Chorus.

But nah I'm goin' to be a reg'lar toff,
A-ridin' in my carriage and a pair,
A top 'at on my 'ead, and fevvers in my bed,
And call me-self the Dook o' Barnit Fair:
As-ter-ry-my-can rahnd the bottom o' my coat,
A Piccadilly winder in my eye;
Oh, fancy all the Dustmen a-shoutin' in my yer,
"Leave us in yer will before yer die."

The same humour is shown in the song of the postman who on his day off took his children around the City. When he came to Newgate Street, he gave the kids a treat and showed them "where their uncle 'e was 'ung"! But Gus Elen could, and still can, wring facile tears from his audience almost with the skill of Chevalier. He is still able to pull the heartstrings of Cockneys with Le Brunn's song *The Coster's Muvver*, 1894:

She's just the sort a muvver that a bloke wants, eh!
Ah, when she's tooked away I won't feel werry gay.
As far as me and 'eaven's concerned I don't put on no side
But if muvver ain't a-goin' in, Well, this bloke stops outside.

As a last example of his and Le Brunn's work, we may take the first verse and chorus of *It's a Great Big Shame*, which expresses in delightful fashion the coster's indignation at a not uncommon domestic situation:

I've lost my pal, 'e's the best in all the tahn,
But don't you fink 'im dead, becos 'e ain't.
But since he's wed, 'e 'as 'ad ter nuckle dahn,
It's enough ter wex the temper of a saint!
'E's a brewer's drayman, wiv a leg of mutton fist,
An' as strong as a bullick or an horse.
Yet in 'er 'ands 'e's like a little kid,
Oh! I wish as I could get him a divorce.

Chorus.

It's a great big shame, an' if she belong'd ter me,
  I'd let her know who's who,
Naggin' at a feller wot is six-foot-free,
  And her not four foot two!
Oh! they 'adn't been married not a month nor more,
  When underneath her fumb goes Jim.
Isn't it a pity that the likes ov 'er,
  Should put upon the likes ov 'im?

Kate Carney, another of the old coster singers who are still performing, specialised in expressing the joys of Cockney life. More than any of the men "pearlies" she sang the delights of Cockney music, the barrel-organ and the mouth-organ. It is perhaps just that her songs should be more remarkable for their tunefulness than for the happiness of their words. *When the Summer Comes Again*, the song of the coster flower-seller to his girl, is characteristic of her work:

When the summer comes again,
  And the pretty flow'rs are growing,
The sunshine after rain,
  The summer breezes blowing;
Then to roam around the country,
  With a girl who's ever willing—
I can buy, and she can cry,
  "Three pots a shilling."

Banal words, but the simple and charming melody endeared it to Cockneys, so that it is still one of the favourite songs at Cockney gatherings.

Marie Lloyd, although the greatest of Cockney comediennes, was quite different from Kate Carney and her male counterparts. Their performances were stylised, a heightening of reality. Marie Lloyd expressed herself, the quintessential Cockney. Born in 1870 at Hoxton, she made her first appearance at The Royal Eagle music-hall in 1885. Her subsequent career was triumphant, and until her death in 1922 she was the most beloved of artistes, not only for her entertainment but also for her open-handed kindliness. It has been admirably suggested that she was the Victorian Nell Gwynne. Her brazen vulgarity and impudent good humour, her vitality and good sense, were transferred without modification from the gutter to the stage. The double-entendre of her lines wittily paralleled the crudity of Cockney speech, and her pronunciation was uncontaminated by finesse. Thus, her songs were cyphers, stones which she adorned with the superfine nacre of Cockneydom:

> Come, come, come and make eyes at me,
> Down at the old Bull and Bush.
> Come, come drink some port wine with me,
> Down at the old Bull and Bush.
> Hear the little German band,
> Fol de ridle-i-do,
> Do let me hold your hand, dear,
> Come, come, come and have a drink or two,
> Down at the old Bull and Bush,

runs one song. In itself it belongs to no class. But when Marie Lloyd sang it, the East End was made vocal.

This is true of Harry Champion, too. He is not a coster comedian, but for over forty years he has been expressing in his songs the spirit of the Cockneys among whom he was born. The Cockney gusto finds utterance in *Ginger, you're Barmy*, and *Whatcher me Old Brown Son*, the Cockney's Gargantuan love of eating in *Boiled Beef and Carrots*, and his perkiness in *With the End of My Old Cigar* or *Any Old Iron!* Gusto is the outstanding quality of

Harry Champion, and even now, when he is well over seventy, his vitality is remarkable in such a song as:

> I'm Henery the Eighth I am!
> Henery the Eighth I am, I am.
> I got married to the widow next door,
> She's been married seven times before.
> Ev'ry one was a Henery,
> She wouldn't have a Willie or a Sam,
> I'm her eighth old man named Henery,
> I'm Henery the Eighth I am!

The Cockney artistes of the present day vary in style. Some of them retain the 'Arry and 'Arriet quality in all its raucousness. Such an artiste is Lily Morris. Max Miller, although less blatant in manner than some of his predecessors, refines upon the perkiness of the Cockney. But the favourite style is domestic Cockney. Elsie and Doris Walters in their Dais and Gert dialogues, and Mabel Constanduros in her Buggins sketches, are brilliant exponents of the maudlin garrulousness of some Cockney women.

These stages may be deduced, therefore, in the treatment of Cockneys upon the music-hall stage. First, the burlesque of Cockney sentimentality as it was expressed in the old broadsides, then character-songs about flash Cockneys in which the slang and cant of some Londoners were extensively used, then the idealisation of the Cockney and the vogue of the coster song, and finally a more subdued but fairly realistic burlesque of Cockneys in ordinary domestic life. The dialect employed in the Cockney songs follows the ordinary literary convention, with a few differences, the most important being that the slang used in these songs is more up-to-date than that in literary Cockney, and that some of the pronunciations which were jettisoned by novelists when they adopted the new convention are retained for a long time in music-hall songs.

These music-hall songs are the true folk-songs of London. They and the chants which are used by Cockney children. In the music-halls and in the streets Cockneys are at their ease. In any place that smacks of the schoolmaster, the Cockney child is on his guard. But among themselves and in the freedom of the streets—playgrounds which the Cockney child prefers to the regulation-tied parks and commons—the children of London shed their artificialities, and drop into the language natural to them, the Cockney dialect they have learned from fathers or mothers, grandfathers or grandmothers. With the inventiveness natural to children who for their amusements are left to their own resources, they run through unending repertoires of games, original and traditional, in which the only implements are ropes, rubber balls or balls of paper and string, hats, coats, cigarette cards, screws, date stones (date ogs is the Cockney name), cherry stones or anything else that comes easily to hand. The very names of some of these games reveal the Cockney's linguistic genius, "Blue water lapping" or "Dead Man's Dark Scenery". Many of the games are accompanied by chants and songs, some of them curious corruptions of old ballads or nursery rhymes, others reminiscences of songs learned in schools, music-halls or even Sunday schools, and others original verses composed for new games. I cannot reproduce the tunes, unfortunately, but some of the verses demand quotation:

Sally go round the moon,
  Sally go round the sun,
Sally go round the omlibus,
  On a Sunday afternoon

is an engaging chant that accompanies a ring game. A skipping game played by girls is accompanied by this charming song, sung to a simple musical phrase repeated in varying tempi:

Eight o'clock bells are ringing,
  Mother may I go out?
My young man's a waiting
  For to take me out.
First he buys me apples,
  Then he buys me pears,
Then he gives me sixpence
  To kiss him on the stairs.

I don't want your apples,
  I don't want your pears,
I don't want your sixpence
  To kiss me on the stairs.

Many of the songs are so corrupt that they are now nonsense rhymes, but their inconsequentiality—and their frequent coarseness—does not prevent their being delightfully quaint. The following chanty-like song, sung to a tune that borrows from the folk-song "Richard of Tauntondene", accompanies a processional game:

As I was going to the Fair,
Who should I meet but an old banker there.
The banker's name was Brass,
His old woman's name was old Mother Bottle-Arse.
There was Brass, old mother Bottle-Arse,
There was Whack, old mother Paddy-Whack,
  And Johnny and Billy and Teddy,
  Oh Liza, lay close to me now!

Of the commoner chants, this is one of the most popular:

Hush-a-larly, hush-a-larly,
  Lost the leg of my drawers,
Hush-a-larly, hush-a-larly,
  Will you lend me yours?

although its popularity is rivalled by these insulting verses shouted by Cockney urchins at any boys or grown-ups whom they wish to torment into the indiscretion of running after them:

Dicky Dicky Dirt, your shirt's hanging out,
Four yards in, and four yards out,

or:

Sam, Sam, Sam, you dirty old man,
Washed your face in the frying-pan,
  Combed your hair
  With the leg of a chair,
Sam, Sam, Sam, you dirty old man.

It could hardly be expected that such games would pass off without dispute, and the quarrels that result afford some of the best examples of pure Cockney dialect, when all the carefully inculcated rules of schoolmasters are forgotten and the disputants lapse into Cockney, native but not unadorned, for swear-words flow naturally from the lips of Cockney children.

I fear that the Cockney dialect will not long survive the common London music-hall, the costermonger's barrow, and the street-game. All of them still exist, but they are getting fewer every year. Multiple-shops, cut-price shops, and police regulations are driving the costermonger from the London streets. The music-hall is succumbing to the empire of Hollywood. Motor-cars make even back streets unsafe for children's games. Good arguments may be brought forward to justify the changes. The music-hall was often coarse: both the costermonger's barrow and the street-game were unhygienic. But unlike the films the music-halls expressed the spirit of a great people; the costermonger's barrow compelled the Cockney housewife to use judgment, not merely to read the name on the packet; and the street-game stimulated the Cockney urchin's imagination to a degree that the schoolmaster's exercises in self-expression have never attained.

CHAPTER V

COCKNEY MANNERISMS AND SLANG

BESIDES a characteristic pronunciation, a dialect should have a characteristic vocabulary. Cockney certainly has a characteristic pronunciation, but it differs from the county dialects in its vocabulary. Country dialect words are for the most part words of country life, names of trees, flowers, and beasts, technical terms of farming and country crafts or old words that have dropped out of normal speech. Most of these words are old; they have endured with the things themselves. They have therefore that respectability that comes from antiquity and accordingly have been the subject of careful study. Cockney is less fortunate. Its characteristic vocabulary is slang. The population of a large town has few things peculiar to itself. In a country district a certain kind of cart may be peculiar to the district and its name will be a dialect word that will be treasured by scholars. But the name of a London cart will not be thought worthy of special notice. If it be used by literary men it will come to be regarded as a standard English word; if it be a popular name it will be dubbed "slang". In the latter case the only people who will honour it will be those philological amateurs whose love of the language is not hampered by academic or social conventions.

Cockney is doubly unfortunate. It is robbed by

standard English and it is condemned for employing those words that standard English does not want. But although standard English does not want all the Cockney words, even people of good education will constantly use them in speaking colloquially. Therein lies a third injury of Cockney. Although slang is characteristic of Cockney it is not easy to tell what is characteristic Cockney slang. In this chapter I have endeavoured to surmount the difficulty and to trace some of the chief Cockney traits since the sixteenth century, other than in pronunciation and grammar. I cannot pretend to completeness, because preceding studies of Cockney have been restricted to notes on pronunciation, but from plays, novels, dictionaries of slang, and occasional comments, I have tried to trace the chief Cockney mannerisms and to analyse the extent and characteristic elements of Cockney slang at various periods.

In the early period the best information may be obtained from the plays of Elizabethan and Jacobean dramatists. They may have been remiss about some Cockneyisms, but they took a delight, often too great a delight, in burlesquing other characteristics of London speech. Above all, they loved to poke fun at the Londoner's love of impressive words and his habit of getting them a trifle mixed either in meaning or pronunciation. It was as inevitable to use malapropisms in characterising a Cockney as to reiterate "fait and trote" when drawing an Irishman. Although comparisons are odorous, it must be confessed that the dramatists are not equally successful in using the device. Shakespeare himself employs it tediously with Elbow and Froth and, heresy as it is to say so, he does not seem to me to employ it much better with Dogberry and Verges, who too frequently use such mechanical blunders as "suffer salvation" or "the most desartless man". But with Mistress Quickly, he is more convincing if only because he uses the blunders sparingly and is not intent on making her say exactly the reverse of what she means—"you are both, i' good truth, as rheumatic as two dry toasts; you cannot one bear with another's confirmities". But for the happy use of malapropism no other play can hold a candle to *The Knight of the Burning Pestle*:

> *Wife.* Now, sweet lamb, what story is that painted upon the cloth? the confutation of St. Paul?
> *Citizen.* No, lamb, that's Ralph and Lucrece.
> *Wife.* Ralph and Lucrece! which Ralph? our Ralph?
> *Citizen.* No, mouse, that was a Tartarian.

One need have no doubt that the Cockneys of the time were prone to these errors. The period, like all periods of great literature, was one of philological enthusiasm. Fine sounds were floating about the earth, and the Cockney loved to hum the tunes even if he could not read the score. Sometimes, as Firk said of Margery Eyre, they spoke like a new cart-wheel, and sometimes the wheel squeaked excessively, but one may excuse them on the score that the words they deranged were, like "occupying", excellent good words before they became ill-sorted.

The justification for the dramatists is easy to find in some of the London records. Two genuine malapropisms at least are as amusing in their setting as anything in the plays:

> This day at a vestry was taken into consideration the complaint of Mr. Phipp who was chosen cunstable in which complaint he made appear his imbecilities both in his body and purse. (St. Alphage Minutes, 1653.)
>
> But yf any Churchwarden shall hereafter expend in any of ye sayd dinners more then is herein expressed it is uppon his owne Apperrill. (St. Mary-at-Hill Minutes, 1624.)

Machyn, when he speaks of "the prynse of Condutt" (p. 298), refers to the Prince of Condé in a style more suiting an Elizabethan conduit, and he frequently confuses prefixes, as in "the menyster wold nott (church a woman) owt-sept she wold com at vj in the mornyng", 249, "the abbott of Westmynster and the monkes was reprevyd", 204, when they were actually "deprived"; he speaks of the parliament being "regornyd" and uses "to dysgratt" for "to degrade", and as companion to the Citizen's wife "Jone and the Wall" he speaks of "the crest of a bluw *porpyntyn*". Similar gaffes occur now and then in the Church records. The St. Barts accounts have a familiar error in their reference to "one boocke of Statues", 1658, and in the Minutes of the same church we find these entries: "Mr Crowshaws 50^{ll} formerly given to our poore wch was not distributed as was *pretended* according to the donors will", 1640, and "she haueing promised forty shillings or double *reparrell* to the childs m^{rs}", 1643. Of the similar errors in the records of St. Margaret we need quote only these: "yt was *erecktyde* by most voysses that Mr Rychard Stubes is chosen", 1583, "without the least *predyges* of the paryshe", 1600, and the note that James Browne was to lose his pension "If he falle into his old Sourse of Deboysnes", 1626.

The perilous affectation of a little latinity was another

aspect of this fondness for impressive words. Everyone will remember Dogberry's "palabras, neighbour Verges" and his threat to "drive some of them to a non-come", or Mistress Quickly's "burning quotidian tertian" or the gravedigger's "argal" in *Hamlet*. The same fondness for tags is shared by Cob and other characters in the plays, and Machyn is as pedantically incorrect in his reference to the persons who got "clen remyssyon of all ther synes tossyens qwossyens of all that ever they did", 94. The popularity of sermons and the compulsory service as churchwardens brought many Londoners who had no classical training into an uneasy familiarity with the Latin tags of law and church. One cannot doubt that the people who dared the perils of mouth-filling English words must have been often tempted beyond discretion by the impressive solemnity of Latin phrases.

It appears paradoxical to suggest that the Cockneys of the sixteenth and seventeenth centuries were more influenced by literature than their descendants are, in view of our pains to inculcate the arts in all our citizens. But it is unfortunately true that our system of education has not led to any general improvement of taste. But at a time when the poorest form of literature was the romances of Palmerin and his fellows, when Lord Mayors' processions were modelled upon "that writer Metamorphoses", when even Bartholomew Fair had its plays and puppet-shows on classical themes, and when apprentices went to see *Hamlet* instead of Bing Crosby, the speech of Cockneys must have been shot with reminiscence. Anyone who recollects how eagerly Londoners caught up the phrases of Marie Lloyd and the other stars of the music-halls will understand why the early dramatists put so many quotations into the mouths of their Cockneys—often with such delightful inappropriateness as in Doll Tearsheet's loving words to Falstaff, "come on, you whoreson chops: ah, rogue! i' faith, I love thee: thou art as valorous as Hector of Troy, worth five of Agamemnon, and ten times better than the Nine Worthies: ah, villain!" It is improbable that they were so romance-stricken that they spoke like Ralph, the knight of the burning pestle, but we may well believe that many of the apprentices were ready, like Ralph or Quicksilver, to spout the rhetorical flourishes of Hotspur or Hieronimo or to apply to current events phrases from ballads and broadsides. And anyone who knows how large a part such music-hall phrases as "Watcher me old brown son" or "one of the ruins of Cromwell" played in the Cockney speech of a few years ago will not challenge the suggestion of the early dramatists that the Cockney speech of the time was patched with "go by, Jeronimo, go by", "but me no buts", "prince am I none yet am I nobly born", and the like. And as evidence of the influence of the Church we have that diverting passage in the *Knight of the Burning Pestle* where the Citizen's wife is so upset by old Merrythought's ill-treatment of his wife that she preaches him this sermon:

> "I had not thought in truth, Master Merrythought, that a man of your age and discretion (as I may say) being a gentleman, and therefore known by your gentle conditions, could have used so little respect to the weakness of his wife: for your wife is your own flesh, the staff of your age, your yoke fellow, with whose help you draw through the mire of this transitory world: nay, she's your own rib. And again——"

Nell had patently been impressed by the theological clichés of the preachers. The theological element in present-day Cockney hardly goes further than "would you Adam and Eve it", but one need only go to a professional football-match to realise how great a part other people's clichés play in Cockney.

The City's love of respectability had an effect on the language of merchants and his wives that never failed to amuse the wits. Every schoolboy knows Hotspur's adjuration to his wife to "swear like a Lady as thou art" and to shun such protests of comfit-makers' wives and Sunday-citizens as "in good sooth", "as true as I live", "as God shall mend me", and "as sure as day". The *locus classicus* for these mincings is *The Knight of the Burning Pestle*, in which George and Nell are for ever saying "beshrew me", "I' faith", "a' God's name", "I prithee", "by my faith", "by my troth", "i-wis", "o' my conscience", "by the faith of my body", or "as I am a true man", and in *The Shoemaker's Holiday* we find "as we are mortal", "God's pittikins", and the unusual "upon some". Shakespeare even gives some similar oaths to Mistress Quickly, "I warrant you", "in truth", "by my faith", "what the good-year", "tilly-fally", etc. We may doubt whether such mild-mannered adjurations satisfied even the merchants, except when they were on their best behaviour. One cannot bring the charge of being mealy-mouthed against Simon Eyre or Quicksilver—whose oaths "by God 'slid", "sfoot", "sblood", "slife", and so on are posed against Touchstone's respectable "as I am a citizen and a tradesman". And part of the humour of *The Knight of the Burning Pestle* lies in the citizen's backslidings. For while Ralph complains that "there are no such courteous and fair well-spoken knights in this age" since they will call people "the son of a whore" or "damned bitch" instead of "fair sir" and "right beauteous damsel", the Citizen is only too free with his "whoreson halter-sack" and "whoreson gallows". The church records are naturally free from oaths of all kinds, but we may find a pointer to the grain of Elizabethan Cockney in Machyn's habit of describing the tail of a cart as "the cart-arse".

The terms of endearment used by the Citizen and his wife are the product of the bourgeois instinct to reduce life and language to comfortable proportions. Dol Tearsheet's amusingly ill-sorted compliment to Falstaff, "thou whoreson little tidy Bartholomew boar-pig", is almost on all fours with those farmyard terms of endearment beloved of George and Nell, "bird", "duckling", "chicken", "duck", "cony", "good lamb", "mouse", "honeysuckle", and so on. Even the robust Simon Eyre occasionally addresses his Maggie as "cony" or "honey". Simon's usual manner of expressing his fondness for Mistress Eyre, "Madge Mumble-Crust" or "midriff-swag-belly-whore", may seem strange unless one is familiar with the Cockney's habit even now of using the terms of lechery as endearments, "he's not a bad old sod", or "the poor little bugger".

It would appear from the Cockney dialogue in the plays that Londoners had a liking for well-worn proverbs and platitudes. This sententiousness is often met with in Cockneys now—one may depend upon hearing "honesty's the best policy", "what can't speak can't lie", or "it never rains but it pours", or "seeing's believing"—and the trait was probably stronger at a time when the Cockney community comprised many fairly prosperous tradesmen bent upon proving their moral and social integrity. Mrs. Touchstone speaks almost like the late Mr. Tupper:

> "Never whimper for the matter. *Thou should'st have look'd before thou had'st leap'd.* Thou wert afire to be a lady; and now your ladyship, and you, may both *blow at the coal*, for aught I know. *Self do, self have. The hasty person never wants woe*, they say." (*Eastward-Hoe*, V. i.)

Most of the Cockneys in the plays occasionally speak in this style, and it is therefore possible to collect a short list of the proverbs and traditional phrases most popular in London speech at the time, viz.:

Light gains make heavy purses.
Keep thy shop and thy shop will keep thee.
'Tis good to be merry and wise.
Enough is as good as a feast.
Drunken men never take harm.
Your ladyship hath fish'd fair and caught a frog.
Fair words never hurt the tongue.
Hunger breaks stone walls.
The leg of a lark is better than the body of a kite.
Fish is cast away that is cast in dry pools.
The ragged colt may prove a good horse.
I will save my breath for my broth. (*Eastward-Hoe.*)

There be more maids than Mawkin.
All flesh is grass.
Naked we came out of our mother's womb and naked we must return.
Set the hare's foot against the goose giblets.
A pound of care pays not a pound of debt. (*Shoemaker's Holiday.*)

You are a fine man, an' you had a fine dog.
As proud as a dog in a doublet.
As merry as mine host.
I tremble (as they say) as twere an aspen leaf. (*Knight of the Burning Pestle.*)

Comparisons are odious.
When the age is in, the wit is out.
The ewe that will not hear her lamb when it baes, will never answer a calf when he bleats.
An two men ride of a horse, one must ride behind.
All men are not alike. (*Much Ado about Nothing.*)

A good heart's worth gold. (*Henry IV*, Part 2.)

Dogberry's speech, from which the examples from *Much Ado* are taken, admirably illustrates the habit of using conversational tags which cannot be classified as proverbs, but which are almost as well-worn—"as they say", "God help us! it is a world to see!", "God's a good man", "God is to be worshipped", and "an honest soul as ever broke bread". Usually the stage Cockneys use one favourite catch-phrase, in addition to the parenthetical "as they say" made necessary by the proverbs and platitudes. Among these are Mistress Quickly's "What the good year", Touchstone's "Work upon that now", and Margery Eyre's "But let that pass". Apparently these catch-phrases were formerly as popular as the more modern "Bob's your uncle", and this may also have been true of two more of Mistress Eyre's phrases—"Away she flung, never returned, nor said *bye nor bah*, and Ralph, you know, *ka me, ka thee*", for the latter phrase, in which *ka* stands for "kiss", is also used by Touchstone. Other phrases worth mentioning are the Citizen's wife's parenthetical exorcism "(God bless us!)" whenever she mentions the Devil, and Cob's short list of slogans against the doldrums, "Helter skelter, hang sorrow, care'll kill a cat, up-tails all, and a louse for the hangman".

Cob is most interesting, however, for his inveterate

punning. In accordance with Jonson's theory of comedy, this habit becomes in Cob a humour rather than a mannerism. But, to judge from the frequency with which all the stage-Cockneys use the pun, Jonson was deliberately ridiculing a Cockney habit, especially in that gigantic pun which turns upon the resemblance between Cob's name and that of a young herring. This form of word-play has sunk from the exalted status of Cleopatra to Shakespeare to the humble level of Drury-lane duchess to red-nose comedians, but it is comforting to realise that, whatever its shortcomings, it has lost few of its attractions for Cockneys.

Cob also suggests a Cockney pleasantry analogous to punning, the practice of capping a word with a rhyme. It is perilous to say "he's a poet" to a Cockney lest he "come out with" the time-honoured riposte "but he doesn't know it", and one runs a grave risk in saying "What?" forcibly of being assailed with "Catstails all hot". Cob's dialogue with Tib runs on similar lines in this passage:

> *Tib.* It's more than you know, whether you leave me so.
> *Cob.* How?
> *Tib.* Why, "sweet"!
> *Cob.* Tut, sweet or sour, thou art a flower,
> Keep close thy door, I ask no more.

Apart from Cob's phrase "I have paid scot and lot" we may find corroboration of this habit in Margery Eyre's unexpected turn from prose to:

> You sing, Sir Sauce, but I beshrew your heart,
> I fear for this your singing we shall smart.

and also in Machyn's jovial entry:

> The xxv day of September (my wife) was browth a' bed with a whenche, be-twyn xij and on at mydnyght, wher-of my gossep Harper, servand unto the quen grace was dyssesed of *rest of ys nest*, and after he whent to ys nest a-gayn. (p. 153.)

The mannerism is analogous with the rhyming slang which enjoys bursts of popularity every now and then in present-day Cockney speech.

Mistress Quickly has two mannerisms which are shared by present-day Cockneys. She is prone to repetitions of a phrase, especially when she is excited, "I have borne, and borne and borne, and have been fubbed off, and fubbed off," or "Do your offices, do your offices: Master Fang and Master Snare, do me, do me, do me your offices". And her narrative style has that needless circumstantiality and reiteration of "he said" and "she said" which one may observe at any time in the conversation of Cockney women:

> "Tilly-fally, Sir John, ne'er tell me: your ancient swaggerer comes not in my doors. I was before Master Tisick, the debuty, t'other day; and, as he said to me, 'twas no longer ago than Wednesday last, 'I' good faith, neighbour Quickly,' says he; Master Dumbe, our minister, was by then; 'neighbour Quickly,' says he, 'receive those that are civil; for,' said he, 'you are in an ill name!' Now a' said so, I can tell whereupon; 'for,' says he, 'you are an honest woman and well thought on: therefore take heed what guests you receive: receive,' says he, 'no swaggering companions.' There comes none here: you would bless you to hear what he said: no, I'll no swaggerers."

The same passage admirably illustrates the tendency to parenthetical explanations, which is productive of many a bracket in the churchwardens' minutes.

The London documents contain many colloquial phrases such as *ill speed* (bad luck), *day of doom*, *after the old fashion*, *huntyd and kyllyd tage and rage*, *the wyff of the Grayhond* which occur in Machyn's diary, but little upon which one can base generalisations upon Cockney colloquialisms, apart from the tendency which is revealed in Machyn's diary of expressing enthusiasm in a *non plus ultra* style:

> he was a nobull captayne as ever was.
> the goodlyest collers as ever youe saw.
> Ther was a grett dener as you have sene,
> the grett pykkepurs as ever was.
> ther was syche a cry and showtt as has not byne.
> she was a fayre a lade as be.
> the goodliest sermon that ever was hard.

and many more phrases to the same effect, if not in the same formulas.

But although words and phrases belonging to the respectable colloquial vocabulary of the Elizabethans and Jacobeans occur now and then in the London records, one may search in vain for anything more familiar. There are references to occasions when language was unseemly, but the unseemliness is never allowed to sully the reporter's page. And as the churchwardens preserved a due decorum in their minutes it is impossible to assess the slang element in the Cockney speech of the time. There is plenty of information in the works of Harman and Awdeley, as well as in the pamphlets of those writers who borrowed from them, Dekker, Greene, Middleton, Brome, and others, about the thieves' cant of the time, but we have no reliable information about the non-technical slang used by more respectable people. The dialogue of the Elizabethan and Jacobean plays, in comedies especially, makes use of a varying element of general slang, without ever suggesting any extensive use of it. In any case, slang is always a very variable element in language. Although it is commonly regarded as one of the chief elements in present-day Cockney for example, many people who use the sounds of Cockney employ only a very few slang words, although other Cockneys use so many that it is difficult to understand them. One would need very careful linguistic studies as a basis for a detailed discussion of early slang, and the plays which are our only evidence upon this element in Cockney speech are far from being that.

The slang of the Citizen and his wife is very limited, consisting mainly of terms of disparagement, *an old stringer* (lecher), a *gallows* or *halter-sack* (gallows-bird), *groutnol* (blockhead), *springald*, *saucebox*, and *sprig* (coxcomb), *flirtgill* (whore), and *lungies* (louts). For the rest, when they are offended they tell the offender to *go snick up*, sometimes adding *with a wanion*, they accuse the actors of seeking to *play the Jacks*, they urge Ralph to **knock them* when there is a fight, and they try to prevent Ralph from being *capped* for debt—a Cockney would now say "nabbed". This is not a very informative vocabulary, but it is as extensive as we should expect from a respectable merchant and his wife. People of this type had such a wealth of new words to attract them that they would not have needed slang as a linguistic stimulant, and there was no reason at all why they should have been familiar with cant.

Because of the nature of its characters, the slang in

* The asterisks preceding some of these slang words indicate that they are still used in Cockney.

The Shoemaker's Holiday is more extensive and much more boisterous. Neither Simon Eyre nor his journeymen were so respectable as George and Nell, and the pools from which they drew their words, especially their terms of abuse, were a little muddier. They describe chatter as *pishery-pashery*, *gibble-gabble*, **tittle-tattle* or *yawling*; they speak of worthless things as *trullibubs*, *flip-flap* or *wash*; brave lads were *bullies* and a coward was a *flincher*. In their slang a *butter-box* was a Dutchman and *basa mon cues* were Frenchmen. The woman who sold pigsheads was a *souse-wife*, and sluts, whores, and fat men were at various times called *drabs*, *aunts*, and *swag-bellies*. A *back-friend* was false and a *gull* foolish. A *firking* fellow was lively and a *penny-pinching* one mean. To **lamb* anybody was to beat him, to **take down* was to abuse, and might get rid of a person by telling him to *go rub*, to *sneck up*, to *trudge* or to *scud*. To avoid anything was to *hold out tack*, to dupe was to *cony-catch*, to smarten up oneself was to *smug up*, and to surprise anyone was to **catch him napping*. A man might be *as fit as a pudding* or contrarily *have no maw to the gear*. Finally, they employ the following miscellaneous slang words: *tipple* (drink), *Mother Bunch* (water), *slops* (breeches), *flap* (cap), **stretchers* (lies), and *sheep's eye* (ogle), while *aurium tenus* and *genuum tenus* represented ten pieces of gold and silver respectively.

The slang element in Cockney is most strongly represented in these two plays. Even *Bartholomew Fair* has only a sprinkling of general slang words, *punk* and *pinnace* (whore), *provender* (food), *froth* (beer), *jacobus* (guinea), **beak* (nose), *muss* (scramble), and one or two more.

One may notice in these lists the tendency towards onomatopœia and descriptive substitution which accounts for so much of modern slang and the influence of sailors' speech, but there is little evidence in the plays that the vocabulary of cant had much effect upon Cockney and no evidence at all that the ordinary Londoner used any special type of slang or, indeed, much slang at all.

The only satisfactory way of estimating how great a part slang played in the speech of the early period is to examine the whole of the writings of some highly colloquial writer. So far as I know, none of the Elizabethan and Jacobean authors can be relied upon for this purpose. Greene, Dekker, and Nashe, who are usually used for evidence upon the slang of the time, are too prone to take their slang from Harman and too apt to indulge in neologisms, which may easily be confused with slang, to be reliable guides to the colloquialism of the period. For my own part I prefer to take for this purpose the work of a later writer who did not need to borrow his slang and who was fairly free from stylistic intent. This writer is Edward Ward (1667–1731), the quondam landlord of the King's Head Tavern near Chancery Lane and the author of *The London Spy* and an imposing array of prose pamphlets and Hudibrastic verse. The literary quality of Ward's work is by no means high, but he may fairly be claimed as among the most colloquial of English authors. His principal work, *The London Spy*, is particularly interesting as it describes in boisterous fashion a sight-seeing ramble through London, commenting upon the London characters and the places where they met. Most of Ward's work deals with the same scenes, and although he does not attempt to analyse London speech or even to give specimens of it, his descriptions abound in slang words and phrases which he must have acquired in the course of his work and rambles in London, particularly in his profession of victualler. It was this quality in his work which appealed to Pierce Egan, whose *Real Life in London* is partly modelled upon *The London Spy* and emphasises the colloquialism of its model. But whereas Egan, like Grose and the other early devotees of slang, was inspired by philological enthusiasm, Ward used his slang as a natural means of expression, without attempting to collect the language of rogues or cliques. The style of his work suggests that he spoke much as he wrote, in the slangy, coarse style suited to the landlord of a popular pub on the bounds of Alsatia. It is reasonable, therefore, to take his vocabulary as representative of the extreme use of slang in the later part of the seventeenth century. If the Citizen and his wife may be allowed to stand for the most respectable section of the Cockney community at the beginning of the seventeenth century, Ward may well represent the other extreme at the end of it.

As one might expect in a man who spent most of his time in taverns, Ward's slang is richest in terms for drink and drinkers. The tavern itself he usually calls a *Boozing-Ken* and less frequently a *Tippling-Office* or *Tipling-Ken*, and its landlords were either *Rum-Droppers* or *Nick and Froth Victuallers*. The terms for liquor vary from metaphorical phrases, such as *Porter's Guzzle*, *Carmen's Comfort*, and *Politician's Porridge*, all meaning "beer", or *Adam's Ale* for "water", *Ninny-Broth* for "coffee", and

Slip-Slops for "soft" drinks, to the less decorative but more popular terms for beer, *belch*, *guzzle*, *tipple*, *stitch-back*, *nappy*, *bibble*, *bub*, **bouze*, *rum-bouze*, *brewer's fizzle*, and *humming tipple*. What are apparently brand names are sometimes used in a slang sense, viz. *stingo*, *old Nog*, *Pharaoh*, and *old October*, and the terms *Cup of the Creature* and **Half and Half* are each used once. The drinkers were styled the *Guzzling Society*, the individuals being *Fuddle-Cap*, *Toper*, and *Maltworms*. They were said *to toap* their drink or *guttle* it in such quantities as a *sneaker*, a **whet*, **soaks*, *rum-gutlers* or large *go-downs*. Too much tippling made them **boozy* or **half Seas o'er*. The slang-terms for tobacco and smoking should be included in this section. Tobacco had not yet become so accepted that it promoted graciously sentimental encomiums, and Ward's slang terms are inclined to be abusive. Thus tobacco is styled *Sotweed*, *Mundungus*, *Oronoko*, *Funk* or *Mundungus weed*, the smoker being a *Mundungus-puffer*, and the smoke of his pipe *Funk*.

A glance at any dictionary of slang will reveal that the main branches of slang describe drink, rogues, and women. Ward's slang is no exception: his slang words for the sex are almost as numerous as his terms for liquor and hardly more respectable. All the following words are general slang terms for women of doubtful morals: *punks*, *jilts*, *wagtails*, *trugmoldies*, *trull*, *bang-tails*, *lady-birds*, *madams*, *Belfa's*, **doxies*, *blowzes*, *blowzabella*, *fireships*, *frowes*, *does*, *drab*, *Mother Knab-Cony*, *Mother Midnight*, *bunter*, *punchable nuns*. He also uses a few slang terms for respectable women, but they are all inclined to be contemptuous or suggestive, viz. *straw-hats* and *flat-caps* (fishwives), *hussiff*, *petticoat*, *pug-nancy* or *pug* (girl), *maukin*, *poppets* (girls), *giglers*, *drozel*, and *honest trout*.

Many of his slang words are terms for craftsmen and officers, in which the tendency of slang towards descriptive substitution is clearly shown, cf. *Cony-fumble*, *City Bull-dog*, *Catchpole Raparee*, and *Trap* for "constable", *pull-guts* and *stripp-eel* for "fishmonger"; and *pulpit-cacklers*, *hum-drums*, and *tubsters* for "parsons". Among the other terms of this kind are: *lubber* or *tar* (sailor), *hour-grunters* (watchmen), *tongue-padders* (lawyers), **bum* (bailiff), *slab-dabs* (glovers), *lick-fingers* (cook), *sheep-biter* (butcher), *crispin* (cobbler). The terms for various nationals include, *Teague* and *Boglander* (Irishman), *Sawney* (Scotchman), **Tike* (Yorkshireman), *Taffy* (Welshman), and *Butter-Box* (Dutchman). More general terms for men were: *chaps* or **chums* (friends), a *merry grig*, *merry snob*, and *jolly tit* (pleasant companion), *hug-booby* and *the smug* (husband), *squab* (fat man), *muckworms*, *swabs*, and *scabs* (unpleasant fellows), **grizzles* and *grumbletonians* (complainers), *blab* and *whiffler* (gossip and boaster), and *love-penny* (miser).

Although Ward's vocabulary is not swamped by the technical vocabulary of cant, he has naturally a large vocabulary descriptive of the various types of rogues, their dupes and their practices. Thus he occasionally employs the following cant names for rogues: *mumpers*, *mump*, *stroler*, *clapperdudgeon* (beggars), *pads* and *wods*, *gentlemen outers*, *light-horse* (highwaymen); *gentlemen of the nig* ("vulgarly call'd Clippers"), *divers* (cut-purses and pickpockets); *sweetner*, *tongue-pad*, and *cadators* (confidence men), and *clickers* (touts). More general terms meaning "rogues" are: *Dark engineers*, *Canary-birds*, *Newgate-birds*, *clip-nits* (dirty ruffians), and the *sharping tribe*. Some of these terms belong to cant, but they are very few compared with the rich vocabulary of that lingo, and the limitations of Ward's knowledge of the thieves' language, despite the proximity of his tavern to Alsatia, is emphasised by the fact that although his books deal mainly with the malpractices of the London rogues, he employs very few of the canting terms for their practices, *bubble* (cheat), *smoke the cheat*, *cut sham and wheedle*, *file the cly* (pick a pocket), *nimmed* (stolen), and *nimming*. And for burglars' tools he has but three terms: *Jack*, *Crow*, and *Betties* (jemmies). It may be fairly assumed, therefore, that even in the seventeenth century when the language of thieves was fairly well known by some writers and hearers of plays, cant had not greatly influenced the speech of Cockneys. The slang element in Cockney seems to have greatly increased during the seventeenth century, but the contributions to the vocabulary had come from general slang rather than from cant.

Of the terms for dupes, some were originally canting terms but they had long formed part of the general colloquial vocabulary and are not used technically by Ward. The most common type of slang compares the dupe to a fish: they are *gudgeons*, *chubs*, *golden chubs* or *cods-head*. The companions of courtesans are styled *Rum-Cullies*, *Rum-Culls*, *Cully*, and in more general senses *old snuffler*, *young fumblers*, *town stallion*. General terms meaning "dupe" or simply "fool" are: *bubbles*, *loobies*, *tom-doodle*, *ninny-hammer*, *coniwobble*, *zany*, and *nisey*. The country fool was called *slouch*, *hobbaddyboody*, *country* *put*, *country hick*, *country cokes*, or *buttered bun*. The fops and gallants also had their share of contemptuous slang descriptions, among them **pilgarlick*, *cracks*, *tom-essences*, *butter-boxes*, *skip-jacks*, *jack of dandy*, and *sprag*.

A further large group of slang words describe the body, which has always been represented by a plethora of words in slang. Most of the following words—many are omitted because of their coarseness—are frequently used in Ward's books: **noddle* (head), **peepers* (eyes), **beak* (nose), **handle* (nose), *stumps* (teeth), **clapper* (tongue), **fizes* (faces), *puddings* (guts), *pedestals* (feet), *pettitoes* (feet), **paw* (hand).

Miscellaneous nouns presenting points of general interest are the following: money was **cole*, **rino* or **brass*; a guinea was a *Jacobus*, *yellow-boy* or *smelt*; half a guinea was a *meg*; sixpence was a *sice* or *tester*; a penny was a *copper-john*, and a farthing was a *jack*. Bribes and tips were styled *garnish* or *sweetning*—the process was called *greasing a palm* or *dropping*. Various names for horses were *tits*, *scrubs*, *jades*, *hobbies*; a rabbit was a *puss*, a dog, **towzer*, and a flea was ennobled into a *gentleman's companion*. Many other words do not fall into any definite class and they include: *snoaring kennel* (bedroom), *jakes* (privy), *kill-devils* (guns), *ripp* (sword), **bounce* (impudence), **elbow-greese* (energy), *belly-timber* (food), *muckender* (swab), *nabs* (hats), *jimcracks* (curios), *ratstails* (pigtails).

As is usual with slang, the colloquial terms in Ward's writings are mostly substantives. The discrepancy in the proportion of nouns to other words is in fact even more marked in Ward, whose slang adjectives are confined to a few abusive terms, such as: **lousie-look'd*, *smug-faced*, *dub-snouted*, *goggle-eyed*, *baker-legged*, *tut-mouthed*, *two-handed* (capable, especially for trouble), *maggot-brained*, *clod-skulled*, *sap-head*, *doodle*, **cocksure*, **swanking*, **nitty* (lousy), *peery* (suspicious). As for verbs, it has already been observed how slight was his acquaintance with the verbs in cant, and even when one considers slang in a general sense it is remarkable how few slang verbs are to be found in his writings. The whole of them, so far as my collection goes, is comprised in this short list: **to pig in* (share quarters), **knock off* (cease), *mumble* (chew), *tiffle up* (dress up), **swop* (exchange), **dop down* (duck), *to tick* (have credit), *huckle* (chatter), *conjobble* and *brim* (copulate). He occasionally employs a verbal phrase in a colloquial manner, as: *stand the bears* (suffer), **sav'd his bacon* (escaped), *paid our shots* (settled our bills), *ty'd the nooze* (married).

The habit of shortening words, which seems to have been popular about this time to judge from the condemnations of Swift and others, is responsible for a number of forms in Ward's writings, *mob* (elsewhere he has *mobility*), *cits* (citizens), *non-con* (nonconformist), *mump* (mumper), *skip* (skipper), *blab* (blabber), *bub* (bubble), *strum* (strumpet), *fizes* (physiognomies), *rep* (reputation), *qual* (quality, gentry). And finally, we may include his considerable array of queer-sounding ejaculations and oaths. Most of them turn upon some corruption of "God's", such as *Ads*, *Cats*, *Uds*, *Cuds*. The forms I have noted are: *Ads-heart*, *ads-bleed*, *Adshearti-wounds*, *Ads-flesh*, *Cats nouns*, *Udslidikins*, *Udsbobbs*, *Uds Niggers Noggers*, *Uds lidikins*, *Uds-bodkins*, *Cuds-bobs*, and a few forms shortened by omitting this representation of the deity: *Wounds, Bloody-Wounds, Nouns.* It is obvious that in Ward's time some Cockneys were not limited to the adjurations of Sunday-citizens.

This is quite an impressive vocabulary of slang for one man, and we may assume that the slang element in Cockney had grown during the seventeenth century. Ward does not use the terms so frequently as this list might lead one to think—they are sprinkled throughout his works—but he had a vocabulary which, when occasion demanded, must have enabled him to speak in a very slangy style. Many of his words, it will have been noticed, are used by the Cockneys in Elizabethan drama, and many of them survived into the nineteenth century and are found in the Cockney dialogue of Egan, Mayhew, and others. If most of them have been supplanted by newer slang in present-day Cockney, a few are still popular and serve to maintain the Cockney tradition.

As we have previously suggested, the Cockneys in eighteenth-century plays continue the habits of Elizabethan Cockneys. Maw-worm, Sneak, the Pentweazels, Soapsuds, and Tom Tug all commit malapropisms of a familiar kind. Some of them have the Elizabethan love of maxims and proverbs, and others preserve the old fondness for Latin tags. Jerry Sneak preserves those farmyard endearments, "dove", "chicken", "chuck", with which Elizabethan citizens liked to soothe their spouses. Except perhaps for proverb-mongering, not one of these habits is a marked feature of Cockney to-day. You would wait many a long day before you heard a Cockney speak a word of Latin, although the Great War has left a legacy of incorrect French terms like "sanfarian". Cockneys certainly blunder over scholarly and technical words, but as they rarely employ such words their malapropisms are occasional and not habitual. The farmyard terms which Cockneys now apply to their spouses are by no means endearments, and the animals with which the comparisons are made are apt to be larger.

Malapropisms are among Pegge's themes, and as he was not attempting to be funny his observations on the subject are truer to Cockney habits. The Cockneys of Pegge's time, the latter part of the eighteenth century, erred principally because they confused various prefixes and suffixes and because they were apt to mix up words of similar pronunciation but different meaning. Other gaffes were the result of pretentiousness in the formation of an imposing word to replace a more familiar one. Judging from Pegge's comments, these seem to have been the most familiar errors: *commonality* (commoners), *successfully* (successively), *despisable*, *stagnated* (staggered), *ruinated*, *solentary*, *eminent* (imminent), *luxurious* (luxuriant), *jocotious*, *vulgularity*, *aggravate* (irritate), *mislest* (molest), *unpossible*, *argufy*, *discommode*, *scrupulosity*, and *conquest* (concourse). A few of these errors occur in Machyn's diary and the churchwardens' records, and the resemblance is emphasised by Pegge's citation of a few muddled Latin tags which he had heard in London, *nolus bolus* (nolens volens), *nisi prisi*, and the Cockney pickpocket's *haporth of copperas* (Habeas Corpus).

Pegge singles out a few Cockney idioms for comment and justification. He cites *a-dry*, *a-hungry*, *a-cold*, etc., as strong Londonisms, and justifies them as analogous to "afoot", "ashore", and parallel to Shakespeare's "much ado", "a-weary", etc. The Cockney, like Shakespeare and the Bible, used *learn* and *remember* instead of "teach" and "remind", and *anger* in the sense of "to make angry". He also said *least-wise* instead of "at least" and *the t'other* for "the other", and called the whole of a thing the *whole-tote*. He would *fetch a walk* rather than "go for a walk" and stay *a few while* rather than "a little while". And in enquiring what had happened to a person he would ask *what is gone with him*—if the person had died, the Cockney reply was that *he went dead* at such a time.

Finally, Pegge gives a few interesting remarks on Cockney conversational mannerisms. "If a Londoner wishes to give a reason for anything," he notes, "he very politely precludes you from the trouble of asking it and goes on by adding, 'and for why?' or 'because why?' " Again, "when a Cockney speaks confidently of some future circumstance, his expression is 'If so be as how' as in 'If so be as how that Mr. A comes to town, I will speak to him on the subject; but if so be as how he does not, I will write to him' ". The Cockney was also apt to use "and so" with damnable iteration, especially in telling a story, "*so* he said, *so* I said, *so* this passed on, *so* then as I was telling you", and finally, "*so* that's all". Lastly, "another superfluous way of telling a London story is, by the interpolation of a reflective verb, generally following the so—'and so says me, I, etc. . . .' Then we come to action, 'Well; what does me, I . . .' "

Most of the Cockney habits that Pegge recognised are familiar to us as the habits of Cockneys in the sixteenth and seventeenth centuries. Not all of them have survived. The idioms which Pegge mentions have passed out of the dialect. But one has only to listen to a Cockney conversation to realise that these conversational mannerisms are still mainstays of vulgar London speech.

The author of *Errors of Pronunciation*, 1817, confirms many of Pegge's observations and even quotes some of the same examples. The additional examples of malapropisms are: impopular, information (inflammation), prejudiciary (prejudice), and statute (statue). The most interesting notes in the book, however, are the comments on Cockney slang. The writer was the first critic to regard slang as a Cockney trait and the "very low" words which he condemns are our first examples of characteristic Cockney slang words: *bamboozle*, "a very low word, too frequently used"; **to blackguard*—"this expression is very low"; **do*, as in "he's done for", "he's done up", "I'll do your business for you"; **half an eye*, as in "I saw it with half an eye"; *lingo*; *mulligrubs*, "a very low word used for a complaint in the stomach"; *muckenger*, "popular expression for handkerchief"; *inexpressibles* (breeches); *smell out*, as in "he smelt out what I was doing"; *smoke* (to abuse); *thingum*, *thingummy*, and **what d'ye call him*. The author also informs us that the favourite Cockney ejaculations were *Law!* or *Oh Law!* and *Lawk!* or *Lawk A Mercy!* We suspect that he neglected more characteristic but less refined ejaculations.

In Jon Bee's *Slang*, 1823, a little dictionary compiled by John Badcock, we are occasionally enlightened as to the milieu of the words discussed. The principle is not consistently applied. We cannot tell, therefore, whether the Cockney terms were the most characteristic slang words of the dialect. *Three *bobs and a bende*, he says, "is real Spitalfields for 3*s*. 6*d*.", a sovereign was called either a *legitimate* or a *mellish*, and *wood* was a tavern term for money. Fourpence-worth of grog was called a *grumbler*, a *duffy* was a quartern of gin, *faddee* was "Billingsgate" for stale fish, and potatoes were wryly called *poor creatures*. A Cockney would jocularly address a friend as *My myrtle*, and if he said *nix deberr* he meant "no my friend". *Mr. Wiggins* was a general term for a nincompoop, a *nincum-noodle* was a noodle with no income, a *veighty-von* was a fat lady, the man who wore "a canary or belcher fogle round his twist", that is, his neck, was called a *gillyflower*. A prostitute might describe her profession as *the way of life*, the *Flesh-Market* was a general term for those places where such ladies abounded. A challenge to fight was opened by saying *Take it out of that!* "accompanied by showing the elbow and patting it"; the **mawlies* were hands, and to *take a licking* was to be beaten. An *Egyptian charger* was a donkey, a **try-on* was an attempt to cheat, a **go* was a state of affairs—"here's a h——l of a go", to ruin a man was to **upset his apple cart*, an impressionable man was said to *have a nose of wax*, and *to flog* a man was to excel him in something.

The Vulgar Tongue, 1857, by Ducange Anglicus is in two parts, the first being "A dictionary of slang words and phrases collected in London, 1856 and 1857". This little book is remarkable among the slang dictionaries of the time in that it is independent of Grose's dictionary of slang. Ducange Anglicus is, therefore, a pretty reliable guide to the slang of London. He divides his words into various sections, one of them being the slang of "low life". These are the most characteristic Cockney terms. They are: *First of May* (tongue); *Potatoe-Trap* (mouth); *Scotch Peg* (leg); **Kegmeg* (tripe); *Staff-naked* (gin); *Twist* (brandy and gin mixed); **Kick* (pocket); *side-boards* (shirt collar); *Sneezer* (pocket-handkerchief); *Pipe* (to weep); **Shoot*, as in "shoot the moon", "go away"; *Shoot the cat* (to be sick from drink); *Stall* (to walk off); **Shut up!* or *Stow your mag!* (hold your tongue!). The much lengthier list of general London terms includes such familiar Cockney slang as: **choaker* (neckcloth); *fadge* (farthing); *blunt* (money); **nix* (nothing); **slap-up* (fine); **screwed* (drunk); **stand sam* (to treat); and **up the spout* (in pawn); etc.

The second part of the book gives a list of rhyming-slang terms. This type of slang seems to have originated among Cockneys about 1840; Hotten, writing in 1859, says it was originally the language of ballad-sellers and apparently introduced about fifteen years before. Mayhew, however, was informed that it was "the new style of cadgers' cant". It, therefore, seems to have begun as a secret language, but from the fact that it so quickly became a characteristic of Cockney slang we may assume that it began in London. Its use in music-hall songs and in sporting journals diffused rhyming slang beyond the speech of costermongers, but the natural use of it has always been a characteristic of London speech. Some of the examples cited by Ducange Anglicus have become obsolete, but many others are still used, cf. *apple and pears* (stairs), *Cain and Abel* (table), *cows and kisses* (missus), *linen draper* (paper), *mince pie* (eye), *round me houses* (trousers), *lord of the manor* (tanner), *cherry ripe* (pipe), *artful dodger* (lodger). The long life of some of these rhyming terms is remarkable in view of the brief existence of most slang words.

In 1859, J. C. Hotten first published his *Dictionary of Modern Slang, Cant and Vulgar Words*, further editions appearing in 1860, 1864, 1872, 1874. The first edition gives an account of rhyming slang, from which it is evident that the experts had begun their practice of shortening the term by omitting the rhyming word. He cites *Nose-my* as rhyming slang for "tobacco"—the full term being *Nosey-me-knacker*. This perverse ingenuity later resulted in such phrases as *Do you Oliver?* meaning "Do you understand?", *Oliver* being a shortening of "Oliver Cromwell", the rhyme for *tumble*, "understand". Hotten also describes another type of slang, back slang, in which words are pronounced backwards. Hotten regarded back slang as the secret language of costermongers, used principally for trade and for confounding the police. His examples include: *egabac* (cabbage), *edgenaro* (orange), *ekom* (moke), *helpa* (apple), *luracham* (mackerel), *neergs* (greens), *pinurt pots* (turnip tops), *rape* (pear), *rutat* (potato), *shif* (fish), *starps* (sprats), *torrac* (carrot), **yenep* (penny), **eno* (one), **owt* (two), **erth* (three), etc. Although a few back slang words have been general in Cockney at various times, *slop*, *traf*, *yob*, among the rest, this type of slang has usually been restricted to costermongers for trade purposes.

In the various editions of Hotten's book many miscellaneous words are marked as characteristic of the speech of costermongers and low Londoners. The costermongers' terms for money were derived from Lingua Franca, e.g. *oney saltee* 1*d*., *dooe saltee* 2*d*., *tray saltee* 3*d*., *quarterer saltee* 4*d*., *chinker saltee* 5*d*., *one beong* 1*s*., *A beong say saltee* 1*s*. 6*d*., *madza caroon* half a crown, etc. Other costermongers' terms were: *bunts* (perquisites), *couter* (sovereign), *huxter* (money), *teviss* (shilling), *tusheroon* (a crown piece); **dab* (a flat fish of any kind); *floater* (dumpling); *legs of mutton* (sheeps' trotters); **topper* (cigar end); *hand-saw* (seller of cutlery), **dona* (woman), **mate* (friend), *patterer* (man who sells last dying speeches), *shake* (harlot), *timber merchant* (match-seller), *touzery gang* (mock-auction swindlers), *chovey* (shop), **The Lump* (Marylebone Workhouse), *The Pan* (St. Pancras Workhouse), *toad in the hole* (sandwich board). A coster greeted his friend as *My Tulip*, a loud greeting was a **chy-ike*, and rapid talk was *barrikin*. A *kings man* was the coster's coloured neckerchief, and the lock of hair which he liked to train over an ear was a *Newgate knocker*. To *chuck a jolly* was to praise an inferior article, **mike* (to loiter), *nammous* (to depart furtively), **to be sold* was to be deceived, **snuff it* (to die), *vardo* (to look at), and **tumble* (to understand). With a few exceptions like *mauley* (signature) and **plant* (swindle) these are the terms which Hotten thought it necessary to describe as characteristic of the slang of costermongers and low Londoners.

Henry Mayhew's *London Life and the London Poor* is the most reliable guide to the extent of slang in the speech of costermongers and other street-folk of London. The great number of his reports of Cockneys' stories and his honest attempt to retain their actual words ensure that he sweeps into the net of his great work practically all the slang words which were commonly used by Cockneys about the middle of the nineteenth century.

As Mayhew was not aiming at literary effect, his reports lack many of the characteristics of the Cockney dialogue in plays and novels. His subjects are not remarkable for malapropisms, although humorous blunders occur now and then—"there's constant men and casualties", "a lemoncholy tone", "handed down to prosperity", or "the lord mayor's blanket". Nor was Mayhew concerned to make his Cockneys into "characters": he has no sententious or lachrymose Cockneys and few humorists. Traditional phrases and proverbs are, therefore, thinly sown in his book, although those which are used are the more convincing because of it—"as deaf as a beadle", "as poor as a church mouse", "tell that to the marines", "I wasn't born yesterday", "yearns their money like horses and spends it like asses", or the proverbs, "an old fiddle makes the best music", "half a loaf is better than no bread", and "what can't be cured must be endured".

A larger vocabulary of slang might be culled from Pierce Egan's *Real Life in London* than from Mayhew's book, and the slang dictionaries of the time contain a multitude of words unrepresented there. But although Mayhew's slang words do not number more than a few hundred, their frequent use gave to Cockney speech that slanginess which is one of its chief characteristics now. He, like Hotten, regarded back slang as the root of Cockney speech, and such terms as *flatch* (halfpenny), *top o' reeb* (pot of beer), *on doog* (no good), and *dillo nemo* (old woman) are occasionally used by most of the people he interviewed. They do not seem to have yet adopted rhyming slang, this was still a secret language; but their general slang words, derived from many sources, were numerous.

The terms for people and tradesmen are numerous: *cheap Jack* or *Cheap John* (hawker), *running patterer* (seller of news-sheets), *pinner-up* (seller of broadsides), *penny-swag* (hawker of penny lots), *chummy* (chimney-sweep's boy), **nipper* (costermonger's boy), *gumbler* and *querier* (chimney sweep), *mudlark* and *bonegrubber* (scavenger), *brass-plate merchant* (seller of poor coal), *screever* (writer), *swag-barrow man* (costermonger), *pug* (pugilist), *counter-hopper* (shop attendant), *catgut-scraper* (fiddler), **bobby*, *peeler*, *johnny*, and *crusher* (policeman), *crocus* (quack doctor), *driver* (employer). General terms were: **bloke* and **cove* (fellow), **swell*, *screw* (miser), **fancy man* (lover), *sharp* (cheat), **flat* (dupe), *lushington* (drunkard), *kid* (child), *duffer* (fool), *brick* (good fellow), **nobs* (well-off people), **strapper* (big man), *mucksnipe* (ruined man), *moocher* (beggar), **twicer* and **bester* (cheat), *Christ-Killer* (Jew), *corner cove* (loafer), *doll* (woman), *doxy* (wife), *dolly-mop* (harlot), **cully* (fellow), **scab* and *scurf* (low fellow), *prig* (thief), *bunter* (harlot), *jolly* (confederate), and *flat-catcher* (swindler). The beggars and thieves whom Mayhew interviewed used many other terms, but as these belong to the vocabulary of cant and were not generally used by Cockneys, I have thought it best to neglect them. Mayhew mentions one other point of some interest on this subject. Costermongers were hardly ever known by their real names:

> They are all known one to another by nicknames, which they acquire either by some mode of dress, some remark that has ensured costermongering applause, some peculiarity in trading, or some defect or singularity in personal appearance. Men are known as *Rotten Herrings*, *Spuddy* (a seller of bad potatoes), *Curly* (a man with a curly head), *Foreigner* (a man who had been in the Spanish Legion), *Brassy* (a very saucy person), *Gaffy* (once a performer), *The One-eyed Buffer*, *Jaw-breaker*, *Pine-apple Jack*, *Cast-iron Poll* (her head having been struck with a pot without injury to her), *Whilky*, *Blackwall Poll*, *Lushy Bet*, *Dirty Sal* (the costermongers generally objecting to dirty women), and *Dancing Sue.*

Adjectives applied to people were: *green* and *balmy* (silly), *cracky* (mad), *screwy* (stingy), *rusty* and *riled* (angry), *queer* and *all-overish* (ill), *fly* (clever), *lushy* (drunk), *bounceful cut-up* (downcast), *seedy* (shabby), *beaten-out* (impoverished), *out of collar* (unemployed).

In addition to the back slang and Lingua Franca terms for money mentioned by Hotten, Mayhew records these general terms: **tin* and *rust* (money), **browns* (pence), *flag* (fourpence), **tanner* and **kick* (sixpence), **bob*, *gen*, and *peg* (shilling), *bull* and *quarter* (five shillings), **sov* and *King's picture* (sovereign), *monarch* (guinea), and **finuff* (five pounds). The slang words for food and drink are surprisingly few: **inside lining* (meal), **grub*, **block ornaments*, and **cagmag* (odd pieces of meat), *scran* (broken victuals), *jemmy* (sheep's head), *winks* (periwinkles), **murphy* (potato), *lush* (beer), **ruin* (gin), and *pale* (brandy). Nor are the terms for the body and its members as numerous as we should expect. Probably the crudity of this branch of slang explains the few terms which the costers used in speaking to Mayhew. **Nut* (head), **gob* (mouth), **trotters* (feet), and **mauleys* (hands) are the only words I have noticed. Terms for clothes and finery are more numerous: *dunnage* (clothes), *duck* and *broady* (cloth), **togs*, *slops*, and *toggery* (clothes), *benjamin* (coat), *kicksies* (trousers), *gallows* (braces), *trotter-cases* (boots), **kick* (pocket), *colour* (handkerchief), *kingsman* (coloured neck-cloth), *fawny* (ring), *belcher* (thick ring), and *mush* (umbrella).

Many slang words related to trade: *paper-fake* (ballad-selling), *busk* (to sell indecent songs in pubs), *cock* (a story sold in the streets), *griddle* (to sing in the streets), **gag* (to tell the story), **racket* (line of business), **pitch* (the hawker's place of trade), *swag-barrow* (coster's cart), *moke* (donkey), **patter* and **barrikin* (hawkers' talk), **carney* (blarney), *squib* (head of asparagus), *specks* (decaying oranges), *scuttle-mouth* (small oyster with a large shell), **slang* (short measure), *work* (to hawk), *cutting* (underselling), **bunts* (easily earned profit), **swop* (exchange), and *crack a crust* (make a living). Whether it was because of the dubious nature of some of the practices covered by these words or no, slang words for fighting are also pretty common in Mayhew's pages: **let into* (attack), **do for* (beat severely), *jacketing* (thrashing), *ferricadouzer* (knock-down blow), **pasting* (beating), **whack* (blow), *noser* (blow on the nose), *prop* (to hit), and *muzzle* (to hit).

Few of Mayhew's subjects were very prosperous and it is therefore natural that many of their words should relate to hard times: *cracked up* (ruined), **licked* (beaten), **hard-up*, *taper* (wretched), *gallows* hard (very hard), **pop* (pawn), *the *big house* (workhouse), *cadge* (beg), *pulled-up* and **pinched* (arrested), **stir* (prison), *the Start* (Old Bailey), *drag* (term of imprisonment), *topped* (hanged), and **the sack* (dismissal). It is a sign of the natural optimism of the coster, however, that the words for enjoyment and good times are as numerous: **spree*, **lark*, **boozing*, *lushing*, **hops* (dances), **penny gaff* (theatre), **gods* (gallery), *jerry* and *shofull* (tavern), *flash* (smart), **slap-up* (fine), **stunning* (excellent).

The miscellaneous words may be grouped into verbs: *prig* (steal), **palm off* (deceive), *mooch* (pilfer), *mug* (rob), **kid on* (persuade), **come it* (impose upon), **bowl out* (find out), **mizzle* and **hook it* (run away), *kick the bucket* (die), *hop the wag* (play truant), *hump* (botch), **mooch* (slouch), **knock about* (roam), *muck* (excel), *cook* (ruin), **tumble* (understand), **bang* (surpass). Nouns: *fudge* (nonsense), **cheek* and **bounce* (impudence), **slop* (rubbish), **all my eye* (nonsense), **dodges*, *lurks*, and **capers* (tricks), *fakement* (a cheating trick), *flam* (lie), *cocum* (cleverness), **doss* (lodging), **snooze* (sleep), **crib* (house), *humbox* (pulpit), *prad* (horse), **monekeer* (name), *catch 'em alive* (flypaper), **specs* (spectacles), *pure* (dung), **row* (noise). Adjectives: *gammy* (useless), **no go* (useless), **rum* (strange), **that's the ticket* (correct).

Not all of these terms were restricted to Cockney speech: some of them, legacies from seventeenth-century cant or contributions from the jargon of beggars, pugilists, and men-about-town, were also used in the colloquial speech of other classes. But most of them are Cockney terms, words which the costermonger applied to his trade and the ups-and-downs of life.

In *Real Life in London*, Pierce Egan had commented

on the popularity among Cockneys of such catch-phrases as *that's the time of day*, *that's the barber*, *go along Bob!*, and so on. Phrases of this kind, meaning little in themselves but helping to express the Cockney's perkiness, have always been a feature of the dialect. We found them in Elizabethan plays, and they are equally popular now. The most noteworthy contributors to this part of the Cockney treasury have been the song-writers and comedians of the music-halls. It would be impossible to trace the brief popularity of all the catch-lines from music-hall ditties. But these are some of the tags which were the Victorian counterparts of the Elizabethan "but me no buts" or "Go by Jeronimo"—the derisive "all round my hat!" and "Where did you get that hat?"; Arthur Lloyd's "Not for Joseph!", "It's naughty but it's nice", and "Just to show there's no ill feeling"; James Fawn's "fair, fat and forty", "You couldn't tell t'other from which", and "If you want to know the time, ask a policeman"; the Great MacDermott's "We don't want to fight, but by Jingo if we do!"; Dan Leno's "You must know Mrs. Kelly!"; Herbert Campbell's "All very fine and large!", "Getting a big boy now!", and the insulting term "Queenie!" addressed to stout women because Campbell, the monumental opposite of the frail Dan Leno, had played the Queen in a Drury-Lane pantomime; Albert Chevalier's "Knocked 'em in the Old Kent Road" and "My Old Dutch"; Gus Elen's ironic "A nice quiet day", "'E dunno where 'e are", and "It's a great big shame"; Marie Lloyd's "Twiggey-voo?", "knocked abaht a bit", and "a little of what you fancy"; and Harry Champion's "Whatcher me old brown son", "Any old iron!", and "Ginger, you're barmy!" Some of these catch-phrases have outlasted the popularity of the songs themselves. Hundreds of others must have faded with the songs themselves.

Although Heinrich Baumann's *Londonismen*, 1887, is not reliable on Cockney pronunciation, it is valuable on slang. Many of the words he quotes are suspect as the current slang of his day, since they are derived from literary works. But the greater part seem to have been collected, as he claimed, from actual speech. The slang words characteristic of Cockney speech do not belong to any type of slang, apart from the rhyming phrases and back slang, but are miscellaneous terms used more by vulgar Londoners than by other speakers. A Londoner would express contempt by saying "It's all my eye and my grandmother", that relation taking the place of the more familiar Betty Martin. He would say that bad food was "enough to make a black man choke", that intimates were "as thick as two Jews on a pay day", and that an ignorant person had as much idea of a subject "as a donkey has of Sunday". For various people he had his own slang terms, most of them contemptuous, **Clever Dick*, *crusty gripes* (grumbler), *gutter kid*, *house-knacker* (landlord), *ink-spiller* (clerk), *Jemima* (servant-girl), **tart* (girl), *dabs* (expert), *dusty* (dustman). A drunkard was said "to be fond of his drops" or "to overheat his flues", and to fall in love with anybody was "to knob on to" him or her. Food, as always in Cockney, accounts for numerous slang words, *drainpipes* (macaroni), **goosgog* (gooseberry), *fish-fosh* (kedgeree), *meat-fosh* (hash), etc. And the Londoner's way of arranging his hair, which had produced so many new words during this century, "aggerawator" being the most famous, still stimulated the Cockney's vocabulary; curls were called *tobacco pipes* or *meat-hooks*, and a girl's fringe was an *idiot fringe*.

J. Redding Ware's *Passing English of the Victorian Era*, 1909, has for our purpose an interest surpassing all dictionaries of slang save only Eric Partridge's great work. Although he, like all lexicographers, was assisted by printed slang, he was more interested than most in spoken slang. He records local slang with more consistency than any previous writer and he is careful to record the status of his terms. From the many words which he designates, "Common London", "low London", "people's", "costermongers' ", it would be possible to compile a small dictionary of Cockney slang. This chapter is no place for such a dictionary, and to represent Ware's work we may quote a few characteristic words which illustrate some of the principles which control the Cockney's linguistic creation. A single conception will often give rise to a group of words: that love is "sweet" prompted the Victorian Cockney to such developments as, *Barrel of Treacle* (love), *Jammiest bits of jam* (perfect young females), *pennorth of treacle* (charming girl), and of course **tart*. Commercial relations with a group of "foreigners", Romanies, Jews or even countrymen, tempts the Cockney to borrow words from their language and to give them a more general application: thus Ware records these Yiddish words used as Cockney slang (mostly in the East End), **clobber* (clothes), **gonoph* (thief), **kosher* (undefiled)—it is now extended to mean "legal" or "above board", **shool* (church), *triper* (unclean), etc. A striking event or a famous person will suggest to the Cockney a general application of its or his name and characteristics: *binned* (hanged) from Binns the hangman appointed in 1883, *'Awkins* (a severe man) from Sir Frederic Hawkins the judge, and a little later in 1905 "a princely costermonger" from Albert Chevalier's character-song "And 'Enery 'Awkins is a first-class name", *do you to wain-rights* (treat you to rights) from Wainwright the murderer, *St. Lubbock* (an orgy) from the bank holidays secured by Lubbock. New descriptions for striking people and striking descriptions for insignificant people account for many new formations: *gal sneaker*, *tottie all colours* (a brightly dressed girl), **Mud Island* (Southend), **basher* (a rowdy), *never squeedge* (a passionless youth), *Ally Luja Lass* (Salvation Army girl). More striking and far more numerous are the metaphorical words, **cock linnet* (a dapper boy), *flight of steps* (slices of bread and butter), *Fountain temples* (public W.C.'s), *beer bottle* (stout man), *Dutch cheese* (bald-headed person), *five-barred gate* (policeman) since he usually was a yokel, *gaspipes* (trousers), *Hyde Park railings* (breast of mutton), *geranium* (red nose). In this type of creation the Cockney best expresses that humour, perky or sardonic, which is the best quality of his language, *gone to Abney Park* (dead) from the name of the cemetery, *virgin's bus* the ironic description of the last bus from Piccadilly, *cold cook* (undertaker). The same perkiness made the Cockney seize upon the catch-phrases of the music-halls, often for the purposes of cheerful insult, and invent similar phrases, *keep yer 'air on!*, *getting a big boy now!*, *all very fine and large*, *queenie!* an insult to fat women. New compound names for craftsmen were formed with the old cant words "faker" and "fencer", *tog-fencer* (tailor), *wig-faker* (hairdresser), *letter-fencer* (postman), and the analogous *water-dona* and *washer-dona* (washerwoman). Finally, London places and London customs account for many slang words characteristic of the Cockney dialect, *tramfare* (twopence), *Sluker* (a St. Luke's harlot), *Angel* a similar lady from the Islington district, *Decker* a dweller in "the Deck", that is Seven Dials, *Barner* (a roaring blade) from the entertainments at Highbury Barn, *waterloo* (halfpenny) from the toll once charged to cross the bridge.

Before the wealth of present-day Cockney slang we stand aghast! From what part of this Niagara shall we fill our two-inch phial? As we have examined the records of Cockney words in past generations we have marked those which survive in present-day speech, and in the two thousand odd columns of Eric Partridge's great dictionary will be found many thousands more. Not all of them are characteristic of Cockney speech. Unlike the countryman, the Cockney shares the words he has created with other people—and is often abused for doing so. The Cockney is remarkable in that he creates slang from philological enthusiasm, he propagates words as horticulturalists propagate flowers. Nor is his enthusiasm restricted to the flowers of his own fancy. He is as enthusiastic over other people's blooms, no matter in what soil they grew.

Cockney slang is often charged with being ephemeral, the worthless product of a day. This is true of a great many slang words, although one might defend them as

Jonson defended the lily. But slang often enjoys a surprising longevity. These words, mostly terms for food, money, parts of the body, stealing and fighting, have been used for two centuries or more: sixteenth century—*lam* and *lick* (to beat), *lift* (steal), *paw* (hand), *pins* (legs), *brass* (money), *peck* (food), *go to pot* (to be ruined); seventeenth century—*prog* (food), *cole*, *rhino*, *the ready* (money), *hog* (shilling), *quid* (guinea) now a pound, *nob* (head) or *noddle*, *phiz* (face), *peeper* (eye), *smeller* and *snitch* (nose), *trotters* (feet), *kid* (child), *nab* (to catch), *make* (to steal), *pinch* (to steal), *sock* (to hit), *neddy* (donkey); eighteenth century—*kick* (sixpence), *nix* (nothing), *bread basket* (stomach), *napper* (head), *mug* (face), *poke* (a blow), *chum* and *pal* (friend), *splificate* (thrash), *clink* (prison), *mizzle* (to run away), *snaffle* (to steal), *cop* (to capture). Other early words have been noticed in the discussion of the slang used in Elizabethan plays and by Ned Ward. The words which survive from the nineteenth century are much more numerous, a Cockney might still rub along very well with them alone. The Cockney cannot claim like the countryman that most of the characteristic words which he uses have a respectable antiquity. There are several reasons for that. The countryman's words apply for the main part to things which are themselves perennial, crops, flowers, animals, birds. The Cockney's vocabulary applies to city customs, places, people, opinions, which change from day to day. The Cockney creates words because he loves creation. He is a Don Giovanni in a world of words, loving them and leaving them. Moreover, many of the Cockney's words gain respectability, some of them even pass into standard

English, and so are lost to him. If the Cockney's language lacks the venerability of the countryman's, it has beyond doubt contributed far more than the county dialects to the language, both literary and colloquial, of good speakers.

Another charge that has been made against the Cockney's vocabulary is that it is mostly derived from the language of thieves. There is just enough truth in this comment to save it from absurdity. A fair number of Cockney words may be traced back to cant, the secret language of thieves, *doss* (to sleep), *gelt* (money), *shice* (worthless fellow), *moll* (girl), *nark* (spy), *nab* (to catch), *lift* (to steal), *mizzle* (decamp), *rum* (strange), *pinch* (steal), *sneak* (steal), *split* (betray), *snooze* (sleep), *bloke* (fellow), *busy* (policeman), *booze*, *crease* (to kill), *croak* (to die), *snaffle* (steal), and some others. Even rhyming slang and back slang have a dubious origin, they seem to have been at first the secret language of beggars. But a great many of these cant words have been used in Cockney for nearly two hundred years. They may have been thieves' words at first, but nobody who now uses them thinks of them as canting terms. Some of them have even gained such respectability that they are used colloquially by the best people. It is as absurd to tax Cockney with the origin of such words as to confront the aristocracy with their ancestors.

The borrowings from cant are only one facet of the Cockney's acquisitiveness. He rivals Autolycus in his fondness for these trifles, wherever he finds them. Cockney slang is made up primarily of his own inventions, enriched by borrowings from many diverse sources. The

Cockney comes into contact with the countryman in many capacities, as costermonger, as entertainer, as tripper: hence such dialect words as *chap*, *chisel* (cheat), *guiver* (pretentiousness), *gab* (mouth), *gumption* (intelligence), *swank*, *whack* (blow). At fairs and racecourses, the Londoner picks up numerous terms from the language of gypsies, *parnee* (rain), *pal* (friend), *ponk* (stink), *cosh* (to hit), *cove* (man), *couter* (sovereign). Various terms from Lingua Franca may be attributed to the same source, although some such terms have come via cant, *donah* (woman), *screeve* (write), *bivvy* (beer), etc. Contact with Jews, in trade and in the life of the East End, has enriched the Cockney's language by many words, *kosher* (fair), *oof* (money), *kye* (eighteenpence), *mazuma* (money), *cady* (hat), *goy* (Gentile), *gonoph* (thief), *clobber* (clothes), *shemozzle* (disturbance).

The slang and colloquialisms of other classes and cliques have proved as attractive. The strength of their contribution varies with the Cockney's familiarity with the people who use the words. The slang of pugilists has proved a rich hunting ground, the Cockney uses many words besides the following derived from this source, *kisser* (mouth), *knock out* (a surprise), *bread basket* (stomach), *boko* (nose), *hammer* (to punish), *conk* (nose), *floored* (beaten), *pins* (legs), *take the shine out of* (to snub), —wrestling only accounts for *get a half-nelson* on, "grapple with". The army has naturally provided many words, old terms like *swing the lead*, *come the old soldier*, *pongelo* (beer), and *buckshee* (free). The Great War contributed hundreds of words and phrases, words of the soldier's invention and words from foreign languages and Colonial slang: many of them barely survived the war itself, but some have persisted, *squiffy* and *blotto* (drunk), *conk out*, to *wangle*, *Jerry* (German), *gasper* (cigarette), *cooshy* (comfortable), to *scrounge*, *muck in* (to share), *sanfarian*, and others. Sailors have not proved so generous, but the Cockney is nevertheless indebted to them for some phrases and words, *shove one's oar in* (interfere), *palaver* (talk), *cut up a dido* (make a noise), *shove off* (go away!), and possibly *push the boat out* (stand treat) and *sling one's hook* (decamp), and of course *Sweet Fanny Adams* (nothing at all). From the racecourse come many terms, among them, *the office* (hint), *no odds* (unimportant), *welsher* (cheat), *it won't run to it* (insufficient). More exalted circles have provided fewer words, but those that have come from such sources are not unimportant, *Rugger*, *Soccer*, *chum* from the Universities, *swell* (dandy), *hop* (dance), *flapper* (girl) from Society. Some Cockney words may even claim the ultimate respectability, the state of seedy gentility; these words and some others were once standard English, *cocksure*, *guts*, *tick* (fool), *swop* (exchange), *peach* (betray)—the other words include some of those blunt words for the body and its functions which are thought by many people to be typical of the crude vulgarity of Cockney and Cockneys.

So one might pursue this theme. From trades and The Trade, from arts and crafts, from professions and pro's, from a thousand and one sources, familiar and unfamiliar, the Cockney borrows the words that strike his fancy. To follow him in his acquisitions would be to reproduce much of what Mr. Partridge has already collected. We need only touch on one further aspect of the subject. Since the arrival of the talkies and the recent fashion of writing newspapers in the style of American journals, hundreds of American slang terms have been adopted by Cockneys, *Oke*, *phoney* (spurious), *tough guy*, *boy friend*, *girl friend*, *spill the beans*, *joint* (place), *pep*, *slick*, *gold digger*—it is unnecessary to continue the list. However irritating the vogue of these words may have been, it was characteristic of Cockney, for the Londoner cannot resist the attraction of new and sprightly words. American slang was a Cleopatra for whom he fell as soon as he heard her first nasal boomings. Most of the terms scarcely outlived the films that introduced them: a few have proved valuable and seemingly lasting contributions to the Cockney's vocabulary. One interesting aspect of this fashion is that it revived the popularity of many old English slang terms: such words as *sock* (hit), *moll* (woman), *swell* (fine), *moocher* (beggar), *skirt* (girl), had been used by Cockneys long before Art had migrated to California. Nor is it a new tendency for Cockneys to borrow from American slang: words which are attributed to the influence of the films have in some cases been used by Cockneys for fifty years or more. Among the borrowings from the U.S.A. used in the last half of the nineteenth century are such familiar words as: *goner* (dead man), *sucker* (dupe), *squirt* (paltry person), *crook* (thief), *bunk* (nonsense), *pile* (fortune), *suck in* (deceive), *spondulicks* (money).

The Cockney's slang vocabulary is large: if he be an expert he probably knows considerably more slang words than standard words. In some subjects, drink, venery, crime and sharp practice, he can draw upon a vocabulary far exceeding that of accepted speech. He has a word, often many words, for every situation and condition, living and dying, sleeping and waking, eating and drinking, for success and failure, happiness and misery, dullness and brightness. He can match with a slang synonym the names of people, birds, beasts, objects, or opinions. His vocabulary enables him to be witty and humorous, crude or coy, enthusiastic or cynical. His words are primarily materialistic, and so is the spirit which creates them. It is this aspect of Cockney speech which usually shocks genteel observers: they are horrified to find even Cockney children expressing blatant cynicism and on speaking terms with the crudest bodily functions. The Cockney's vocabulary, although far richer and more expressive than the countryman's, certainly lacks the charm with which the pastoral tradition has endowed the country dialects. But it is a vocabulary natural to townspeople living in poverty. When poverty forces people to live in verminous, insanitary slums, when starvation wages dignified by the approval of the Board of Trade lead girls to prostitution, when want and the attitude it breeds lead men and women and even children to covet their neighbours' property, a materialistic attitude is to be expected. But the cynicism of the Cockney differs from the cynicism of more prosperous people. It is natural and not the result of disillusionment: it is cheerful rather than sentimental. When the Cockney pricks the bubbles of idealism it is not from bitterness: when he is crude it is not because he finds crudity repellent. This attitude is as natural to him as his shadow. As the Cockney climbs in the social scale he changes his outlook and his vocabulary. Slang is used extensively only in the slum areas and among the poorest people (excluding tradesmen). Cockneys in reasonably paid jobs and living in decent conditions use little more slang than the lower middle class. Perhaps the chief reason why the ambitious Cockney rivals the pedagogues in his aversion to the dialect is that it is the symbol of the conditions of life in the slums.

Because the Cockney borrows so freely from the slang of other groups, and particularly because other groups borrow even more freely from Cockney slang, it is almost impossible to isolate those words which are used solely by Cockneys. The attitude to life natural among Cockneys is adopted in the humour of more prosperous classes. The crude and materialistic vocabulary which the Cockney employs as his natural expression is, therefore, adopted in the humour and banter of smoke-rooms and clubs. A distinction of this kind would apply to many hundreds of words. Many other words may be characterised as far more familiar in Cockney than in the speech of other classes.

Rhyming slang, which originated in Cockney speech, has always been characteristic of the London dialect, except during the Great War, when it was taken up generally by the army. Its use varies even in Cockney. Some Cockneys use it as an exercise in wit and ingenuity, others are not conscious of it as a distinct species of slang and their few rhyming terms are used naturally as part of the ordinary slang vocabulary, *pot and pan* (old man or husband), *half inch* (pinch or steal). The best rhyming slang unites the rhyme with a social commentary, *artful dodger* (lodger), *trouble and strife* (wife), *Gawdforbids* ("kids" or "Yids"). Other rhymes, of which the following are among the most familiar, are less inspired, *round the houses* (trousers), *skin and blister* (sister), *tit for tat* (hat), *plates o' meat* (feet), *Dicky Dirt* (shirt), *apples and pears* (stairs), *Harry Tate* (plate), *four by two* (Jew), *lord o' the manor* ("tanner" or "sixpence"), *daisy roots* (boots). The expert use of rhyming slang consists in the abbreviation of the terms by the omission of the rhymes. The most familiar example is the term for that derisive noise given wider popularity by some American films, *raspberry*, short for *raspberry tart* (fart)—a further shortening is *ra*. Other widely used abbreviations are *titfer* (hat), *daisies* (boots), *platesers* (feet). Back slang, which in Mayhew's time was the secret language of the costermongers, never seems to have gained wider popularity among Cockneys. A few inverted words have found common acceptance, *slop* (police(man)), *yob* or *yobbo* ("street rough", an inverted form of "boy"), *traf* and *sip* which need no explanation. But back slang is still commonest among tradesmen: the inverted numbers *eno*, *owt*, *erth*, and so on are sometimes used by card-players in the East End, but it is among butchers and other dealers in raw foodstuffs that this type of slang is commonest. In Smithfield and Spitalfields they still use such apparent gibberish as *delo woc* (old cow), *tib o' the delo* (bit of the old), *erf yennep* (threepence). The experts use this type of slang with extraordinary facility, inverting every other word in rapid conversation.

Of the miscellaneous words more frequently used by Cockneys than by other groups it would be possible to compile a dictionary far too long for such a sketch as this.

The scope of this book will not permit of more than a representative selection. I diffidently suggest the following words as the most familiar slang terms rarely used except by Cockneys:

acid, impudence
basin-full, specimen, trial
beano, jollification
boozer, public-house
cag-mag, rough meat
carve-up, swindle
chivvy, face
clean, to scold, abuse
cooty, verminous
cop a packet, to be injured
cosh, to hit
crown, to hit
cully, friend (in greetings)
dekko, glance, look
dutch, to cheat
erb, wag, humorist
faggot, fool
freemans, costing nothing
guts, a greedy person
geezer, old person
gorblimey, rakish cap
guiver, pretentiousness, "blarney"
hank, nonsense
hog, shilling
josser, fellow
jossop, gravy
lay on to be, claim to be
lovely dripping, excellent
lump, in the, hard-up
mivvy, a marvel
mouldies, pence, coppers
muck about, to handle
nark it! stop talking!
old china, old dear
perisher, unpleasant person
ruck on, to betray, quarrel with
shonk, nose, Jew
splosh, money
swiz, swindle, to swindle
tea-leaf, unpleasant person
wallop, beer.

Even some of these words may be more widely used than I think they are.

Another traditional feature of Cockney is the fondness for catch-phrases, ready-made tags which are applied to anything and everybody, often with maddening frequency. Some of them are not capable of definition, terms of exuberance or phrases analogous to those damnable snatches of melody which do not quit the mind until it has been worn out by recollection. Such phrases are these, *have a banana!*, *come up and see me sometime*, *Archibald certainly not*, *how's your poor old feet?*, *the same to you with knobs on!* The provenance of some of these phrases is obvious: they mostly come from the music-halls, less frequently from the cinemas. Many catch-phrases serve the same purpose as so many slang words, to express contempt or insult, *after the Lord Mayor's show comes the dungcart*, *do you see any green in my eye?*, *get your hair cut!*, *was your father a glazier?* (to a person blocking the view), *put a sock in it!*, *keep your hair on!* Readiness is expressed by saying *Bob's your uncle!*, a hint that a borrower should return his loan is *It's got a back to it*, a child whose nose is running is told *Wipe your nose, your chin's bleeding!*, and one person staring at another is rebuked by the query, *Got your eye full?* Some catch-phrases are mechanical answers to questions, often intended as rebukes. The query "How far are you going?" is met with the answer, *There and back to see how far it is*; the person who interjects "I thought . . ." is snubbed by *You know what thought did*, the query "What?", which many Cockneys consider a vulgar form of expression, is rebuked by the rhyming catch-phrase, *Cats'-tails all hot*; if an accidental rhyme is made in speaking the person who observes it will say *He's a poet* and will promptly be capped by *But he doesn't know it.* This form of prop and cop is traditional: some examples of it may be found in the Cockney dialogue of Elizabethan plays.

Many other Cockney mannerisms of the sixteenth, seventeenth, and eighteenth centuries have survived, as we have already seen. It is not necessary to repeat former comments on them. Only two other aspects of the dialect need be discussed, the Cockney oaths and intensives.

The desire for emphasis has always been a source of colloquialism, not only in Cockney. The Cockney's intensive adjectives are not many, but the frequency with which they are used richly colours the dialect. They range from the mild and meaningless *blinking* and *blooming* to the stronger *bloody* and *bleeding* and the very forceful *s—dding* and *f———ing*—it is perhaps necessary to note that the last two adjectives are rarely used in this way with any sexual significance; they are even used by children and are prompted by the desire for vividness and strength. The intensive adverbs are formed simply by the addition of "well" to these adjectives, *blinking-well*, *bloody-well*, etc. Cockney oaths have a similar forcefulness. The bourgeois oaths burlesqued by the Elizabethan playwrights must have been confined to the Sunday citizens. It is hard to imagine that the Elizabethan Cockneys would have used such mealy mouthed asseverations as "By my faith" and "O' my conscience", when their descendants, whose speech habits are in other respects so similar, use such mouth-filling oaths as *Gawd Blimey*, *Blimey*, *By Christ*, *B—gg—r me*, *F——k me*, *Strike me pink*. The aristocratic characters of the early plays swear with conviction and impressiveness. One can hardly doubt that the Cockney must have been just as impressive.

CHAPTER VI

COCKNEY PRONUNCIATION AND GRAMMAR

THE most striking feature of any dialect, although it may not be its most characteristic trait, is the pronunciation. In the historical study of pronunciation only one aspect of pronunciation can be traced with any certainty, the nature of vowels and diphthongs and the treatment of consonants. Intonation, pace, quality of voice are all dialectal features which impress the ordinary listener, but students of dialect have until recently not considered them worth description. The comments upon dialectal vowels and diphthongs and the phonetic spellings of people who spoke dialect enable the historian to reconstruct this part of historical pronunciation, but the more subtle elements do not reveal themselves in spelling. So is it with Cockney.

Unfortunately, however, there has been no Cockney "dialect literature". The student of county dialects may base his discussion of nineteenth- and perhaps eighteenth-century pronunciation upon poems and sketches written in elaborate phonetic spelling. The writers were proud of their dialects and eager to display them in all their broadness. The Cockney dialogue in eighteenth- and nineteenth-century novels was conventional. The novelist was content to represent a yokel's dialect by a few odd spellings like *wool* (will) or *Zunday*, no matter where he was supposed to come from, and he thought it sufficient to represent a Cockney by misplacing a few *h*'s or by interchanging *w* and *v*, consistently or inconsistently. This convention also served to represent general vulgarism. Dickens, for example, uses this "Cockney" dialect as the speech of several country characters, Peggoty for example. This convention, as Shaw says, was copied from book to book by authors who never dreamed of using their ears.

The literary convention for Cockney prior to 1880 is superficially so unlike present-day Cockney and the present literary convention that ordinary readers assume that the dialect has completely changed. In the report of the Conference on the Teaching of English in London Elementary Schools issued by the London County Council in 1909 it is alleged that:

> When a boy or girl in Devonshire, Lincolnshire, or Yorkshire is taught to acquire the constructions of the King's English at the expense of his native forms of speech, there is a balance of loss and gain in the process. But with the pupil in the London elementary school this is not the case. There is no London dialect of reputable antecedents and origin which is a heritage for him to surrender in school. The Cockney mode of speech, with its unpleasant twang, is a modern corruption without legitimate credentials, and is unworthy of being the speech of any person in the capital city of the Empire.

Even scholars have been led to the same opinion by a comparison of Sam Weller's dialect with present-day Cockney. Georg H. Höfer, in his dissertation published in 1896, declared that a Cockney of Dickens's time would not be able to understand a modern Cockney, and Joseph

Saxe, in a comparison of Bernard Shaw's Cockney with that in *Punch* about 1860, finds that those vowels and diphthongs which are most characteristic of present-day Cockney are for the main part new developments.

The scholars who take this view have been strengthened in their opinion by the fact that these vowels and diphthongs are not mentioned by the early commentators on the dialect. Thus, Alexander J. Ellis, writing to A. W. Tuer in 1885,[1] gave this testimony:

> I was born in the N. district (of London) over seventy years ago, and I do not recall the ī pronunciation of ā in my boyish days, nor do I recollect having seen it used by the older humorists. Nor do I find it in "Errors of Pronunciation and Improper Expressions, used frequently and chiefly by the Inhabitants of London," 1817, which likewise does not know any pronunciation of ō like *ow*. Hence I am inclined to believe that both are modernisms, due to the growing of London into the adjacent provinces.

He might have added that *i* for *a*, and *ah* for *ow*, are unrepresented in Elphinston and Walker, too.

In my enquiries about the dialect from old people, I have always found that educated people and non-Cockneys had the same view. But they always relied on quotations: none of them seemed able to separate his own observation from what he had read or been told. On the other hand, the Cockneys who have discussed the subject with me do not recollect any change in the dialect. The oldest of them—and some of them were over eighty—are certain that when they were boys and girls Cockneys were using the same "aht-and-abaht" dialect that they do now.[2]

[1] Letter dated 24th April, 1885, reprinted in Tuer's *Old London Street Cries*, 1885.

[2] My enquiries were made mostly in Hoxton and adjacent districts.

Some people were free from it—it is a remarkable fact that some Cockneys now are almost free from the characteristic vowels and diphthongs, although they have brothers and sisters who use the broadest Cockney. Most of the old Cockneys clearly recollect the use of *w* for *v* (never *v* for *w*, however), but they agree that it was not general: some people used it naturally, but it was most familiar as a comic pronunciation. The Cockney music-hall comedians, not only Chevalier and Gus Elen, but their predecessors, all used the modern sounds, I am told, even if the printed versions of their songs suggest that they spoke "good English" with the addition of a few Victorian Cockneyisms. Moreover, the oldest Cockneys I have found, some of them nearly ninety, all speak the broadest form of modern Cockney. The B.B.C. programme "In Town To-night" has often brought to the microphone old Cockneys practising unusual crafts: so far as I recollect they all spoke that "modern corruption without legitimate credentials" of which the L.C.C., of all bodies, was so ashamed.

Modern Cockney must have been going strongly at the middle of the nineteenth century, despite Dickens and despite Ellis and other philologists. A dialect does not change overnight: these old Cockneys must have been reared in the sound of *piper* and *tahn* as well as of Bow Bells. The most remarkable change has been in the literary representation of the dialect. Barry Pain, Whiteing, George R. Sims changed suddenly from Dickensian to modern Cockney. Was it because they had noticed a change in the dialect or because they had all come across another class of Cockneys? I think not. A more probable explanation is that Tuer's criticism had made the inadequacies of the old convention so obvious that to continue to use it would be to run the risk of being called old-fashioned.

The Dickensian style of Cockney was a literary convention and it is dangerous to take it as an adequate representation of the dialect as most scholars have done. The 'Arry ballads in *Punch* are a striking example of the danger of relying upon the observations of literary men. These ballads, which give up the old interchange of *w* and *v* but do not represent the modern diphthongs and vowels, have been treated as an interesting half-way stage between Victorian and modern Cockney. But when E. J. Milliken published a selection of them in 1892, he said in his preface:

> As regards 'Arry's diction, his orthography, it is hardly needful, perhaps, to observe, that no attempt has been made to be accurately phonetic. No possible combination of letters will really render 'Arry's pronunciation of such words as "lady", "game", "Charlie", "daisy", "down", or "trousers". To besprinkle these pages with such orthographic combinations as "lidy", "goime", "Choarlee", "doisy", "daoun", or "trersers" would (in my opinion) make them a perplexing, eye-wearying, phonetic puzzle, without attaining absolute orthoepical accuracy. It would, of course, be quite possible to approximate more closely to 'Arry's actual pronunciation, but only, I think, at the cost of making my version hideous to look at and hard to read. Rightly or wrongly, I have deliberately abstained from the attempt.

This, as a Cockney would say, blows the gaff. It would perhaps be ungenerous to suggest that Milliken did not adopt the phonetic spellings for the simple reason that when he began to write the ballads the old convention had not been challenged. The essential fact is that what might be taken as a very different dialect from modern Cockney is, in fact, merely an old literary convention for the same thing. I have not the least doubt that Dickens would have made the same apologia had he been questioned about Sam Weller's dialect. The question for consideration, therefore, is how far back these characteristic sounds of modern Cockney really go.

The diphthongs which Cockneys use instead of long *ee* and long *oo*, by introducing a slight *er*-glide before the normal sound, are not represented in any of the early documents or indeed in modern Cockney literature. It is a testimony to the originality of Shaw's observation of the dialect that he was the only writer to notice these Cockneyisms. The earliest evidence of their existence that I have found is Shaw's description of the Cockney alphabet he had heard while passing a London elementary school—"I, Ber-ee, Ser-ee, Der-ee, Er-ee, Aff, Jer-ee, Iche, Awy, Ji, Ki, Al, Am, An, Ow, Per-ee, Kioo, Aw, Ass, Ter-ee, Yer-eoo, Ver-ee, Dabbleyew, Ax, Wawy, Zad". Shaw was also the first writer to recognise the Cockney tendency to darken and vocalise *l*: he uses the spellings *'eolth* (health), *teoll* (tell), *weoll*, etc. The slight advancing of long *oo* which accompanies the diphthongisation is represented by Shaw by *ew*, as in his spelling of the Cockney "W". This is also the device used by Barry Pain, *tew* (two), etc. Similar spellings may be found in earlier Cockney records: *yewve* (you've), *shews* (shoes) in *Punch*, 1850–60,[1] and *shewes* (shoes) 1597, *conclewded*

[1] Quotations from Shaw and *Punch*, 1850–60, are taken from Saxe's study.

1605, *Hewgo* 1622, etc., in the churchwardens' records,[1] although one cannot be sure that these are not inverse spellings prompted by the pronunciation of "dew", "few", etc.

There is better evidence, however, for the existence in early Cockney of the other pronunciations which we regard as characteristic of the modern dialect.

The raised pronunciation of short *a*, which resembles the ordinary sound of short *e*, has always been a feature of the dialect. Machyn spells *messe* (mass), *then* (than), *Crenmer*, and among the many forms of the church records are: *gellon* 1492, *gedderyng* 1512, *wex* 1530, *seckes* 1577, *keche* 1599, *aperill* 1617, *texes* 1662, *bellancs* 1671. Even the later orthoepists and novelists regard this vowel as a Cockneyism. Yeomans suggests the raising was a general Cockneyism; Sharp and Walker cite *belcony* and *ketch* respectively; Jeames Yellowplush spells *drenk*, *ren*, *Jennuary*; Mayhew's Cockneys use *kerackter*, *reddishes*, *ratketcher*, *lemontation*; and Baumann cites *keb* and *ketch*.

There is similar authority for the antiquity of *aw* for short *o*. Early phonetic spellings which illustrate this variant include: *ffauster lane* 1487, *chorst* (cost) 1573, *shoopes* (shops) 1661, *loose* (loss) 1658. Walker gives these examples: *brawth*, *frawth*, *mawth*; Yellowplush writes *intawsicated*, *tawsing*; Mayhew has *cawfee*, *corfin*; *Punch*, *nawn-sense*, *corck*, *horficers*; and Baumann, *dawg*.

The pronunciation of *th* as *f* and *v* is also represented at all periods. Early examples are: Machyn, *Frogmortun*, *frust*, *Quenheyffe* (Queenhithe), *Garlykeheyffe*, *Feverstone*

[1] Quotations from the churchwardens' records are taken from my article: *The Vulgar Speech of London in the XV–XVII Centuries*.

(Featherstone) 1634, *Redriff* (Rotherhithe) 1641, *tiues* (tithes) 1671. Elphinston notices *loph* (loth) and *Redrif*; Yellowplush writes *mouf*, *Goffick*, *oaves*, *cloves*; *Punch* gives *nuffen*; and Baumann *nuffin*. Similar spellings are frequent in the Cockney music-hall songs which we have quoted previously.

The addition of *t* and *d* after certain consonants has always been prevalent among Cockneys. Among the many early spellings are: *Regyment* (regimen) 1564, Machyn, *surgantt*, *orfunt* (orphan) 1603, *margent* 1671, *ostbitall* 1579, *Lost* (loss) 1640, *Elest* (else) 1698, *knifte* (knife) 1637, *gallande* 1579, *winde* (wine) 1612, *eindmate* 1630, *Sermond* 1662, Machyn, *Cold Harbard* 300, *gerrelds* (girls) 1630, *Trenchard* (trencher) 1691. Elphinston instances *bacheldor*, *wonst* (once), *gownd*, *sermont*, *drownd*, *scollard*; Pegge adds *verment* (vermin), *surgeont*, *regiment*, *paragraft*, *nyst* (nice) and *nyster*, *sinst*; Yellowplush has *moond*, *half-a-crownd*, *wind* (wine), *skreend*, etc. Many other examples may be found in nineteenth-century Cockney dialogue or in modern representations of the dialect.

The Cockney practice of omitting initial *h* and inserting it at the beginning of words that normally start with a vowel has always been used by novelists, and it is unnecessary to quote their examples. Earlier examples include: *Inges* 1494, *alywater* 1494; Machyn, *alffe*, *Amton*, *ede* (head), *ard*, *untyng*, *olles*, *erbes* 1579, *ospitall* 1635; and *hould* (old) 1548, *hallallan* day 1549; Machyn, *Hambrosse*, *hundershaft*, *Hyslyngton*, *hanswered*, *helder* 1571, *hawght* 1593, *height* (eight) 1627. The addition of *h* has probably always been much less common than the omission of it: as Tuer says, Cockneys prefer to save their energy on *h*'s. Walker gives the true explanation of these unwarranted *h*'s: they arise from a consciousness that it is incorrect to drop the aspirate, so that in attempting to talk fine Cockneys were apt to insert *h*'s before all initial vowels. It is typical of literary Cockney that it should have extended this mannerism into a general practice.

It is true, as Ellis says, that the substitution of *i* for *a* is not recorded by the early orthoepists. But I am afraid that they, like the literary men, were content to copy from previous books and to neglect their ears. The modern diphthong seems to have been used by some Cockneys in the sixteenth and seventeenth centuries, to judge by these spellings: Machyn, *chynes*, *obtyninge* 1589, *Rile* (rail) 1623, *Cordwyners* 1636, *acqintance* 1645, *ordined* 1655, *Byes* (bays) 1655, *strynge* 1657, *exchinng* 1671, etc. This diphthong is neglected in the following two centuries, but there are a few indications that it was actually used. In the 1814 edition of Pegge's *Anecdotes* there is this note: "Amongst some people bottles are 'libelled' as well as Ministers of State." The isolated spelling *Purvyor* in *Punch*, 1850–60, may be a slip, but there can be no doubt about the word *Nire* which occurs in Hotten's slang dictionary, 1859: it is back slang for "rain". The slang-term *silver-laced* (lousy) given in Grose's *Lexicon Balatronicum*, 1811, may pun on "lice" and so reflect this diphthong inversely. There seems no reason to believe that a pronunciation used by seventeenth-century Cockneys and by their descendants in the middle of the nineteenth century should have disappeared in the interim. The more reasonable assumption is that its use did not occur to the writers who first formulated the literary convention, with the result that it was neglected until Tuer was shocked by its omission.

The rounding of long *i* which accompanies this form of long *a* is similarly recorded. The early London documents contain such spellings as: *ploying* 1614, *hoye* (high) 1633, *loyne* (line) 1635, *Oylle* (aisle) 1661, *point* (pint) 1679. After Tuer had changed the fashion similar spellings are commonly used in literary Cockney, but in the intervening period there are only a few scattered records which testify to the existence of the sound. Deborah Hornbeck addresses Peregrine Pickle as *Coind Sur*; *Punch* spells *toime*, *foight*, *Eloiza*, *whoy*, *oi*, *oi'll*; the form *pervoided* occurs in G. W. Hunt's Cockney song *The Doctor's Boy*, 1873. There is more justification for the novelists and critics in this case: the rounding is hardly sufficient to call for such a spelling as *oi*.

Before 1880 I have found no representation of the Cockney pronunciation of *ou*, *ow* as *ar* or *ah*. But in the early London documents there are a number of spellings which replace the normal spelling by *u*: *Hundeslowe* (Hounslow) 1486, *ffundacyon* 1487, *Acunt* 1503, *grvnd* 1503, *vnce* (ounce) 1504; Machyn, *bune* (bound), *Brune* (Brown), *cuncil*, *fundation* 1579, *Acuntant* 1621, *Acunt* 1622, *Cunsel* (counsel) 1662, *ffunlin* 1694; and Machyn, *shutt* (shout), *shrudes* (shrouds), *fulles* (fowls), *justes* (jousts), *wood-husse* 1593, *Suthe* (South) 1595, *vtter* (outer) 1622, *abut* (about) 1633, *vt* (out) 1665. The first group of spellings may reflect a shortening of Middle English *ū* before *n*—such Cockney pronunciations as *pun'* (pound) are legacies of this process. But this explanation does not apply to the other spellings, which patently represent either the short *u* vowel or a sound akin to it. It is quite possible that this sound may be that used in present-day Cockney. As I have previously stated, the Cockney sound in such words as "town" and "out" is either a vowel with the quality of short *u* or a diphthong which begins with that sound. It would represent Cockney pronunciation better if writers were to use *u* instead of the conventional *ar* or *ah*: *ut* (out), *shutt* (shout), etc. It may seem to be special pleading to suggest that the sixteenth- and seventeenth-century writers were prompted by the present-day Cockney sound, but it is difficult to suggest any other explanation.

The Cockney pronunciation of long *o*, which Tuer and his followers represent by such spellings as *rowd* (road), *now* (no), *towld* (told), *ould* (old), *stoun* (stone) may be traced back with more certainty. This value of long *o* is recognised even in the eighteenth and nineteenth centuries before *l*. Thus, Elphinston writes *behould*, Walker complains of the vulgar pronunciations *mo-oold*, *co-oold*, *bo-oold*, etc., and spellings like *ould*, *cowld*, *rowld*, are common in novels. Similar spellings are very common in early London records: *towle* (toll) 1567, *howld* 1572, *owlde* 1584, *rowlers*, 1642, *gowlde* 1602, *howldfast* 1648, etc. Apart from Pierce Egan's representation of the old-clothes-man's cry, *Clow*, *clow*, I have found no evidence in eighteenth- and nineteenth-century documents of the use of this diphthong except before *l*. But, although they may possibly be inverse spellings due to the normal pronunciation of "row", "sow", etc., the following typical spellings from early Cockney records may very well be evidence of its existence much earlier: Machyn, *Rowse*, *howme* 1562, *lowde* 1579, *house* (hose) 1593, *goue* (go) 1612, *Nouble* 1657, *bouth* 1681, etc.

The rounding of the *a* in such words as "father", "park", "ask" is represented by Tuer and some of his followers as *aw*, *fawther*, *pawk*, *awsk*. Apart from Jeames Yellowplush's spellings, *chawms*, *Chawls*, *Jil Blaw*, I know of no similar spellings in eighteenth- and nineteenth-century documents, and even they may be intended to burlesque an affected pronunciation imitated from the beaux. But it is pretty clear that the rounded vowel must have been used by Cockneys long before the modern period. I have found these early spellings which reflect it: *raughters* (rafters) 1610, *churchyorde* 1499, Machyn, *portesans*, *maurqwes*, *Morten Colledge* 1630, *mawsey* (mercy), *Aurther* 1654, 1662. The *er* in "Merton" and "mercy" had been previously retracted to *ar*, as in "clerk".

Finally, there is some little evidence that the glottal stop was used in early Cockney. The popularity of the glottal stop is rapidly increasing: even Mr. McEager's parable does not reveal the completeness of its usurpation of *p*'s and *t*'s and *k*'s. In 1882 Professor D'Orsey spoke of the difficulty of distinguishing between "life", "like", and "light" in Cockney pronunciation, and Whiteing's spelling *Hy' Par'* confirms that it was replacing some of the plosive consonants at the end of last century. I am also inclined to think that it must have replaced *t* and *d* in *Punch's* spellings, *coont* (couldn't), *dint* (didn't), and in these forms from the churchwardens' records: *woostreet*

(Wood Street) 1677, *Statues* (statutes) 1658, *ffleestreete* 1624, *Lighfoots* 1635.

There is sufficient evidence, therefore, to justify our claiming for these characteristic pronunciations of modern Cockney an antiquity which has been hitherto denied. The evidence of their existence in the sixteenth and seventeenth centuries is fairly strong, and the evidence from the two succeeding centuries is striking if not abundant. The neglect of these Cockneyisms in the eighteenth and nineteenth centuries is easy to explain. When the Cockney convention was first evolved it was as a burlesque of the speech of City merchants, the Pentweazels, Sneaks and Maw-worms. The merchants would have been fairly free from the grosser forms of the dialect, and the omission of *h* or the use of *w* for *v* might have been more striking in their speech than the pronunciation of *a* or *ou*. And once the convention had been settled it was copied mechanically.

Ellis's suggestion that these pronunciations are modernisms due to the extension of London into Essex is therefore very improbable. Ellis shows that the Essex sounds of long *a* and *i* were approximately *i* and *oi*, but I very much doubt whether that is more than a coincidence, for Ellis's own account of the Essex dialect suggests no other strong resemblance to Cockney and the two dialects are certainly very different now—even the Essex *oi* for *i* is very different from the Cockney diphthong. I cannot believe that the densely populated areas which grew out into Essex can have been greatly influenced by the dialect of a comparative handful of countrymen. Moreover, the districts where Cockney is strongest,

Hoxton, Bermondsey, Lambeth, and so on, have been appendages of London for many centuries.

It is possible that the broader form of Cockney may not have been so general before the middle of last century. The apprenticeship system and the close and constant contact between servants and craftsmen and their employers may have kept the pronunciation of many Cockneys much nearer to accepted speech than it is now. Although it cannot be proved, the diffusion of broad Cockney may have been due to the decline of the apprenticeship system and the growth of the factory system, whereby the modifying influence of the middle class was removed and a coarser form of Cockney which had been associated with the courts and alleys was enabled to become general.

The continuity of Cockney by no means rests solely upon the evidence we have been discussing. Present-day Cockney shares a multitude of minor variant pronunciations with the Cockney speech of the preceding four centuries. They tend to be overlooked because they are less striking and less consistently used by novelists than the interchange of *w* and *v* or the substitution of *i* for *a*, but they are very important to the philologist as showing the persistence of Cockney speech-habits. These are most of them:

Instead of short *e*, Cockneys often pronounce short *i*, *git*, *kitch*, *cimetery*, *stiddy*, *kitchup*, *gint* (gent), *whilk*: the popularity of the pronunciation varies from speaker to speaker, some Cockneys using it almost as consistently as Irishmen. The variant was very common in early Cockney. Among the churchwardens' examples are:

chistes 1553, *erikting* 1581, *Inquist* 1621, *Riddy* 1630, *spicified* 1641, *Rigester* 1679, *pibbles* 1683, and its use in the following centuries is shown by these forms: Jonathan Wild, *sinsibil*; Pegge, *Kingsington*; Yellowplush, *gintleman*, *confision*, *inymies*, *spissymen*, etc.; Mayhew, *ivver*, *riglar*, *gits*, *Siven*, *depinds*, etc. On the other hand, Cockneys sometimes lower the *e* and pronounce it like *a*: this is the usual pronunciation in "yellow" and "celery" and Shaw notices it in the Cockney alphabet, *Aff*, *Al*, *Am*, *An*. There is abundant evidence of the existence of this variant in earlier pronunciation: Machyn, *Fanchurche*, *whan* 1592, *manding* 1621, *saxtons* 1631, *sauerall* 1648, *Lacctorer* 1673, *Tarris* (terrace) 1691, *Squarill* 1696; Wild, *haven* (heaven); Elphinston, *sat* (set); *Errors of Pronunciation*, *arrant* (errand), *salary* (celery); Yellowplush, *saminary*, *jallowsy*, *exparrymence*, *sallybrated*, etc.; Mayhew, *yallers*, *pratty*, *arrand*.

In a number of words Cockneys replace short *i* by short *e*, *ef*, *sence*, *set*, *sperrit*, *toothpeck*, *erritation*, *meracle*, *tell*, etc. This pronunciation, which is more popular among some groups than among others, was very prevalent in early periods of the dialect. It was one of the most striking traits of early Cockney, the sixteenth- and seventeenth-century forms including: *belles* (bills) 1444, *Meneris* 1487, *Sesterns* (cisterns) 1490, *weddo* 1531, *tembar* 1549, Machyn, *denner*, *menyster*, *Eslyngtun*, *consperacy*, *tell* (till) 1585, *wretten* 1587, *sette* (sit) 1609, *stell* 1643, *chelldren* 1696, *Ef* 1698. Later examples are not so abundant, but the continuance of the variant is proved by numerous forms: Elphinston, *sence*, *set*, *tell*; Walker, *sperrit*; *Errors of Pronunciation*, *set*, *meracle*;

Yellowplush, *disperryted*, *consperracies*; *Punch*, *sperrit*, *mester*, *set*; etc.

A number of words normally pronounced with short *u* are sounded by Cockneys with *i* or *e*, *sich*, *sech*, *jist*, *jest*, *kiver*, *skittle* (scuttle), *kim up*, *kiver*, and (by older speakers) *inguns* (onions). The variant was commoner in the early periods. The churchwardens have these spellings, among others: *breshes* 1623, *brish* 1641, *keveringe* 1577, *kiveringe* 1607, *Incerrag* 1674, *shitt* (shut) 1518, *syche* 1558, *myche* 1579, *Cretched ffryers* 1628, *seche* 1568, *Shettleworth* 1618, *shetting* 1643. Among the later forms are: Lowe, *kiver*; Pickwick, *jist*, *sich*, *adjestin*; Yellowplush, *skillery*, *kipple*, *jest*, *shet*; Mayhew, *inguns*, *kivered*; Baumann, *sech*, *jest*, *kimplete*.

The pronunciation of short *u* in such words as "first" is a minor characteristic of the dialect, *fust*, *bust*, *cuss*, *wuss*, *nuss*, *pufficklу*, etc. This variant was employed at least as early as the seventeenth century, cf. *nusse* (nurse) 1676, *Reinbust* 1680, and it is recorded later by Sharp, *thusty*; Yellowplush, *dutt* (dirt), *suttinly*, *pufficklу*; Mayhew, *pusses*, *nusses*, *cussing*, *suckus*; *Punch*, *fust*, *wuth* (worth), *pusn* (person), *suvvent* (servant), etc.

In a few words spelt with *er* but pronounced with *ar*, Cockneys keep the *er*-pronunciation, *fur* (far), *clurk* (clerk), *Durby*, *Burkeley*, etc. Spellings in early London documents show that Cockneys used to retain the old Middle English pronunciation in many more words, even those where the orthography had been changed to *ar*: *sterres* (stars) 1489, *yerd* (yard) 1496, *fermere* (farmer) 1500, *fer* (far) 1513, *skerlett* 1531, *person* (parson) 1563, *merke* (mark) 1581, *perchment* 1648, *Mergaret* 1673, etc.

The Cockney *fur* (far) is recorded by most later writers, but only Yellowplush suggests any extensive use of the old sound; he writes *purt* (part), *durk* (dark), etc.

The pronunciation of long *u* as *oo* is common in present-day Cockney, *dook* (duke), *toon* (tune), *soot* (suit), *noo* (new), etc. I have not noticed any spellings which reflect this pronunciation in London records of the sixteenth and seventeenth centuries, but it has certainly been used since the middle of the eighteenth century, for all the critics and novelists notice it: Walker, *noo*, *doo* (dew), *dook*; Elphinston, *toon*, *doo*, *dook*, *soo*, *toonic*, *resoom*, *dooly*; Pickwick, *constitootional*, *commoonicate*; Yellowplush, *delooded*, *noosance*; *Punch*, *Toosday*, *noospapers*, *prodooce*, *delooged*, etc.

Many of the Cockney habits in relation to unaccented vowels are of long standing. The omission of initial unaccented syllables, *'stead*, *'cept*, *'cos* (because), *'leven*, or a medial vowel as in *b'leeve*, *fam'ly*, *s'pose*, which is so popular now, was just as common earlier. The churchwardens spell *tachmente* 1594, *leven* 1594, *greed* (agreed) 1611, *parell* (apparel) 1619, *longs* (belongs) 1536, *gester* (register) 1598, *paringe* (repairing) 1620, *Straine* (distrain) 1645, etc., and *perticklers* 1633; and they anticipate the reduction of final *-ow* by such spellings as *bellys* (bellows) 1548; Machyn, *gallus* (gallows). Similar spellings occur in later Cockney: Sharp, *potticary*, *riccolas*; Pickwick, *'sterics*, *'spectable*, *'pinion*; Mayhew, *'suade* (dissuade), *'timidation*, *'stead*, *'Straliar*, etc.; Elphinston, *cur'osity*, *immater'al*; *Punch*, *bleeve*, *reklect*, *cumpny*, etc.; and Walker, *winder*, *feller*; *Punch*, *tomorrer*, *Tremoler*, *narrer*.

The introduction of a glide vowel in unaccented positions is familiar in such forms as *Henery*, *umberella*, *mischievious*; and it is occasionally used in such plurals as *postis* (posts). These glides seem to have been more frequent in eighteenth- and nineteenth-century Cockney than now. Peregrine Pickle is the first to record *postis*; Walker condemns a similar pronunciation in "posts", "fists", "mists", etc., and he is followed by Pegge and the author of *Errors of Pronunciation*. Elphinston mentions the introduction of a glide before *r*, *countery*, *umberella*, *propperietor*; and Pegge the *i*-glide before *-ous*, *coveteous*, *grieveous*, *mischieveous*, *stupendious*. *Punch* records a similar glide before *-al* and *-ant*, *morttial*, *Crystial*, *gallient*. Similar spellings may be found here and there in most Cockney novels of the nineteenth century.

The omission of *t* and *d* after certain other consonants, particularly *n*, *r*, *l*, *s*, *f*, *p*, and *k*, is a commonplace of vulgar speech, as is evident from the frequency in literary Cockney of such spellings as *blin'*, *Lor'*, *kep'*, *fack* (fact), *gen'leman*, *breckfus*, etc. Abundant evidence of the same and similar omissions is available from the early sixteenth century. The many illustrations in the churchwardens' writings include: Machyn, *Brenford*, *St. Clemens* 1620, *inhabytons* 1647, *nex* 1560, *Baptis* 1677, *kep* 1603, *imperfeck* 1630, *Lef* 1666, *Harford* 1659; and *hammon* 1601, *stipen* 1620, *Lanlady* 1675, *allgatt* 1583, *arnoll* 1599, *Richar* 1555, *Lumber streat* 1686. It is hardly necessary to quote more than a few of the many later spellings: Sharp, *Ilan*; Jonathan Wild, *amirer*; Peregrine Pickle, *hussban*; Pickwick, *kep*, *gen'lm'n*, *funs*; Yellowplush, *subjick*, *fack*, *slep*, *Swiff*, *abruply*, *Bon Street*, *beesly*, *swinler*; Mayhew, *Lunnon*, *ole man*, *toll* (told), *recollec*, *Ack*; Baumann, *dreffle*, *breckfus*, *fac*, *wep*; etc.

Voicing of normally voiceless stop consonants is a feature of vulgar speech. Such spellings as *pardner*, *beedle*, *eggspect* are frequent in literary Cockney and they are symbols for a much more extensive reality: the Cockney tends to "dull" or voice voiceless consonants in many other words, *prodestant*, *samwidge* (sandwich), *mizzletoe*, *carpender*, *'Obkins*, etc. Unvoicing is not so prevalent, although such pronunciations as *leaf* (leave), *errants*, *mannitch* are often used. As we have already noticed, voicing and unvoicing was a characteristic of early Cockney. Among the abundant examples in London records are: *debytie* 1579, *Hobkins* 1654, *Babtist* 1672, *opteyned* 1557, *Apsent* 1621; *Cristover* 1572, *provete* (profit) 1577, *leafe* (leave) 1496, *festrye* 1563, *Skaffinger* 1645, *weefer* 1697, *Robard* 1492, *carpendar* 1558, *statude* 1618, *Stradfourd* 1652; Machyn, *reverentt*, *ballit* (ballad) 1578, *agreet* 1630; Machyn, *sagbottes*, *tangerdes* 1582, *signesse* 1629; Machyn, *vacabond*, *necklect* 1630; *voyze* 1585, *apprentize* 1632. The habit continued in the following centuries. Elphinston declares that in vulgar London speech, *p*, *k*, and *f* were pronounced *b*, *g*, and *v*, and cites the following examples: *padrole*, *pardner*, *proddestant*, *prespyterian*, *prizes* (prices), *vew* (few). Other illustrations are: *Errors of Pronunciation*, *beadle* (beetle), *arrant* (errand), *gobble* (cobble), *leef* (leave), *figary* (vagary); Yellowplush, *sallit* (salad), *errint*, *usitches*, *nollitch*, *cribbitch*, *seffral*, *instructif*, *abuff*, *narratif*, *enfy*, *natiff*; Pegge, *skrimidge*, *radidges*, *rubbidge*, *furbidge*; Mayhew, *chewlry*, *beadle*, *pardner*, *mizzletoe*, etc.

The effect of *y* or *i* following *d* and *t* in Cockney is to transform the groups into *dge* and *ch*: *didger* (did you), *Indgan*, *betcher* (bet you), *immejit*, etc. The same process accounts for *jook* (Duke), *hijus* (hideous), *choon* (tune), *Choosdy*, etc. This vulgarism is an extension of the normal pronunciation in words like "soldier". Strangely enough I have found no examples of the process in the churchwardens' documents except *sawgear*, etc., although Professor Wyld has found spellings like *tejus* in the writings of good speakers in the seventeenth century. There can be little doubt that this pronunciation was used by Cockneys much earlier than the eighteenth century when we find our first evidence of it: Walker, *o-jus*, *te-jus*, *juke*, *rejuce*; Yellowplush, *introjuices*, *higeous*, *jewtiful*, *East Injine*, *obeajance*, *corjally*, *Chewsdy*; *Punch*, *hintermejet*, *tejus*, etc.

Cockneys often omit *w* in unaccented positions, *allus* (always), *summat*, *awkurd*, *innards*, *ekal* (equal), etc. This practice is reflected in many early spellings: Machyn, *Camurell*, *Woodard* 1587, *muzel hill* 1689, *bancket* 1550; Machyn, *condam* (quondam); Sharp, *aukurd*; Pickwick, *markis*, *for'ard*, *up'ards*, *in'ard*; Yellowplush, *antickety*; Mayhew, *backards*, *Nor'ud*, *arter'ards*, *some'at*, *sum'ares*. The omission of the initial *w* in "woman" by the Wellers and other literary Cockneys is anticipated by Machyn's *Odam* (Woodham): incidentally, *'ooman* is still used by many old Cockneys.

Metathesis of *r* is another common Cockneyism which has a long history. The Cockney pronunciations *purtest*, *perdooce*, *childern*, *hunderd*, *permisc'ous*, etc., are foreshadowed in the churchwardens' spellings, *chil-*

dern 1487, *hundered* 1550, *sakerment* 1557, *parsecuted* (prosecuted) 1662, *percinct* 1680, etc., and by many forms in eighteenth- and nineteenth-century records: Jonathan Wild, *purtest*; Foote, *perdigious*, *purfarment*, *purtend*; Pegge, *perdigious*, *perwent*; Mayhew, *purty*, *permiscuous*, *purcession*, etc. The omission of *r* in *Lord*, etc., which is apparently regarded as a Cockney vulgarism by modern novelists is, of course, common to standard English: good speakers as well as Cockneys have omitted the consonant since the seventeenth century at least.

The pronunciation of *in* and *en* as *ing* is prevalent in Cockney, although it is perhaps used mostly by older speakers, e.g. *garding*, *kitching*, *capting*, *millingtary*, *parding*, *skelington*, etc. This pronunciation has been used by Londoners since the fifteenth century, cf. *kechyng* 1477, *lynyng* (linen) 1568, *brethering* 1593, *tomlingson* 1595, *cushings* 1631, *coffinge* (coffin) 1630, *chamberlinge* 1676, *wardings* 1692; Foote, *sarting*; Yellowplush, *muffing*, *virging*, *childring*, *satting*, *foring*; Mayhew, *Hatting Garding*, *Golding-lane*; Baumann, *capting*, *skelington*; etc.

On the other hand, Cockneys more frequently "drop the *g*" in *-ing*, *takin'*, *runnin'*, *mornin'*, *lodgin'*, etc. This, too, is an ancient practice, cf. *remaynyn* 1496, *Ringin* 1558, *belongyn* 1591, *Billinsgate* 1597, *diggin* 1643, *newinton* 1676, *bleadin* 1691, etc., and Pickwick, *takin'*, *hurtin'*, *lodgin'*, *mornin'*, *somethin'*; Baumann, *nuffin*; etc. Some Cockneys, however, pronounce this group as *-ink*: the pronunciation is pretty general in "something", "nothing", "anything", etc. The application of it to other words is illustrated by Shaw's spelling *awskink* (asking). It is difficult to determine how old this variant is. It was certainly used in the eighteenth century, cf. Elphinston, *anny think*; Yellowplush, *everythink*, *somethink*, *nothink*, *swarink*, *hummink*, *mornink*; *Punch*, *playink*, *wavink*, *wishink*. It may have been used by Londoners much earlier. I have noted the spelling *tonkes* (tongs) 1531, and Wyld quotes the example *brinkinge* from Queen Elizabeth's letters.

The intrusive *r* which annoys so many provincial observers of Cockney, in *jawring*, *idear of*, etc., is another old Cockney habit to facilitate pronunciation. The first example I have noticed is in Clarinda's letter to Roderick Random, *your aydear is*; Elphinston cites "a low feller of the causey"; the author of *Errors of Pronunciation*, in discussing the pronunciation of "idea" as *idear*, says, "many people are guilty of this error when the following word begins with a vowel, as, I have not the least idear of it—Is Mariar out? Is Louisar at home?"

It was formerly a Cockney habit to replace voiced *th* by *d* and, less frequently, voiceless *th* by *t*, cf. *gadered* 1455, *leddir* (leather) 1477, *fadym* (fathom) 1492, *odur* 1498, *togeder* 1541; Machyn, *anoder*, *fardyng*, *Bednoll Grene*, *der* (there), *doys* (those), *fardar* 1572; and *terd* (third) 1556, *tursday* 1556, *Artor* 1615, *Smitt* 1644. This pronunciation seems to have become less popular later, although it is recorded in a few words: Foote, *furder*; Mayhew, *farden*; Baumann, *furder*, *farden*; and Jon Bee, *vid* (with) and *dere* (there). At the present time it is common in *farden*, *furder*, and is often used in many other words, *de* (the), *dis* (this), *dere* (there), *dese*, *dose*, *tree* (three), etc. The reverse substitution of *th* for *t*, *d*, which was very common in Elizabethan Cockney, seems to have passed out of the dialect.

The pronunciation beloved of Mrs. Gamp, *dge* for normal *z*, is not generally used by Cockneys, although many of them continue to say *squeege*, *dispoge*, *compoje*, *exscuge*. Besides Mrs. Gamp's pronunciations, there are these examples of its use in early Cockney; Pegge, *squeedge*, *refuge*; Mayhew, *Pancridge*; *Punch*, *egscuge*, *compoje*, *cristalliged*; I have found no exact prototypes in the churchwardens' records, but the following are very similar: *Rubidge* 1620, *Portchmouth* 1691.

Cockneys often substitute *m* for *n*, *se'em* (seven), *brem-butter*, *basilicum*, etc. This, too, is an old habit, cf. *francomsense* 1594, *Varnam* (Vernon) 1614, *Chrisome Child* 1620; and *Errors of Pronunciation*: *burgamy*, *basilicum*; Yellowplush, *mellumcolly*, *Bottomy Bay*, *Mrs. Siddums*, *millium*. The introduction of *m* into *-soever* also goes back to the sixteenth century, cf. Machyn, *whatsomever*, *what man somever*.

Many miscellaneous pronunciations used by Cockneys may be traced back for several centuries. The use of a *y*-glide in *yere* (here), *yer* (ear), *beyind*, etc., was commoner in early Cockney; cf. *yester* (Easter) 1528, *yerbes* 1538, *yendid* 1543, *yerthe* 1550, *Yeades* (Edes) 1649; Lowe, *yerb*; Mayhew, *yarn* (earn); *Punch*, *Yar-sparrer-grass*, *Yeaprul*; etc. The *s* which some Cockneys now tack on to words like "anyhow", "somewhere", was also added by their ancestors; cf. Mayhew, *sum'ares*; Baumann, *somewheres*, *anyhows*; and there is similar antiquity in the occasional transformation of *t*, *d* into *r*: Pegge, *moral* (model); Mayhew, *Piccirilly*; Yellowplush, *imperence*; Baumann, *imperent*, *comforable*, *wirrout* (without). The omission of *f* in "after" is commonly shown in early nineteenth-century Cockney, cf. Mayhew, *arter*, *arternoon*, *arterwards*; and the Cockney elision of medial *v* was practised at least as early as the fifteenth century, cf. *pament* (pavement) 1477, Machyn, *sennet* (sevennight), *Graisend* 1651. The substitution of short *o* for *a* in *wrop*, *codger*, *stomp* is anticipated by: *Notamy* (anatomy) 1581, *Sollery* 1677, *ploncke* 1596; Walker, *codger*; Pickwick, *wropped*; Pegge, *sot*, *anotomy*. Similar authority might be quoted for many isolated pronunciations: Pegge, *summonsed*; *Errors of Pronunciation*, *ast* (asked), *sawder* (solder); Mayhew, *heerd*, *stun* (stone), *grunsel*, *fur'ners*, *soger*; *Punch*, *munce* (months); Pickwick, *owdacious*; Pegge, *obstropolous*, *chimley*; Mayhew, *on'y*, *gal*. Among the odd pronunciations for which still earlier authority may be claimed are: Machyn, *wrastelyng*, *whitt chappill* 1675 (still a common local pronunciation), *trustylls* (trestles) 1531, *Hankerchirs* 1657, *close* (clothes) 1591, *churchard* 1522, *Sandwidge* 1664, *Robbyson* 1601, etc.

Very few of the pronunciations which characterise the dialect now are recent developments. The only important changes in recent decades have been the diphthongisation of long *ee* and long *oo* and possibly the extension of the glottal stop to stop consonants other than *t*. It is possible that even these pronunciations may be older than the evidence suggests. For all the rest there is evidence, abundant in most cases and pretty convincing in others, that they have been used by Londoners for hundreds of years. In fact, although the modern literary Cockney looks so much broader than earlier Cockney, the difference lies only in the representation of some vowels and diphthongs which were not shown in earlier Cockney but which were nevertheless used in actual speech, and in the omission of a few pronunciations which have become obsolete.

These obsolete pronunciations—obsolescent would be a better description, since a few of them are still occasionally employed by old Cockneys—may nearly all be traced back from the Victorian period to the Elizabethan. They are, therefore, interesting testimony to the continuity which Cockney has maintained, despite the efforts of pedants and the incursions of provincials from every corner of the kingdom.

The most evident omission from modern Cockney dialogue is the interchange of *w* and *v*. It is extremely doubtful whether the variant was ever as popular as the novelists suggest. In his *Walker Remodelled*, 1836, B. Smart says: "Few persons under forty years of age with such a predilection for literary nicety as will lead them to these pages can be in much danger of saying that they like 'weal and winegar wery well'—the habit of a more distant generation of Cocknies." Tuer affirms that Sam Weller was exceptional in his pronunciation, and although Professor Weekley, who was born in London in 1865, says that the substitution of *w* for *v*, *wicious*, *wittles*, etc., was perfectly familiar to him in the most venerable Cockneys of the humblest class in the early 'seventies, he never heard the opposite change of *v* for *w*. Several old Cockneys have expressed the same opinion, although they suggest that even *w* for *v* was used only by a few Cockneys, and that in the 'eighties it was regarded as comic. It is often said that the variant is quite obsolete and has been so since the 'nineties. But Gus Elen and other pearly comedians used such forms as *werry*, *wex*, and some of them still do so. Only last year I heard Lew Lake, acting as a guest-artist at Collins's in a modern thriller, use *w* for *v* several times, *wan*, etc., and I have occasionally, though very seldom, heard similar pronunciations from old Cockneys. The pronunciation was, as we have previously stated, characteristic of Elizabethan Cockney, the illustrations including *velewet* 1485, *wacacion* 1492, *Nowember* 1513, *Wawtes* 1517, *Wesmentes* 1549, *westery* 1551; Machyn, *waluw*, *woyce*, *wyolles*, *benewolence* 1586, *wouyd* 1624, *adwance* 1646, *woted* 1658, etc. Substitutions of *v* for *w* are less frequent, but they include *vhich* 1497, *vynddovs*, *vythe*, *vyf*, *voman*, *vappyng* 1503, *vorsted* 1553; Machyn, *Vestmynster*, *Varren*, *vedyng*, etc. After the spelling *wingar* (vinegar) in *Roderick Random*, these variants become the chief characteristic of Cockney dialogue in novels and they are condemned by the critics. Walker suggests that the substitution of *v* for *w* was encouraged by attempts to correct the reverse substitution. The *v* for *w* seems to have been less common than its opposite and it may be similar to the insertion of *h*, the product of confusion as to when to pronounce one and when the other.

The pronunciation of *er* as *ar* as in "clerk" was formerly almost general. Among the myriad examples in the churchwardens' records are *marchaunte* 1485, *Bar-*

mondsey 1487, *sartayne* 1492, *sarvant* 1502; Machyn, *marser*, *sarmon*, *Barmsey*, *vartewe* 1574, *Resarving* 1592, *sarvice* 1633, *marsey* 1641, *sartcher* 1665, *Marmayd* 1673. This variant continued to be common in Cockney speech until late in the nineteenth century, although the examples are fewer than in the early records and the pronunciation is not reflected by all writers of Cockney dialogue. The examples include: Elphinston, *marchant*, *larn'd*; Walker, *sarvice*, *sarvant*; *Errors of Pronunciation*, *sartin*, *sarve*, *larn*; Yellowplush, *concarning*, *Bargymot*; Mayhew, *larning*, *yarn* (earn), *varmint*, *dissarn*, *sartify*, *arly*; *Punch*, *desarves*, *narves*, *arnings*; Baumann, *arn*, *sarve*. The pronunciation even extended into the beginning of the "modern" period of Cockney, to judge by Shaw's spellings *consarns*, *concarnin*.

Short *o* and its long counterpart *au* were frequently unrounded by Londoners in the sixteenth century and later. The earliest examples include: *ffastar* (Foster) 1536, *Larymer* (lorimer) 1554; Machyn, *marow* (morrow), *caffen* (coffin), *aspetall* 1575, *ffallowethe* 1618, *map* (mop) 1632; *Throgmartene* 1594, *Yarke* 1604, *Lard* 1646, *Tharpe* 1677; and *sasers* (saucers) 1531; Machyn, *dran* (drawn), *straberres*, *adit* (audit) 1597, *Laa* (law) 1697, *chardern* 1653, *warnut* 1689. Similar forms are regarded as London vulgarisms by later writers: Walker, *beyand*, *yander*, *sassage*, *darter*, *sarce*, *sarcer*, *sarcy*; Pegge, *Saace*, *Saacer*, *Saacy*, *Daater*; *Errors of Pronunciation*, *janders* (which is still used), *grassplat*; Mayhew, *larels*, *sassage*, *harnts*, *sarsepans*, *sarcy*, *a'most*, *warnuts*; Baumann, *Arleens*.

The pronunciation of *oi* with the sound of long *i*,

particularly before *n* and *l*, is still occasionally used by old Cockneys, *ile* (oil), *spile*, *pint* (point): a few illustrations will be found in the passages of modern Cockney quoted in Chapter III. The variant was formerly a normal Cockney pronunciation. It is illustrated by the churchwardens' spellings, *Ryall* 1501, *yelle* (oil) 1563, *vyage* 1579, *giner* 1587, *appyntment* 1637, *pints* 1671, *Surline* 1688; and its use is recorded in all the Cockney records of the two succeeding centuries. Walker condemns it as a vulgarism in "boil", "toil", "spoil", "joint", "point", "anoint"; and it is frequently shown by such spellings as, Yellowplush, *sirline*, *pizon*, *appinted*, *imply*; Mayhew, *bilings*, *highsters*, *ile*; Baumann, *ile*, *hist*.

The shortening of long *a* to short *a* and of *oo* to short *u* is shown by many early spellings, e.g. *macken* (making) 1570, *gatte* 1533, *latte* 1626, *tacke* 1646; and *futt* (foot) 1574, *buckes* (books) 1604, *hudd* (hood) 1633, *Huckes* 1658. Similar shortenings are recorded as Cockneyisms in the eighteenth and nineteenth centuries: Mayhew, *bab* (babe), *babby*; Baumann, *babby*, *craddle*; *Punch*, *mad* (made), *tak*; Walker, *sutt* (soot); Mayhew, *shuggar*, *buzzum*; *Punch*, *stud* (stood), *tuk* (took). The forms *stud* and *sutt* are still used by some of the older Cockneys. On the other hand the lengthening of *i* in *leetle* (*Punch*, etc.) was a solitary survival from a fairly common early variant, cf. *weedow* 1592, *breeklayers* 1582, *Candellweeke* 1623, *Smeeth* 1695, *seex* 1698, etc.

Various pronunciations of unaccented vowels which are now obsolete or obsolescent were used in Cockney for at least four centuries. The reduction of final *ue* and *a* to *i* or *e*, and of medial *u* to *i* or *iv*, and the pronunciation of final *-ture* as *ter*, are repeatedly shown in eighteenth- and nineteenth-century Cockney dialogue, e.g. Pickwick, *eddication*, *ockipy*, *sitivation*, *Samivel*, *continy*, *walley*, *Wultur*, *natur*, *picter*; Walker, *sing-e-lar*, *reg-e-lar*; *Errors of Pronunciation*, *creater*, *feater*, *chaney* (china); Mayhew, *stattey*, *influenzy*; Baumann, *extry*, *bony fide*, etc. An abundance of similar forms may be found in the churchwardens' writings, *debyty* 1571, *monimente* 1619, *Janyver* 1581, *Samvell* 1617, *newys* (nephews) Machyn, *Barthelemys* 1597, *vergeney* 1618, *taffity* 1634, *lecter* 1576, *venter* 1625, *indenter* 1658, etc. The use of *in* and *il* instead of sonant *n* and *l* had a similar antiquity. It is used in, Yellowplush, *orgin*, *surpint*, *merchints*, *morrils*, *equill*, *pebbils*; *Punch*, *coachmin*, *lemmin*, *marshil*, *bridils*, etc., and also in the church records, *gardyn* 1479, *wardins* 1583, *Allin* 1608, *surgins* 1674, *dubbill* 1583, *parsills* 1622, *utinsills* 1677, etc.

The substitution of *sh* for *s* is familiar in the Cockney pronunciation of "liquorice" as *lickerish*. This variant was formerly more widely used. There are many illustrations of it in the church documents besides these: Machyn, *granshyr*, *shepter*, *shuche* 1565, *shogers* 1596, *nursh* 1659, *Sherchers* 1662, *Lewish* 1674, *Morrish* 1696. It was also fairly common later, cf. Elphinston, *cutlash*, *nonplush*, *frontishpiece*; Pegge, *nonplush'd*; *Errors of Pronunciation*, *lickerish* (liquorice); Yellowplush, *mattrapolish*, *Imprimish*, *dishcord*, *neagush*, *shinycure*, *dishconslit*; *Punch*, *gashly*. The pronunciation of *su* as *shoo* has a similar history, cf. *shute* (suit) 1585, *Sheward* 1621, *Ishewe* 1633, *Shusan* 1661, etc., and Yellowplush, *shoot*, *preshume*, *purshuits*, *ishew*; Mayhew, *shewer* (sewer). On the other hand, although *s* is substituted for *sh* in *srub* and *srimps*, Mayhew (the latter is still occasionally heard), the variant seems to have lost the popularity it had earlier, cf. Machyn, *flesse*, *fysse*, *marssys*, *Extinguisers* 1626, *bussell* 1628, *paris* 1636, *Sroud* 1690, etc.

Pegge observed the Cockney's use "of the letter *w* in the place of the letter *h* in compound words, for instead of neighbourhood, widowhood, livelyhood, and knighthood, they not only say but often write *neighbourwood*, *widowwood*, *livelywood*, and *knightwood*". Earlier evidence of similar pronunciations are the spellings: Machyn, *wysswer* (wizard), *Cornewell* (Cornhill) 1646, *Cornewall* 1657. *Punch* also notices the introduction of a labial glide between *p*, *b*, and *a* following rounded vowel, *puoap*, *bwoy*. This pronunciation is condemned by Dr. Wallis in the middle of the seventeenth century and it is illustrated by two spellings in the church documents, *apwintment* 1662 and *bwoy* (boy) 1697. It is interesting that the latter word is similarly pronounced by Drinkwater in *Captain Brassbound's Conversion*. The palatal glide which appears as a Cockneyism in Mayhew's spellings *ke-ow*, *Kate Kearney*, *black-geyard*, was described by Wallis, 1653, and allowed as correct by Elphinston and Walker.

Just as these pronunciations have practically dropped out of the dialect, so a number of pronunciations which were popular in the sixteenth and seventeenth centuries are not represented in the descriptions and examples of the dialect in the eighteenth and nineteenth centuries. It is possible that some of them were actually used by some Cockneys and a few examples of them actually occur in the later Cockney, but they may safely be regarded as obsolete or obsolescent in the later period. These variants are included in my study of vulgar London speech in the fifteenth to seventeenth centuries and it is unnecessary to discuss them here, but for the purposes of completeness a short summary of them may be given here:

Short a: Short *i* was used in a few words, *hyng* (hang) 1485, *chisible* Machyn, *stynddyng* 1594, *Lindmark* 1676; and *an* often retained the Middle English variant pronunciation *on*, *Sond* 1538, *stondeth* 1556, *londs* 1697. Before labial consonants *al* was sometimes pronounced *aul*, *haulfe* 1558, *Pawmmar* 1570, *Rauff* 1579.

Long a occasionally retained its Middle English low sound, *Paage* 1592, *maade* 1592, *laate* 1592, *plauts* (plates) 1621; but it was sometimes raised to *ee*, *leece* (lace) 1535, *misteeken* 1629, *Manteen* 1676.

Long ea retained its original sound, similar to our long *a*, until the 17th century among some speakers, *prachinge* 1627, *spake* 1662, *Paybody* 1652. In several words where this vowel is normally shortened to *e*, a long vowel was used, *breed* (bread) 1595, *threede* 1605, *steede* (stead) 1664. The value of this vowel before *r* occasionally differed from present values; *spayre* (spear) Machyn, *yares* 1618, *Beerbinderlaine* 1591, *wheereof* 1620, and *berd* (beard).

Short i was pronounced like short *u* in a few words, *Busshope* 1477, *Bushops gate* 1612, *wolle* (will) 1592; Machyn, *jubett*, *sturope* 1599.

Long i was pronounced *ee* before *r* in some words; Machyn, *Greyfreers*, *quere* 1582.

Short o was occasionally pronounced like short *u*; Machyn, *shut* (shot), *cluthe* 1621, *Roungfully* 1662.

Or was sometimes sounded like *ur* or *oor*, *furthwith* 1642, *Osburne* 1650, *boorne* (born) 1643, *ffoord* 1655. Similar pronunciations were apparently used in: *durres* (doors) 1527, *dooer* 1658, *Coorte* 1633, *Jurdin* (Jordan) 1644, etc.

Short u retained its Middle English rounded quality among

some speakers, *loodge* 1509, *Coopes* 1567, *roone* (run) 1611, *soome* (sum) 1623, *Moonke* 1634.

Loss of Consonants. Various minor consonantal elisions are illustrated by these spellings: Machyn, *Camurell*, *lomer* (lumber) 1531, *Asemly* 1638, *bayly* (bailiff) 1531, *Randolle* 1626, *Ratlyffe* 1587, *coletteres* 1604.

Consonantal Changes. (*a*) interchange of *t*, *d* and *k*, *g*, Machyn, *Prykkyllwell*, *gagyn* (garden) 1563, *Bartley* 1674; (*b*) *th* for *t*, *d*, *consither* 1584, *lathers* 1588, *embrotherers* 1599, *bothom* 1633, *wather* 1671; (*c*) initial *g* pronounced *y*, *yeld halle* 1536, *yeven* (given) 1584; (*d*) *gh* pronounced *f* in *dafter* 1650; (*e*) *ch* pronounced *sh*, *trenshars* 1598, *shildren* 1644, *quinshing* 1626; (*f*) metathesis of *s*, *clapsinge* 1581, *hapse* 1602; (*g*) *wh* pronounced *w* in *wo* (who) 1575, *woose* (whose) 1622.

The most important of these variants were old-fashioned pronunciations which naturally passed away as the new sounds became established. Most of the others were confined to a few words. In consequence there was little difference between the Cockney of the sixteenth century and the dialect of the nineteenth century.

Of the miscellaneous pronunciations recorded as Cockney characteristics in the eighteenth and nineteenth centuries some rose and fell within that period, but most have earlier (*) or later (†) parallels. The chief of them are: Sharp, **Crowner*; Lowe, **bushop*, *scrouge*, *squench*; Elphinston, **acs* (ask), *admiraltry*, **alablaster*, **soorce*, **coorse*, **thof* (though); Walker, **chaw* (chew), **drowth* (drought), **sithe* (sigh); Pegge, †*vemon* (venom), *vemonous*, *Common Garden*, *progidy*, *palaretick*, **musicianer*, *intosticated*, *loveyer*, **summonsed*, *squits* (quit), *scrowdge* (crowd); *Errors of Pronunciation*, **burnfire*, *Bishergate*, *chaney*, **noways*, **otherways*, **shore* (sewer), **cowcumber*, *drugs* (dregs), *garp* (gape), **Gracious Street*, *massacree*, *muckenger*; Mayhew, **coorse*, **heerd*, **obleege*, *chisscake*, *chair* (char), *leddies*, *rayther*, **Portingle*, *hask* (harsh), *tremenjous*, **condic* (conduit); Yellowplush, *omlibuster* (omnibus), **frow* (from), *gev* (gave), *cem* (came), **goold*, *goolden*, *twollet*, †*Hamlick*, †*vomick*, †*benefick*; *Punch*, *barnd* (band), *harnd* (hand), **air* (are), **theer* (their), *weer* (were), †*cheer* (chair), †*aweer* (aware), **discoorse*, *rooshins*, *prooshins*, **horlbums*, *momink* (moment); Baumann, *thripund*.

These are the pronunciations which have characterised Cockney at its various stages of development. Those pronunciations in which the dialect agrees with Standard English have, of course, been ignored. Probably several minor pronunciations have escaped our net, either because I have failed to notice them or because earlier observers neglected to describe or utilise them. And some of the variants which I have described as obsolete may better deserve the description of obsolescent. Walking about London I have often been surprised to hear pronunciations like *cheer* (chair), *cowcumber*, and so on, which I should otherwise have said were obsolete. But whatever our omissions, we have established beyond any reasonable doubt that present-day Cockney pronunciation is a lineal descendant of the speech of London in the sixteenth century. So far from the truth is Höfer's suggestion that Sam Weller would be unable to understand a modern Cockney, that it is justifiable to claim that if George and Nell, Jerry Sneak, Sam Weller, and Mr. 'Enery 'Awkins could be introduced to one another they would not only be able to understand one another but would recognise in one another the typical pronunciations of those reared within sound of Bow Bells.

The Cockney tradition is perhaps even stronger in grammar. My provincial friends tell me that when they first came to London they were struck more by the Cockney's grammar, his treatment of verbs, pronouns, and so on, than by his pronunciation. Most of these Cockney characteristics have been used in London speech since the sixteenth century.

The mathematical axiom that the multiplication of two negatives results in a positive has never recommended itself to Cockneys. They incline to use negatives emphatically and not logically, "I don't know nuffink abaht it", "He ain't nobody!", "I ain't never been nowhere near there", and so on. The habit is a traditional Cockneyism. Machyn loved to pile up negatives in bewildering fashion, particularly when he was reporting proclamations—"The ix day of Marche was a proclamacyon that *no* man *or* woman shuld *nott* ett *no* flesse in lent *nor* fryday, *nor* wednesday thrught the yere, *nor* ymberyng days, *nor no* days that is condemned by the chyrche." Among the similar passages in the church records are these: "he shuld *neuer* trobell the p̄ish *no* more" (St. Barts., 1661), and "*not* otherwysse to be ussyde at *noo* tyme" (St. Margaret, 1583). The habit was occasionally burlesqued by the dramatists; the Citizen's wife asks the actor, "Were you never none of Master Moncaster's scholars?" The later critics naturally seized upon the characteristic as a vulgarism: Elphinston quotes, "Presumption i'n't it not in me" and "you had no room to tremble neither", and Pegge chooses for justification on historical grounds the phrases "I don't know nothing about it" and the London citizen's query "if nobody had seen nothing of never a hat no-wheres". The abundance of similar examples in Cockney dialogue makes it unnecessary to quote more than a few interesting examples from Mayhew: "I have nothing to say about nobody that ain't no customers", "Spinach I don't do only a little in", and "They doesn't care nothink for nobody".

Cockneys often indulge in unorthodox comparatives and superlatives, *worser*, *littler*, *biggerer*, *worsest*, *littlest*, and so on. Occasionally they will intensify a comparative or superlative by adding an unnecessary "more" or "most", "the most awfullest fing you ever see" or "it's a bloody sight more lousier than what he said". The Citizen's wife and Cob were fond of this intensification. The former speaks of her husband as "the frowningest little thing" and maintains that Ralph was "the most comfortablest" to her, while Cob alleges that Bobadil did "swear the legiblest of any man christened" and that Clement was "the honestest old brave Trojan in London". A few similar formations may be found in the churchwardens' documents: "he should thinke mooste meteste", "the most discretest" (St. Barts., 1579, 1582), and "the substantialste men" (St. Margaret, 1579). The practice seems to have been very popular in the eighteenth and nineteenth centuries. The unorthodox forms recorded in that period include: Elphinston, *chiefest*, *lesser*; Pegge, *worser*, *endermost*, *biggermost*, *bettermost*; *Errors of Pronunciation*, *highliest*, *shockingest*, *supremest*; Mayhew, *backer*, *blackguarder*, *quickerer*, *worser*, *littlest*, *swellest*; and the double comparatives and superlatives are represented by: Pegge, *most impudentest*, *most ignorantest*, *most particularest*; *Errors of Pronunciation*, *far more superior*; Mayhew, *more tastier-like*, *rather vorser*, *far more ferociouser*, *the most audaciousest.*

Adjectives are commonly used as adverbs in modern Cockney. A Londoner will say "it was done quick", or "it must be done proper", or "he's a reg'lar good bloke". This practice has long been established in Cockney; cf. Baumann, *fairish well*, *talk foolish*; Mayhew, *uncommon severe*, *shocking hard up*, *you've done famous*, *he spoke very kind*; etc.

The habit of some Cockneys of using the ordinary indefinite article *a* before words beginning with a vowel, *a orange*, *a apple*, etc., is also age-old. Among the nineteenth-century examples we may note Mark Lemon's *a aching heart*, *a old maid*, and long before, Machyn often employs similar forms, *a arme*, *a elevant*, *a in* (inn), *a auter*, etc. Machyn apparently also adopted the habit, common among many Londoners now, of attaching the *n* of "an" to the following word, *a nold hore*, *a nebe* (an ebb), *at a nend*, *a nold man.*

The plurals of nouns sometimes differ in Cockney from the normal forms. We have already spoken of such forms as *postis* (posts), *ghostis* (ghosts), and shown that similar formations were used in the eighteenth century and probably even in the sixteenth. Other occasional variants are the omission of the plural termination, "Two pound o' sprout, Ma?", "'Ere's yer fine colliflower!", or the addition of an unwarranted termination, "Look at the lovely deers!", "Bloody lot of swines they was!" Similar formations are occasionally met with in early records, particularly of "corpse", "shilling", and "joist", cf. St. Margaret, *Corpuscis* 1592, *corpusses* 1593; St. Barts., *ten shillingses* 1630; St. Mary Woolchurch, *Joyces* 1577. In the earliest records other variant plurals, more characteristic of Middle English than modern speech, are sometimes found, e.g. St. Mary-at-Hill, *hosen* (hose) 1489, *schone* (shoes) 1489, *chelder* (children) 1505; St. Margaret, *housen* (houses) 1583. And an interesting selection of variant plurals occurs in this sentence of Machyn's, "ther was sent her mony grett gyftes by the mayre and aldermen as beyffes, mottuns, velles, swines, bred, wylld ffulle, wyne, bere, spysys, and all thyngs and qwaylles, sturgeon, wod, and colles, and samons by dyver men".

The Cockney employs many variants from the normal pronouns. He inclines towards the accusative rather than the nominative forms of personal pronouns—"'Im and 'er look like 'avin' a bust-up", or "Them? Why, us 'as got 'em licked any time!", or "Me and old Bill Smiff's bin dust 'oys". The Cockney possessive pronouns are all modelled on "mine", "that ball's ourn, it ain't yourn", *theirn*, *hern*, and occasionally *hisn*. For the reflexives "himself" and "themselves", the Cockney substitutes forms modelled on "myself", "Finks a lot of 'isself, don't 'e?", or "They ain't 'arf doin' theirselves proud!" The demonstrative pronouns "this", "that", and "those" are replaced frequently by "this here", "that there", and "them", "This 'ere dust wants shifting into that there box", or "Them blokes ain't no bleedin' good!" And the relative pronouns "who", "which", "that", are normally replaced by "as" and "what", "a bloke what I knows", "a feller as lives near us", "the money what I earns", etc. Occasionally "which" replaces "that", or "who", "the old faggit, which I know 'er to be a liar, says", etc. Finally, "you" and "your" are apt to be used unnecessarily, "'Ere's yer ripe tomatoes!", "Set yerself down", etc.

All these variants existed in the earliest days of the dialect. Machyn speaks of "the goodlyest collars as ever youe saw", and "Master Edward Halle of Gray in, the wyche he sett forthe the cronnacle", and "a sofferacan, the wyche was sospendyd". The writers of the St. Bartholomew Minutes sometimes employ "which" instead of "who", as in "the wife of Williā Killigain w[ch] is now kept in Bedlam", 1612, and "m[r] Buckner which is of late gonne forthe", 1617. In the same minutes the familiar substitution of "as" for "that" is sometimes used, "I did acquaint ym as there was 2 new peues as did want & was neadfull to be lined", 1650. The Citizen's wife and Cob are both fond of associating a listener with a tale by using "you", "he will act you", "he will fetch you a couraging part", or "there he will sit you a whole afternoon". The Cockney dialogue in these plays, however, suggest a few early habits which seem to have dropped out of the dialect. The stage Cockneys habitually used the second person singular in speaking to relations and friends, and occasionally employed "ye" for "you", while the Citizen's wife is prone to substitute *it* for "he" when she is feeling motherly, "Thou seest the poor gentleman, dear heart, how it labours and throbs", or "by my troth it's a fine child".

But on the whole the early dramatists were not interested in this feature of Cockney, and were usually content to note the habit of reducing pronouns, *y'are*, *th'art*, *'twill*, *h'as*, *in's*, *on't*, *'a has*, *'a shall*, etc.

The whole of the variants are represented in the comments and dialogues of the eighteenth and nineteenth centuries. The following are selected from a multitude of examples. Elphinston, "like *me myself*", "an't *us*", "shall *us*"; Pegge, "can *us*", "shall *us*", "have *us*"; Mayhew, "*me and Carry H*—— carries the little uns", "*me and her's* great frens". Pegge and all later commentators and novelists, *ourn*, *yourn*, *hern*, *hisn* and *hisself* and *theirselves*; Foote, "*them* paintings", "*them* kind of things"; Mayhew, "*them* Crocusses", "*them as* has got things", "*this here* creation", "*them ere* lodging-houses", "*that there* shilling"; etc.; Greenwood, "gents *wot* wins", "*them as* fetches water and *them as* looks arter the empty bottles"; Mayhew, "A man *as* know'd mother", "an old gent *what* I served", etc. One variant of this period, which is rare now, was the use of the nominative forms of personal pronouns instead of the accusative, cf. Elphinston, "'twixt *you* and *I*"; Mayhew, "It aint *we*"; on the other hand, Elphinston's remarks on the use of "who" instead of "whom", as in "from who" and "on who", still apply to Cockney.

One of the most interesting variants is the extension of the *-s* termination of the third person singular present indicative, to other persons, "I goes", "he bets", "we doesn't", "you gives", "they says". This practice, sometimes incorrectly described as using a singular verb with a plural subject, has always been used in Cockney.

Professor Wyld points out that the *-s* plurals do not appear until the *-s* forms of the third singular are already in use, and that the plural forms must be due to analogy with the singular. The early London examples include, Machyn, "the porters that *longes* to the stapull", "these iij *hanges* in chynes", "after them *comys* harolds"; St. Barts., "the pore w[ch] *goes* a begen in the strets" 1579, "the p̄son & churchewardens *makes* the promes" 1603; St. Christopher, "the pour wo *payes* & wo pay not" 1575. Examples are abundant in later Cockney, e.g. Maw-worm, "I says", "the neighbours reviles my wife"; Elphinston, "I dares", "we regains"; *Errors of Pronunciation*, "I does", "I knows", "I goes"; Mayhew, "I recollects", "we says", "we makes", "you speaks", "they quarrels", "the shops shuts up", "the lads goes and lives", etc.

The frequent use of "is" and "was" for the plural forms is probably also due to analogy, "the blokes is going to the pictures", "They was out", "we wasn't there", etc. Occasionally a plural form may be used with a singular subject, "I were going", "he weren't 'alf screwed!", etc. These habits, too, derive from Elizabethan Cockney, cf. Machyn, "the xxij day of October *was* all the craftes of London commandyd to go to ther halles"; St. Barts., "the showgars *was* freyyd" 1593, "ther *was* chosen collectors" 1606; St. Margaret, "the names of suche parishonars as *was* present" 1577, "the paryshonars names *is* on the other syd" 1577. Occasionally "have" is used instead of "has", cf. St. Barts., "the said Parrish *have* sustained" 1614, and "so much as he *haue* disbursed" 1630. Among the abundant illustrations in later Cockney documents are these: Foote, "you was"; Elphinston, "we was", "they was", "otherguess folks was to blame", and "my company were high"; Mayhew, "I never has", *I's*, *you's*, *they's*, "the gals is fools", "they is devils", and "I arn't", "after I were born"; Baumann, "he haves", "you gives", "they'se", "I wur", "I warn't", "he do", "he've".

For the normal preterite forms Cockneys often substitute the normal singular, *I see* (saw), *I give* (gave), *I come* (came). They will often employ weak preterites in strong verbs, *I seed*, *I knowed*, *I gived*, or they will make use of the past participle, *I run* (ran), *I begun*, *he done it*. The following preterites from earlier documents show that these habits are very old ones: Machyn, they *brake*, *ware* (wore), *smytt* (smote); St. Barts., *hould* (held) 1593, *spake* 1636, *I see* (saw) 1644; St. Katherine Coleman, *he Run* 1624; Elphinston, *we see*, *I come*, *I begun*; Pegge, *know'd*, *throw'd*, *draw'd*, *grow'd*, *see'd*; *Errors of Pronunciation*, *crow'd*; Mayhew, *I seed*, *hurted*, *gived*, *knowed*, *throwed*, *bursted*, *catched*, *com'd*, *sweeped*, *runned*, *growed*, *give*; Baumann, *seed*, *heerd*, *keeped*, *begun*, *done*. Among the earlier variant preterites which have dropped out of the dialect we may mention: Machyn, *fochyd* (fetched), *yede* (went); St. Barts., *mought* (might) 1623; Elphinston, *hove* (heaved); Pegge, *mought*, *fit* (fought), *cotch* (caught), *fotch* (fetched); Mayhew, *ris* (rose), *guv* (gave), *catched*; Baumann, *snew* (snowed).

Strong past participles are often replaced by weak forms, *growed* (grown), *sewed* (sewn), *tooked* (taken), etc., or by the normal preterite forms, *broke* (broken), *shook* (shaken), *took* (taken), *tore* (torn). Similar forms in early records are: Machyn, *shud* (shewn), *broke* (broken), and also *byldyd*; St. Barts., *shewed* (shewn) 1603 and *lended* (lent) 1643; St. Christopher, *aboue-writt* 1634, *chose* 1677; St. Barts., *chose* 1626, *gaue* 1650; etc. The Cockneys of this period also frequently extended the *-en* termination of the past participle to words which are normally without it and even to some weak verbs, cf. Machyn, *stryken* (struck); St. Barts., *gotton* (got) 1581, *comen* 1591, *bounden* 1602, *layen* (laid) 1629; St. Christopher, *letten* (let) 1580, *holden* 1671. The modern Cockney variants are often employed in eighteenth- and nineteenth-century documents, cf. Elphinston, *know'd*, *came*, *began*; Pegge, *know'd*, *throw'd*, *draw'd*, *grow'd*, *see'd*, *took*, *rose*, *fell*, *wrote*, *mistook*, *forsook*; *Errors of Pronunciation*, *forgot*, *spoke*, *broke*, *eat*, *wrote*, *beat*, *fell*, *drove*; Mayhew, *seed*, *blowed*, *knowed*, *drawed*, *took*, *beat*, *drove*, *tore*, *fell*, *writ*. Cockneys do not seem to have retained the variant past participles with the *-en* termination at this period, but they occasionally used an unusual form, such as: Mayhew, *ris* (risen), *druv* (driven), *bet* (beaten), *guv* (given); Baumann, *fruz* (frozen); Pegge, *went* (gone).

The *a-* prefix of the present participle, "Warny, I'm a-coming" or "What are you a-doing of?", is of course an old habit. It is occasionally used by Cockneys in Elizabethan plays, "a-making, a-brewing", etc., and it is common in later Cockney—*Errors of Pronunciation*, *a-coming*, *a-doing*, *a-going*; Mayhew, *a-calling*, *a-talking*, *a-watching*. Sometimes Cockneys now use a similar prefix to the past participle, "What have you a-written", etc. This may be a survival of the old prefix *y-*, which passed out of normal English towards the end of the Middle English period.

Infinitives are sometimes prefaced by "for", although this practice is not very common, "What I want for to know", "he went for to go", etc. This habit seems to be less popular than it used to be. Among the early examples are: Machyn, "there was a heretyke ther for to here the sermon", "her grace whent thrugh the parke for to take her barge"; St. Barts., "there was chosen for to be a helpe to our Minester" 1623; St. Margaret, "for to Repayre" 1584, "for to have" 1585, etc.; Elphinston, "Pricks us for to assurt"; *Errors of Pronunciation*, "I was going for to say", "what are you going for to do"; Mayhew, "I'd like for to know", etc.

Cockney occasionally differs from standard speech in the use of prepositions. Sometimes a locution is formed by the addition of a preposition: "I took it off of the stall", "Come along o' me", "It's nigh on a week since I 'ad a wet", "What are you a-doing of?" Sometimes normal prepositions are replaced by others, "on" for "of" is particularly common, "three on us", "take hold on it", "I never does nuffink of a week-day", etc. Similar forms may be found in early Cockney records. The habit of regarding the present participle as a verbal noun accounts for the addition of "of" in such phrases as: Machyn, "ther was on blohyng of a trumpet"; St. Margaret, "Att a Vestry . . . for chosinge of Churchwardens" 1676; St. Barts., "and doeinge of other reparacons" 1628. At this period some verbs, "like", "accept", "allow", "consider", and a few others, seem always to have been followed by "of", cf. St. Barts., "would allow of him" 1630, "to consider of it" 1630, "the p̄ishoners greately dislyke of the interest" 1587; St. Christopher, "The Parish accept of the front of a house" 1676, "he would admitt of him to be Clerke" 1677, etc. Among the other variations used at this time are Machyn's omission of "on" in "the King grace whent a presessyon", and the use of abnormal prepositions in, St. Barts., "gone ffor Holland" 1651; St. Margaret, "in regarde of trobles" 1626, "Discharged for being Church warden" 1665. Later examples of these variations may be represented by these quotations: *Errors of Pronunciation*, "I'm not doing of anything", "there were three on us"; Mayhew, "in course", "what they were a buying on", "a punch of the nose", "to think on it", "two on us", "to speak on", "heerd tell on", "we has meat of a Sunday"; Pickwick, "kitch hold on him", "robbed on it", "ashamed on you".

Other Cockney variants are the use of "more nor" or "more'n" for "more than", "he had more'n me"; the use of "that" as an adverb meaning "so", "'E was that stuck-up, 'e wouldn't call the King 'is uncle"; the circumlocution "what for" instead of "why", "'E pasted me, I dunno what for!" or "I'll give 'im what for when 'e comes in"; the adverbial use of "like", "I sort o' gets along with 'im like"; the locution "as how" for "that", "I don't know as 'ow I cottons on"; and the repetition of an auxiliary verb, "Fair knock-out, it was", "She wouldn't 'arf a' christened 'im she would", "took 'im for a pie-can, 'e did", "Goes like 'ot cakes, they do". Most of these practices seem to be modernisms, although earlier authority may be found for some of them: Foote, "she says as how I bawl worser than the broom-man"; Maw-worm, "saying as how she set no store by me"; Baumann, "like I told you".

In grammar, therefore, as well as pronunciation, there is certain evidence of the continuity of Cockney. Its claim to dialect status cannot reasonably be denied. It may often be inconsistent, but its inconsistencies have historical justification. One may speak of the dialect of London as one may speak of the dialect of Yorkshire. Both contain many varieties of dialect linked together by common characteristics. In Yorkshire it is possible to separate the sub-dialects. London speech has similar variations, but they get confused owing to the movements of the population and the constant contact between the different groups of speakers. With this limitation, Cockney is as worthy of the regard of dialect-lovers as any of the more praised and more studied county speeches.

CHAPTER VII

THE INFLUENCE OF COCKNEY ON STANDARD ENGLISH

THE attempt to unify English speech by fostering an absolute standard of pronunciation was first begun by the orthoepists of the sixteenth and seventeenth centuries. The first definite comments on the most acceptable type of English may be found in books written during the reign of Queen Elizabeth. Thus, in the preface to Hart's *Methode to Read English*, 1570, reference is made to "the Court, and London speaches, where the generall flower of all English countrie speeches, are chosen and vsed". A more extensive and familiar statement of the same opinion appears in *The Arte of English Poesie*, 1589, in which the author advises the would-be poet on his choice of language:

> Our maker, therfore, at these dayes shall not follow *Peers plowman* nor *Gower* nor *Lydgate* nor yet *Chaucer*, for their language is now out of vse with vs: neither shall he take the termes of Northern-men, such as they vse in dayly talke, whether they be noble men or gentlemen, or of their best clarkes all is a matter: nor in effect any speach vsed beyond the riuer of Trent, though no man can deny but that theirs is the purer English Saxon at this day, yet it is not so Courtly nor so currant as our Southerne English is, no more is the far Westerne mans speach: ye shall therfore take the vsuall speach of the Court, and that of London and the shires lying about London within lx myles, and not much aboue. I say not this

> but that in euery shyre of England there be gentlemen and others that speake but specially write as good Southerne as we of Middlesex or Surrey do, but not the common people of euery shire, to whom the gentlemen, and also their learned clarkes do for the most part condescend, but herein we are already ruled by th' English Dictionaries and other books written by learned men, and therefore it needeth none other direction in that behalf.

This view of what constituted acceptable English—much the same as that which is still held—was accepted even by provincials. The Welsh schoolmaster, Owen Price, says in his *Vocal Organ*, 1665, "I have not been guided by our vulgar pronunciation, but by that of London and our Universities where the language is purely spoken", and in the *Practical Phonography*, 1701, of his compatriot, Dr. John Jones, English speech is defined as "the Art of signifying the Mind by Humane Voice, as it is commonly used in England (particularly in London, the Universities or at Court". There has, in fact, never been any serious opposition during the Modern period to this view of what type of English is most acceptable.

London's increasing importance as the focus of the official and cultural life of the country made it inevitable that London English should ultimately become the standard. But it was long before this supremacy was actually attained. The author of *The Arte of English Poesie*, although he admits that London English was written by some people in every county, suggests that most of the writers used dialect in speaking. But the movement towards the unification of the language from which we must date the modern period of English, had begun early in the preceding century. In the Middle

English period, there was no such recognition of the superiority of one type of speech over all others. As W. P. Ker said, "Middle English is not really a language at all, but a great number of different tongues, belonging to different parts of the country. And not only does the language of Yorkshire differ from that of Kent or Dorset, or London or Lancashire, but within the same district each author spells as he pleases and the man who makes a copy of his book also spells as he pleases, and mixes up his own local and personal varieties with those of the original author." The fifteenth century saw the retreat of the dialects, not only among literary men and officials but also among private citizens. From his investigations of personal documents written in that century, Professor Zachrisson perceived that "although dialectal forms occur sporadically in many private letters it is obvious that the writers endeavoured to avoid them and followed as nearly as possible the London style".

The supreme importance of London in governmental, legal, and business affairs was probably the primary cause of the adoption of London speech as the standard. The business connections of country lawyers, officials, and merchants with the capital compelled them to use a common language, which could only be that of London. Official documents written in English even in the fourteenth century do not contain nearly so many dialect forms as the contemporary literature. The diffusion of this speech was ensured by an obvious advantage enjoyed by London speech, that it was used by a large proportion of Englishmen. At the end of the sixteenth century the London population, although numbering only about a quarter of a million, yet formed about a tenth of the total population of England and Wales, and since that time the proportion has gradually increased. The domination of London speech was also hastened by printing. Caxton explained that it was necessary to alter the language of some of the books he printed and to adapt it to the best current usage. In preparing reading matter for the whole country, printers were obliged to adopt that type of speech which was most widely used and understood. In this way London English became the standard language of the printers and so was carried into the remotest parts of the country.

Although the accepted form of English was defined as the English spoken in London and at Court and in the Universities, it is difficult to imagine what influence the Court and the Universities can have had. The Courtiers were too small a community to affect the main stream of the language considerably, and too remote from general acquaintance to serve as a model. The chief linguistic product of such a community is fashion, the phraseology of *Euphues* or the elegancies of *Arcadia*. And although the Universities served to diffuse the new standard, from the schools and pulpits, the University men adopted and diffused the standard rather than formed it. Some of them even retained their dialects. John Aubrey has the following note on some Oxford scholars. "The Westerne people cannot open their mouths to speak ore rotundo. Wee pronounce *paal*, *pale*, &c., and especially in Devonshire. The Exeter College (Oxford) men in disputations, when they alledge *Causa*

Causae est Causa Causati, they pronounce it *Caza*, *Cazae est Caza Cazati*, very ungracefully." And even Dr. Johnson admitted that when he was not careful he was liable to speak with a trace of the Staffordshire accent.

The only type of English which could have served as the model for the accepted speech of the time was the good speech of the London populace. It must have been this type which was used at Court, except by the few who retained their local dialects like Sir Walter Raleigh. It is probable that there were different strata in London speech at this time, even though there can be little doubt that it was more uniform than present-day London speech, with its many varieties of Cockney and its numerous shades of modified standard. London was a small and very compact city and it could not have been the home of many local dialects. But as much as now the capital was the lodestone that drew provincials from all parts of the British Isles. The formidable proportion of provincials who have become Lord Mayor of London is eloquent upon this fact. These provincials, lewd and learned, must have had considerable influence upon the speech of their hosts the Cockneys and have introduced incongruous elements into London speech. Differences of education and scholarship, too, must have resulted in differences of speech between the prosperous and poorer sections of the populace. But because of the apprenticeship system and the close and constant contact between masters and men, these differences cannot have been so wide as they are now. It is this factor that may help to explain the surprising absence of Cockney dialogue from early literature.

But there was one vital difference between accepted English and the English of the London populace in the early modern period. London English when used as the accepted speech by other people was, in the early part of the modern period at least, an artificial speech. The natural speech of a Plymouth man, for example, was the South Devonshire dialect and if he adopted London English it was as a Sunday suit. He probably used it only when it was strictly necessary and dropped into his own dialect at other times. It is impossible to say how long this artificiality continued in the early accepted speech. The author of *The Arte of English Poesie* shows that late in the sixteenth century gentlemen and their learned clerks still "condescended" to the common people in this respect, and my view is that it was not until the habit of sending children of the well-to-do classes to boarding schools had been established in the seventeenth and eighteenth centuries that accepted English became the sole language of the educated classes. The importance of this factor lies in the difference between a dialect and an artificially accepted speech. A dialect is always fluid and develops both by movements from itself and also under the influence of neighbouring dialects. An accepted speech tends to be static, to get its changes at second-hand and to be ruled by authority rather than by normal linguistic processes.

The details of the relationship between accepted speech and London speech in the early modern period can only be studied by comparing the speech of a representative group of good speakers with the speech of the ordinary London populace at the same time. The latter we have already discussed from the evidence of the phonetic spellings in London records. Similar evidence for the speech of the upper classes may be found in many volumes of private correspondence, particularly those relating to the seventeenth century. The ladies of that period were as unfettered by the conventions of orthography as the least literate of the churchwardens.

The misspellings of these ladies bear a remarkable similarity to the misspellings of the Cockneys of the same time. I do not propose to analyse them in detail, that has been done already by Professor Wyld and other scholars. But from a few diaries and collections of letters I propose to quote spellings which indicate the resemblance.

The letters of Lady Brilliana Harley, written between 1625 and 1645, contain many spellings which also appear in the churchwardens' documents, some of them reflecting pronunciations which we have found to be characteristic of the dialect. Yet Lady Harley was not a Londoner. She was born abroad, at Brill in the Netherlands, her father being Sir Edward Conway, a member of an old Warwickshire family. She came to England in 1606 and after her marriage in 1623 lived in Herefordshire. But her letters suggest that she used several London pronunciations, short *e* for short *a* in *Seboth*, *i* for long *a* in *acquinted*, and *f* for *th* in *Meredife's*. Quite often she substituted *w* for *v*, *adwantage*, *sarwants*, *wise counstabble*, *guwornor*. Occasionally she used *th* instead of *t* and vice versa, *Sathan*, *Arter*, etc. She anticipates a Cockneyism mentioned by Pegge in *knightwood*, and voices or unvoices consonants, *sugsess*, *Hasellrike*, *them-*

selfes, etc. Many other of her spellings reflect variants which were Cockneyisms at this period and later, among them: *sparigous* (asparagus), *fraid* (afraid), *papis* (papist), *conduck*, *markis* (marquis), *Assbe* (Ashby), *shuters* (suitors), *shue* (sue), *ramsom*, *hamsom*, *Catterne wheele*, *handcherchers*, *sence* (since), *Sharpshire* (Shropshire), *sarvant*, *desarved*.

Lady Twysden came from a different part of the country, and the Cockney pronunciations shown in her diary, 1645–51, might be explained by her connection with London. She was the youngest daughter of Sir Nicholas Saunders of Ewell in Surrey, and the wife of Sir Roger Twysden, the London historian. She, too, sometimes substituted *e* for *a* as in *spet* (spat). She also used those characteristic London variants, *e* for *i*, *flech* (flitch), *setting* (sitting), and the unrounding of *o*, *Tamme* (Tom), *lard* (lord), *refarmados*. And although she sometimes omitted *d*, she added it elsewhere, as Londoners did, cf. *Arnoll* and *comands* (Commons). Of the many other "London" pronunciations which she used we need only instance the following: *tirriblest*, *undrising*, *Burkly*, *ower* (hour), *bedfortshire*, *defensife*, *huberd's* (Hubert's), *cromill* (Cromwell), *lodgin*, *harinton*, *colshester*, *sholders* (soldiers), *marchant*, *tould*, *fift* (fifth).

The diary and occasional writings of Mary Rich, Countess of Warwick, written in the years 1663–76, are rich in phonetic spellings. But with one or two unimportant exceptions, all of them may be paralleled in the contemporary records of the London churches. Yet the Countess was born and lived most of her life remote from London. She was of Irish descent, the daughter of Richard Boyle, first Earl of Cork. She was born at Youghal and brought up at Mallow. Coming to London in 1638, she married three years later, when she was sixteen, Charles Rich who later became the third Earl of Warwick. After her marriage she lived at Leighs Priory, near Felstead in Essex, passing the later part of her life as a religious recluse. One would hardly expect one of the greatest ladies of the land to speak Cockney, especially if she did not live in London, but there can be little doubt that the Countess of Warwick used many variant pronunciations which were also used by ordinary Londoners of her time. The substitutions of *e* for *i*, *e* for *a*, *a* for *o*, and *a* for *au* are often represented in her spellings, cf. *sperit*, *Lettultone*; *tennett* (Thanet), *creane* (cranny); *fallow* (follow), *classett*, *safter* (softer), *salomly*, etc., and *sharte*, *starme*; *abrade* (abroad), *undanted*, etc. She often anticipated the later Cockneyism of *au* for *o*, *caufe* (cough), *cauke* (cock), *one aclauke*, *flauk*, etc. Sometimes she adds *d* after *n* or *l*, *uild* (vile), *gond* (gown), *tenderdnes*; and she frequently substitutes voiced for voiceless consonants and vice versa, *bublike*, *banked* (banquet), *mititate* (meditate), *atentife*, etc. To follow her spellings to the end would be to repeat much of what we have said in earlier chapters in describing Cockney pronunciation. These examples of her "London vulgarisms" must suffice: *strinth*, *Ibony*, *stid* (stead); *malencally*, *arante* (errand); *King Chorles*, *fother* (father); *sarmon*, *unsartenty*, *mr. harburte*; *could* (cold); *gine* (join); *Emonies* (anemonies); *Emakelate*, *futer*, *verty* (virtue); *respeke*, *Lanlord*; *sithes* (sighs); *pershewde*; *wesmester*; *Claringtone* (Clarendon).

Many of the correspondents in the six volumes of Verney letters share Mary Rich's disregard for conventional orthography. Beginning with the two volumes of memoirs during the Civil War and ending with the two volumes of eighteenth-century correspondence, the Verney letters which are interesting to the phonetician cover approximately the century 1630 to 1730. In the first four volumes the chief writers who are disposed to spell phonetically are Sir Edmund Verney, the standard-bearer to Charles I, his wife Margaret, and their children, Ralph, Penelope, Margaret, Cary (later Lady Gardiner), Mary, and Elizabeth (who married the Rev. C. Adams). Sir Edmund's family had long been settled at Claydon in Buckinghamshire: his wife was one of the Dentons of Hillesden in the same county. The chief correspondents in the last two volumes are Elizabeth Adams and Lady Gardiner, by this time old ladies, and Nancy Nicholas. The Verney letters may safely be taken to represent the accepted English of the time as it was spoken in Bucks. But here, too, we meet with the same variants which we have found in the writings of other good speakers and also in the London records. They often substituted *e* for *i*, *lebberty*, *cheldren*, *stell*, *sperits*, *pell* (pill), *pettyful*; they used *a* for normal *o*, *faly*, *resalefed*, *sassages*, *6 a clake*, *becas*, and *a* for *au*, *janders* (jaundice), *sentarbones*, *lafull*, *Tanton*; they diphthongised *ol* to *owl*, *sould*, *ould*, *Owlney*, *howlds*; occasionally they must have used *i* for long *a* as in *refrine*; in a few words they replaced long *i* by *oi*, *St. Goyles*, *Aloyes*; and *ou* by short *u*, as in *sund* (sound). They sometimes aspirated initial vowels, although at other times they did not pronounce initial *h*, *Hunicorne's*, *hobblegashons*, *houes* (owes), *onest*, *Ospitalls*, *youmer*. Occasionally they pronounced *v* as *w* or replaced *th* by *f* as in *Wioll*, *Wiolls*, and *lofte* (loth). Some of them interchanged *s* and *sh* or *t d* and *th*: *Burgishes*, *shinged*, *shute* (suit), *wissed*, *sillings*, and *fardest*, *farding*, *Chesther*, *Northern* (Norton). Now and then they added *d* or voiced or unvoiced a consonant, *lemonds*, *clendlynes*, or *errant*, *adfise*, *barswad* (persuade). All the characteristic London pronunciations of the time find occasional representation in the Verney letters, and so do many other less characteristic variants, cf. *leetle*; *requist*, *willcom*; *togather*, *yallow*; *thinkes* (thanks) and *thonked*; *merkwis* and *perlement*; *Varney*, *varmin*, *larn*; *luck* (look) and *sutt* (soot); *sich* (such), *implyment*, *Jinter*; *amell* (enamel); *valy* (value), *futer*, etc. The miscellaneous consonantal variants may be similarly represented: *contreydicks*, *gretis* (greatest); *enought*, *mickelmust*; *teges* (tedious), *sogers* (soldiers); *aneythink*, *edgin*, *willinly*, *chickings*, *fashing*; *twellmonth*; *yearnestly*, *yerne* (earn), and *yeare* (ear). A detailed comparison of the Verney letters with a group of London records of the same period would show that the same variants were used by both groups of speakers. The only difference would be that the London records would indicate a few pronunciations not used by the Verneys, and that several variants meagrely represented in the Verney letters are abundantly represented in the London records.

The collection of Strafford Papers indicate that these variants continued to be used by good speakers even at the beginning of the eighteenth century. The letters of Anne Wentworth, wife of the third Earl of Strafford, relate chiefly to 1711 and 1712, although a few letters written in 1724–36 contain some phonetic spellings. The letters of her mother-in-law, Isabella Wentworth, written in the years 1707–14, are still more fruitful in misspellings. The Wentworths were a Yorkshire family, although Anne Wentworth came from Buckinghamshire. The spellings of these two ladies reflect many of the characteristic Cockneyisms of the time, cf. *tell* (till), *veset*, *speritless*, *setting* (sitting); *lemontations*, *telloe*, *ketcht* (caught), *gether*; *sasers* (saucers)—similar spellings of other writers in the Strafford Papers are, *Ardered*, *Lardship*, *Conart* (Connaught); *could* (cold); *pund* (pound); *chiney*, *sparra-grass*, *partment*, *Quitted* (acquitted); *prodistations*, *Provesy*, *Rubidg*, and *excessif*, *chepan* (Japan), *Cupit*; *sinement* (cinnamon), *sarment* (sermon), *Crayands*, *undkynd*, *gound*, *mold hill*; *farden*, *fardist*; *cornish* (cornice), *Blussing*. Other variant pronunciations, less characteristic of London speech, are abundantly represented, the phonetic spellings including these: *Kingsington*, *yallow*, *Assambly*; *caugh* (cough); *jest* (just); *hard* (heard), *sarched*; *distryed*, *Jyne*; *venter*; *Pheasans*, *Utrech*, *foolishis*, *thoussan*, *poun*; *Twittenham*; *drouth* (drought); *shillin*, *drippin*, *Kitching*; *childern's*, *exsterordenary*—similar spellings by other writers in the Strafford Papers are, *perseed*, *persumptions*, *persume*, etc.; *Harlekin*; *Bayly* (bailiff).

Similar evidence might be quoted from numerous other documents written by good speakers in many parts of the country, the letters of Lady Frances Hyde and Elizabeth Butler, Marchioness of Ormonde, in the Nicholas Correspondence, the letters of Anne Finch, Countess of Nottingham, and her relatives, the Hattons of Northamptonshire, the correspondence of the Jervis family of Staffordshire, the letters of Elizabeth Countess of Huntingdon and her mother, Frances, and so on. These documents, and many others which I have examined among the manuscripts of the British Museum, all contain phonetic spellings similar to those we have quoted. The similarity of the variants in all documents proves that they must have been part of the accepted speech of the time, the pronunciation used by the aristocracy and the upper classes generally. There can be no question of their being the result of local dialect influence upon the speakers who used them, for the same pronunciations were used by good speakers from Yorkshire, Northampton, Buckingham, Staffordshire, Essex, Ireland, and so on.

A comparison of the grammatical variants in these and similar documents with the characteristics of Cockney grammar yields the same result. Many of the variants used by Cockneys were also used by good speakers. I do not propose to follow this part of the subject into details, but the following grammatical solecisms taken from the Verney letters and the Strafford Papers will serve to indicate the resemblance.

The Verneys occasionally use the form of the present tense as a preterite, *see* (saw), *right* (wrote), *speake* (spoke), or the preterite form instead of the normal past participle, *spok* (spoken), *took* (taken), *eat* (eaten); and sometimes they employ unusual *-en* participles, *strucken*, *loaden*, *lyen*. Very frequently they extend the *-s* termination of the third person present to the plural, "both sides promises", "My Lady and Sir tomos remembers their sarvices", or they use "is" and "was" with a plural subject, "all hopes of peace is now taken away", "your delayes is out of your goodness", "we was glad", etc. They sometimes use an adjective instead of an adverb, "the weather has been wonderful stormie", "he is reasonable well". And now and then they confuse the nominative and accusative forms of pronouns, "between you and I", or "Sis Peg and me got an opportunity".

The Wentworths used many similar variants, judging by their letters in the Strafford Papers. The Countess of Strafford used emphatic negatives, "I don't see no likelyhood of her dying", and double superlatives, "the most Agreeables things", etc. She and Peter Wentworth were apt to confuse singulars with plurals, "she and I am", "most people thinks", "the Less witt wemen has the Better", "A great many is gon Away", "both you & Mr. Conolly is mistaken", etc. They also varied from present-day standard in their use of prepositions, "went down of his knees", "set fire of the bords", "accept of my sincere thanks", and they inclined to use the *a-* prefix for the present participle, "He is Jest Agoing to be marred", "she was agoing to walk". The Countess substituted "them" for "those", "them things", "there is them of two hundred pound", and used adjectives for adverbs, "extrem delightfull", etc. Occasionally she omitted the *-s* termination of a plural noun, "ten shilling a pound", "three hundred thousand pound". The variant verbal forms in these papers include the following preterites, *ketcht* (caught), *see* (saw), *hope* (helped), *run* (ran), *sung* (sang), and these past participles, *Draw'd* (drew), *bore*, *tore*, *bespoke*, *brock*, *stole*, *trod*, *drank*, etc.

These quotations confirm what was proved by Pegge in 1803, that the Cockney variations from normal grammar may be justified by the example of good speakers in the seventeenth century. They, like the many variant pronunciations, were formerly used both by Cockneys and by the best speakers.

The existence of so many variant pronunciations and grammatical forms among these two groups of speakers may be explained by the fact that although there was an accepted speech, the London speech which was the basis of it was a mixed dialect. Among Londoners this speech, learned from parents and acquaintances of all ages, was used naturally. For centuries new pronunciations had developed in London and gained popularity, without always driving out the older pronunciations. Many dialect forms may have gained a place in London speech and been used side by side with the indigenous forms or with forms contributed by other dialects. Not only was there a continuous flow of dialect speakers into London, but the capital was situated between several dialect areas, the South and South-West, the Midlands, the South-East, and East Anglia. The linguistic problem of London is not dissimilar to the racial problem of the United States. London was the melting-pot. And the contributions to the pot required varying degrees of heat before they fused, and fresh contributions arrived before the last had melted. But although we may be certain that regional dialects have contributed to London speech it would be rash to attribute this pronunciation or that to particular dialects. Much work must yet be done on English dialects in the early modern period before we shall be able to make such attributions with any certainty.

It is even more rash to attribute, as some scholars do, the variants in the pronunciation of upper-class speakers to the influence of the dialect of the places where they lived. It is clear from the congruity of the speech of Londoners and members of the upper classes that the variants came from London speech. This speech with all its inconsistencies, its doublets, triplets, and quadruplets, was accepted by good speakers. New pronunciations and Londonised provincialisms were adopted by the upper classes throughout the country, so that good speakers in Yorkshire or the Midlands began to use such South-Westernisms (?) as our present pronunciations of "broad", "laughter", "one", or such East Anglianisms (?) as our pronunciations of "wash", "quart", "when", "whip", etc. Some of the new pronunciations became dominant in accepted speech, some had little influence upon it, and others were adopted on an equal footing with the older pronunciations. This, I believe, is the explanation of many of the anomalies in present-day standard, "foot", "good" as compared with "blood", "flood"; or "put", "bull" as compared with "butter", "bun"; "break", "great" as compared with "weak", "heat"; "bear", "wear" as compared with "beard", "smear"; "sweat", "dead" as compared with "breath", "lead", etc. Standard speech is now quite independent of London speech and develops in its own way, but the accepted speech of the early modern period was dependent on the speech of London and had no independent existence.

* * * * *

The absolute form of standard English, which allows only one pronunciation of a word, was certainly customary among good speakers early in the nineteenth century, and it is therefore apparent that the absolute standard was settled and largely adopted during the eighteenth century. The grammarians of the seventeenth century were undoubtedly in favour of such a standard, and with the exception of Jones, 1701, they rarely hint at the existence of more than one pronunciation of any word. This uniformity, as we have seen, existed only in the text-books, where it represented an ideal rather than a fact.

When the absolute standard recommended without obvious success by the earlier orthoepists was ultimately adopted, it was as the speech of the middle classes and its arbiters were middle-class grammarians and lexicographers and their disciples the schoolmasters. In the early part of the modern period the middle class did not occupy that assured rank in the social hierarchy that it does now. The disputes between the velvet breeches and the cloth breeches which exercised the Elizabethans, and the touchiness of the merchants about which Beaumont, Nashe, Chapman, and others were so pleasantly satirical, were early signs of a social upheaval which led to the revolution of the late seventeenth and early eighteenth century.

The effect of this social dispensation is plainly reflected

in language. The good speech of the sixteenth and seventeenth centuries may be defined as the speech of the Court and the aristocracy. Members of this class knew no necessity to adhere to a rigid form of speech in order to establish their worthiness and respectability. What is perhaps the chief function of an absolute standard of speech, a badge of good breeding, was meaningless to them, and it was of no importance to them that certain pronunciations which they used were also used by the vulgar or were inconsistent with other pronunciations.

The rapid change from the variety of good speech in the seventeenth century to the uniformity of standard speech in the eighteenth century must be explained by social rather than linguistic causes. During the second half of the seventeenth century the professional classes, the merchants, and the more influential members of the clergy became acutely aware of themselves as a distinct and, as they believed, eminently worthy class, superior to the poor in breeding and substance and intellect, and superior to the aristocracy in honesty, seriousness, and moral worth. The revolution of 1688 was the decisive victory of the middle classes, resulting in a practical reshaping of the social order and the establishment of a new triple order of aristocracy, middle class, and lower class. Within a few years the whole outlook of culture had changed. Jeremy Collier launched his attack upon the amoral brilliance of the courtly Restoration comedy, and Steele, diverted perhaps from his natural tendencies, instituted the do-me-good sentimental comedy which dampened the theatre with its pious tears during the eighteenth century. The spirit of the little Bethels of nonconformity infected the arts as well as the government and life of the nation. Even men's dress and houses assumed a staidness rare hitherto.

Literature became dominated by a social purpose. The poetry of Dryden, the prose of Addison, Steele, Swift, and Defoe, is concerned primarily with political and social problems. As an aspect of this vogue and change in culture there was devised the literary figure of a censor, whose function was to point out and so, it was hoped, to correct the errors in the conduct and taste of his contemporaries. To this new social consciousness and the desire for guidance and authority we owe such creations as Isaac Bickerstaff, the Spectator, the Rambler, and Goldsmith's Chinese philosopher. The spirit of the age demanded a standard, and the spirit of the age was self-conscious in Addison. The *Spectator* was informed primarily by the desire to formulate and popularise a middle-class culture. To this end Addison devoted a large part of his essays, considering the cultural problems of literature, of religion, of sculpture and architecture, of landscape gardening, of education.

The new ideal of life and art was "Nature", a simplicity attained by submission to rule. In the arts it is typified by the completeness and straight lines of Palladian architecture, a style which was adopted for the suburban homes of the new middle class. So strong was the worship of uniformity and simplicity in this form of art that our greatest exponent of the Baroque style, Vanbrugh, was a figure of fun. In poetry the counterpart of the Palladian architecture was the heroic couplet of Dryden and Pope with its straight lines and regular balance. In prose the simple style, a style which was easy, correct, and conversational without being vulgarly colloquial, was adopted by all writers who pretended to merit.

The literary men who were the chief advocates of this new ideal of culture were concerned with language too. They did not address themselves to the formation of a standard of correctness, but they were very desirous of pruning language of its excesses and of stimulating a greater care for the English tongue. In the *Tatler* (No. 234) Steele urged the reformation of English teaching in the schools and recommended that English grammar should be studied before the classical languages —a paper which was in the nature of a preliminary puff to a grammar now styled "Steele's Grammar"—and some years later Colman added the logical corollary in a plea for the institution of a professorship of English language at the Universities (*Connoisseur*, 1754, No. 42). The *Spectator* in one paper deplores the fashionable slang shortenings of the time, *pozz* (positive), *phiz*, *mob*, *rep* (reputation), etc., while Swift in the *Polite Conversations* and other papers satirised the affectations of slang and fashionable colloquialism, the overworked words and phrases, the hoary witticisms and the sententious proverb-mongering which passed for sprightly conversation among the smart set. In his attitude to the speech of the time Swift adopted the same view as Addison and Steele had of its social conduct. "The court," he said, "which used to be the standard of propriety and correctness of speech, was then, and I think hath ever since continued, the worst school in England for that accomplishment; and so will remain, till better care be taken in the education of our young nobility." And he went on to assert that the drama of the previous fifty years had been "filled with a succession of affected phrases and new conceited words, either borrowed from the current style of the court, or from those who, under the character of men of wit, and pleasure, pretended to give the law".

The ideal of speech was shaped, as were the other cultural ideals, by a series of negations. The negative attitude is strong in the *Spectator*, which is largely condemnatory. But the positive attitude was a recommendation of formalisation associated wherever possible with classicism, and a *via media* between two types of negations. The new standards were deliberately evolved as a contrast to aristocratic affectation on the one hand and vulgarism on the other. No better statement of the effect of this attitude on speech can be found than the following passage from the preface to Johnson's *Dictionary*:

> Most of the writers of English Grammars have given long tables of words pronounced otherwise than they are written, and seem not sufficiently to have considered that of English, as of all living tongues, there is a double pronunciation, one cursory and colloquial, the other regular and solemn. The cursory pronunciation is always vague and uncertain, being made different in different mouths, by negligence, unskilfulness and affectation. The solemn pronunciation, though by no means immutable and permanent, is yet always less remote from the orthography, and less liable to capricious innovation. They have, however, generally formed their tables according to the cursory speech of those with whom they happened to converse; and concluding that the whole nation combines to

> vitiate language in one manner, have often established the jargon of the lowest people, as the model of speech. . . . For pronunciation the best general rule is, to consider those the most elegant speakers who deviate least from the written words.

Here the new attitude, opposed to affectation, colloquialism, and vulgarity, and upholding a solemn pronunciation adhering closely to the spelling, finds full expression. The advocacy of the same solemn style is pursued by Johnson's followers, Walker, Kenrick, Nares, and the rest of the eighteenth-century lexicographers, even though they do not always agree in details.

One of the first effects of this new approach to pronunciation was that the dialects became a subject of interest. This interest corresponded closely to the attitude of the *Spectator* to social life and conduct. The broad country dialects were regarded benevolently while they were only the speech of the lower classes. Such dialects titillated the eighteenth-century love of quaintness and eccentricity, and it is therefore no accident that the earliest collections of dialect words were made in this period. But when the dialects infected the speech of members of the middle class they were regarded with strong dislike. In a previous age even Sir Walter Raleigh might speak broad dialect, but we may judge of the attitude of polite society in the eighteenth century by this comment of Lady Mary Wortley Montagu, "'tis as ridiculous to make use of the expressions used, in speaking to a great man or a lady, as it would be to talk broad Yorkshire or Somersetshire in the drawing room" (Vol. 1, p. 303). Such a dialect might even seriously handicap a man in his profession, as we see from one of the letters which Mr. Bramble wrote to his friend Dr. Lewis in *Humphry Clinker*:

> I think the Scots would do well, for their own sakes, to adopt the English idioms and pronunciations; those of them especially who are resolved to push their fortunes in South Britain. I know, by experience, how easily an Englishman is influenced by the ear, and how apt he is to laugh when he hears his own language spoken with a foreign or provincial accent. I have known a member of the House of Commons speak with great energy and precision, without being able to engage attention, because his observations were made in the Scots dialect, which certainly gives a clownish air, even to sentiments of the greatest dignity and decorum.

He proceeded to recommend the employment of a few native Englishmen to teach the Scots a true pronunciation. This was actually done, if we may believe Mr. Vulliamy when he describes the Select Society of Edinburgh as "a choice association for curing gentlemen of the Scotch accent". Certainly many provincial speakers became ashamed of their accents and endeavoured to assume the London speech. The Irishman aping the English accent became a favourite subject of burlesque —of Lady Clonbroney in Maria Edgeworth's *The Absentee* it is said "you cawn't conceive the peens she teeks to talk of the teebles and the cheers" and she was "in perpetual apprehension lest some treacherous 'a' or 'e' would betray her to be an Irishwoman".

In the advocacy of their new standards, the arbiters of the new state, as we have seen, adopted the tactics of condemning as affected or vulgar those habits and practices which were opposed to the new ideals. There is no reason to think that ostentation, gambling, or debauchery were unknown among merchants and professional men, and the *Spectator's* association of them with the aristocracy or the lower classes was merely an attempt to correct the same failings among the middle class by indicting them as characteristic of less worthy members of society. The same strategy was used in language. With Addison and Swift the attack was mainly upon affectations in vocabulary and idiom. But the orthoepists adopted the same tactics in their attempt to enforce the solemn and absolute form of pronunciation. An amusing instance of this attitude, although it does not apply specifically to pronunciation, is found in Vyse's popular *New London Spelling Book* in a lengthy chapter of Directions for an agreeable Behaviour and Polite Address. The following are among its gems of social observation:

> You are placed above vulgar Children (who run wild about the Streets) by being brought up at School.
>
> Be always pliable and obliging; for obstinacy is a Fault of vulgar children, and arises from their not having your advantages of Birth and Education.
>
> Nothing shews the Difference between a young Gentleman and a vulgar Boy so much as the Behaviour in Eating.
>
> Never sing or whistle in company; these are idle Tricks of vulgar Children.

The schoolmasters who used Vyse's book doubtless extended the social commentary to pronunciation.

As the standard speech was that of London, the linguistic vulgarities chosen for condemnation were those of London, too. A significant change may be observed in the definition of good speech. Whereas the earlier commentators described it as the speech of London, the

Universities, and the Court, the eighteenth-century orthoepists are more critical of London speech. Thus, Solomon Lowe, 1770, says, "I have founded my rules upon what I conceive to be the most common way of pronouncing them among the better sort of people at London. Though even among them we find corruptions which one may venture to declare inexcusable." Kenrick limits his London model to "the general practice of men of letters and polite speakers in the Metropolis", and Nares formed his standard upon the speech of "polite speakers in the city of London". Some critics even divorced the standard speech from London: a writer in the *Gentleman's Magazine* for 1798 maintained that the best speech is to be met with "in the mode of speaking of the most celebrated orators, whether of the senate, the pulpit or the bar; in the converzationi of men of letters; and in the habits of pronouncing used in those exalted and numerous circles, where no motive can exist for perverting the sound even of a single letter; and where talents, education, ease, elegance, and leisure, combine to command assent, and to recommend and ensure imitation". The standard speech had passed away from London and been put into the trusteeship of that amorphous body, the best speakers.

As the eighteenth century progressed the animus against Cockney, the speech of the vulgar Londoners, increased, largely because the orthoepists were using the opprobrious tag "London vulgarism" to extirpate variant pronunciations which continued to be used by some members of the middle class. It is for this reason that we get in this period the first comments upon

Cockney speech which we have discussed in a previous chapter.

The earliest definite manifestations of this attitude occur in the lists of vulgarisms which appear in Cooper's *Grammatica Linguæ Anglicanæ*, 1685, and in *The Writing Scholar's Companion*, 1695, which takes over and slightly adds to Cooper's list. The anonymous author of the latter work seems to have been a Londoner, for he speaks of the pronunciation "at *London*, where to avoid a broad Clownish Speaking, we are apt to run into the contrary Extream of an affected way of speaking perhaps too fine". We have a priori reason, therefore, for regarding his chapter of "Words vulgarly spoken" as London pronunciations, and this assumption receives support from the fact that most of the pronunciations occur in the records of the London churches about the same time. But the same forms were also used by many members of the upper classes. Of the vulgarisms noted in these two works, the following may be paralleled in both the London documents and the writings of people of good education:

> except (accept), ax (ask), bushop (bishop), eend (end), fut (foot), git (get), Hankercher (handkerchief), hundurd (hundred), howsomever, lat (let), mought (might), op (up), wun (one), shure (sure), shugar (sugar), sarvice, thare (their, there), wull (will), wusted (worsted), yerb (herb), yerth (earth), yeusless (useless), Chorles, Frankumsense, hild (held), hwutter (hotter), maracle, quawm (qualm), reddish (raddish), sez (says), scrupelous, stomp (stamp), thrash (thresh), want (wont).

Of the remaining vulgarisms, nother (neither), faw (few), gove (gave), chimly, eent (is it not), gim me (give), squirge (scourge) may be paralleled in Cockney spellings in the church records or in later Cockney; furmety (frumenty) and ommost (almost) are allowed by Jones, 1701. Only a few forms, tunder (tinder), extree (axle-tree), wumme (with me), whuther (whither), yau (you) are not corroborated by other evidence.

The manner of achieving the solemn style of pronunciation is plainly revealed by the similarities we have discussed. We need not doubt that the schoolmasters who used these books improved upon their exemplars and launched a general attack upon the "vulgarisms" in their pupils' speech. Their attitude is admirably expressed by Nares—"among enlightened speakers, every deviation from the purity of language is low and vulgar", where purity of language means adherence to spelling and analogy. I do not suggest that this strategy was the only means of extirpating the variant pronunciations from good speech. It was an aspect of the fostering of spelling pronunciations and pronunciations having the authority of analogy. The writers were not attacking the Cockney dialect itself, but in making their attack upon variant and irregular pronunciations they were naturally inclined to abuse the low speech most nearly related to the standard speech, that is, the vulgarisms of London. The dialects of provincial towns and the counties did not greatly concern the writers of orthoepical text-books, even though the regional dialects may have used some of the same irregular pronunciations.

An interesting example of this attack, because it is so very obvious, is Sharp's condemnations of certain pronunciations allowed in Gignoux's *Child's Best Instructor* on the ground that he had too much followed the common London pronunciation. The attack upon Cockney as a dialect did not develop until the institution of compulsory education late in the nineteenth century. The London vulgarisms attacked in the eighteenth and nineteenth centuries were not characteristic of London speech, but had also been used by good speakers. This is evident from the following characteristic vulgarisms noted by the critics of the eighteenth century:

> ef, sence; yit, yisterday; yallow, shipwrack; ketch, wrop; beyand, yander; brawth, frawth; sarce, sarcer; sutt; shet (shut), sich; larn'd, sarvant; laylock; co-oold, bo-oold; bile (boil), spile; gownd, scolard, sermont; Redrif; Bednall; soon (swoon); wile (while); winegar, vill; perdigious; cutlash, nonplush; o-jus, te-jus; childring, nothink, a-gettin'; proddestant, pardner, prizes (prices); sithe (sigh); east (yeast); arter (after), etc.

In fact practically the whole of the "Cockneyisms" of the eighteenth and nineteenth centuries may be paralleled not only in the spellings of the churchwardens but also in the writings of good speakers not only in the seventeenth century, but as I have shown elsewhere in the first half of the eighteenth century, too. I have found such spellings as these used by members of the upper classes in the eighteenth century:

> lettle 1727, senc (since) 1731; spilling (spelling) 1730, frind 1729, Liftenant 1745; wan (when) 1733, elauen 1727; sleept 1732; ketch 1729, Jen.ry 1733, saftly 1733; Lardship 1724, warters 1726; jest (just) 1748, Sheten (shutting) 1745, presarve 1731, consarn'd 1734; sould 1733, tould 1733; disapinted 1726; sevare 1734, apairs 1734;

and many late examples of the consonantal variants we have previously noted.

It is also an amusing fact that many of the pronunciations described by some orthoepists as London vulgarisms are admitted as correct by other writers, and they not Londoners. Among the variant pronunciations allowed by such writers as Sharp, Walker, Sheridan, Nares, Lowe, etc., are such familiar forms as: yallow, yis, squerrel, meracle, brawth, darter, jarnders, larn, sarge, bile (boil), inion (onion), etc. With many orthoepists the thought that these pronunciations were vulgar was evidently fathered by the wish.

A further amusing result of this attitude is that these "London vulgarisms" were sometimes fastened upon people whose natural dialect was quite different from that of London. This is the case with the vulgarisms in *Humphry Clinker*. The two ladies in that book who spell phonetically, Winifred Jenkins and Tabitha Bramble, are alleged to be Welsh of the Welsh, but except for a very few words their phonetic spellings might have been written by that arch-Cockney, Jeames Yellowplush, as we may see from these characteristic passages:

> He was *tuck* up for a roberry, and had before Justuss *Bushard* who made his mittamus: and the *pore* youth was sent to prison upon the fals *oaf* of a *willian*, that wanted to sware his life away for the *looker* of cain.
>
> A *fellor*, who would think for to go for to offer to take up with a dirty trollop under my nose—I *ketched* him in the very *fect*.
>
> *Providinch* hath bin pleased to meke great *halteration* in the *pasture* of our affairs. We were yesterday three *kiple chined* by the grease of God in the holy *bands* of *mattermoney*.
>
> Sattin has had power to *temp* me in the shape of Van Ditton the squire's *wally* de shamble, but by God's grease he did not *purvail*.

It would be easy to over-emphasise the importance of London vulgarism in the formation of the absolute standard of English. One cannot be certain how much of the vulgarism is effect and how much cause in the movement. But we may be certain that it was one of the main factors. The pedagogic abhorrence of vulgarity is still so prevalent that one may readily conceive the eighteenth-century teacher admonishing his pupil, "No, Smith, y-e-l-l-o-w sounds [jelo]—only the vulgar say *yaller*." Even Gray, the Cambridge don, adopted this attitude. In a letter to Horace Walpole he castigated his correspondent's pronunciation of *London*—"if you will be vulgar and pronounce it *Lunnon* . . . I can't help it". With Kemble the actor a vulgar pronunciation was damning. Mrs. Pritchard, he said, "in common life, was a vulgar idiot: she would talk of her gownd". And that the schoolmasters of the time drove out old pronunciations in this way is highly probable from the very fact that their authorities, the lexicographers, adopted the same technique.

But as I conceive the attitude of the authorities, they first examined which pronunciations were irregular because they broke the rule of conformity to spelling or the laws of analogy, and then perceiving that these same variants were used by the vulgar, they decided to label them London vulgarisms. In this way the appeal to the middle-class desire for uniformity was reinforced by playing upon their abhorrence of vulgarity. Law and snobbery went hand in hand, and it is difficult to say which of them bore the greater share in their victories.

Certainly this strategy was highly successful. Practically all the variants which existed in both accepted speech and Cockney in the seventeenth and early eighteenth centuries were driven out of good speech, leaving only those standard forms which we now use, while at the same time they remained in Cockney and eventually became dialect features simply because they were no longer used by good speakers. But in some few cases the orthoepists attacked irregular pronunciations that were too firmly established to be driven out, and it is in these failures that the nature of their strategy is most evident. For example, the orthoepists noted two pronunciations of the vowel in "glass", "grass", "fast", etc., one a lengthened form of the short *a* vowel, the other the present-day back vowel. They chose to condemn the latter, and it is accordingly described as a London vulgarism by Walker and burlesqued by the nineteenth-century novelists through such Cockney spellings as *varst*, *glarss*, *grahss*, etc. Nevertheless, the back vowel, although it is used by Cockneys, has persisted in the standard speech of London and the Southern counties. Again, the etymological pronunciation of *wh* in "when", "what", "where", etc., advocated by Dr. Johnson and his followers led to the description of *wen*, *wot*, *were*, etc., as typical London vulgarisms and they are used to the present day as Cockney spellings. Yet with the exception of the model products of girls' schools, the best Southern speakers continue to agree with the Cockneys. Lastly, according to Elphinston and others, the non-pronunciation of *r* in "lord", "far", "harm", etc., was a vulgarism characteristic of London, and although such Cockney spellings as *Lawd* are still used, standard speech as well as Cockney continues to omit the consonant. If the strategy is less obvious in other cases it is only because it is obscured by its success.

This, then, is the justification for the claim we made for Cockney, that it has been by far the most important of all non-standard forms of English for its influence upon accepted speech ever since accepted speech emerged. In the early modern period the vulgar speech of London served as the model for accepted speech, and later when standard was formulated, vulgar London speech served as a criterion of error by which correct speech could be measured. Accepted speech has bitten the hand that fed it.

BIBLIOGRAPHY

This list of the principal books, etc., quoted or consulted does not include novels, plays and songs discussed in the text.

DUCANGE ANGLICUS: *The Vulgar Tongue*, 1857.
J. ASHTON: *Modern Street Ballads*, 1888.
HEINRICH BAUMANN: *Londonismen*. Berlin, 1887.
JON BEE: *Slang*, 1823.
C. COOPER: *Grammatica Linguæ Anglicanæ*, 1685. Edited by Jones, 1911.
M. W. DISHER: *Music Hall Memories*, 1935.
A. J. ELLIS: *On Early English Pronunciation*, Part V, 1889.
Errors of Pronunciation and Improper Expressions, Used frequently and chiefly by the inhabitants of London, 1817.
W. FRANZ: *Die Dialektsprache bei Ch. Dickens*. Englische Studien XII, 1889.
JOHN GIGNOUX: *The Child's Best Instructor in Spelling and Reading*, 1757.
Letters of the Lady Brilliana Harley, 1625–45. Camden Society, 1854.
J. HART: *Methode to Read English*, 1570.
GEORG HÖFER: *Die Londoner Vulgärsprache*. Marburg, 1896.
J. C. HOTTEN: *A Dictionary of Modern Slang, Cant, and Vulgar Words*, 1859, 1860, 1864, 1872, 1874.
OTTO JESPERSON: *Modern English Grammar*, I, 1914.
DANIEL JONES: *An Outline of English Phonetics*, 1932.
JOHN JONES: *Practical Phonography*, 1701. Edited by E. Ekwall, 1907.
WILLIAM KENRICK: *A New Dictionary of the English Language*, 1773.
W. P. KER: *English Literature, Mediæval*. Williams & Norgate, London, n.d.
SOLOMON LOWE: *The Critical Spelling Book*, 1770.
MACKENZIE MACBRIDE: *London's Dialect*, 1910.
W. MCEAGER: "The Cockney Tongue". *Contemporary Review*, 1922.
HENRY MACHYN: *The Diary of Henry Machyn*, edited by J. G. Nichols. Camden Society, 1848.
J. MANCHON: *Le Slang*, 1923.

WILLIAM MATTHEWS:
"London Slang at the Beginning of the XVIII Century". *Notes and Queries*, June 15, 22, 29, 1935. [Ward.]
"The Vulgar Speech of London in the XV–XVII Centuries". *Notes and Queries*, January 2–April 3, 1937.
"Some Eighteenth Century Phonetic Spellings". *Review of English Studies*, January, April 1936.
"Some Eighteenth Century Vulgarisms", *Review of English Studies*, July 1937.
"Polite Speech in the Eighteenth Century", *English*, November 1937.
HENRY MAYHEW: *London Labour and the London Poor*, 1861.
E. J. MILLIKEN: *'Arry Ballads from Punch*, 1892.
W. H. MORTON and H. C. NEWTON: *Sixty Years' Stage Service*, 1905.
E. MÜLLER: *Englische Lautlehre nach James Elphinston*, 1914.
R. NARES: *General Rules for the Pronunciation of the English Language*, 1792.
H. C. NEWTON: *Idols of the Halls*, 1928.
E. H. PARTRIDGE:
Slang To-day and Yesterday, 1935.
A Dictionary of Slang and Unconventional English, 1937.
SAMUEL PEGGE: *Anecdotes of the English Language*, 1803, 1814.
G. PUTTENHAM: *The Arte of English Poesie*, 1589.
Report of the Conference on the Teaching of English in London Elementary Schools, 1909.
MARY RICH, COUNTESS OF WARWICK:
Diary, 1666–1676: British Museum Additional MSS. 27351–5.
Occasional Meditations: B.M. Add. MS. 27356.
Some Specialities in the Life of M. Warwicke: B.M. Add. MS. 27357.
ST. ALPHAGE, LONDON WALL:
Accounts, 1527–1629: Guildhall MS. 1432/I, II and III.
Minutes, 1593–1711: Guildhall MS. 1431/I and II.
ST. BARTHOLOMEW EXCHANGE:
Accounts, 1596–1698. Edited by Edwin Freshfield, 1895.
Minutes, 1567–1676. Edited by Edwin Freshfield, 1890.
ST. CHRISTOPHER-LE-STOCKS:
Accounts, 1575–1622. Edited by Edwin Freshfield, 1885.
Minutes, 1562–1660. Edited by Edwin Freshfield, 1886.
ST. KATHERINE COLEMAN:
Accounts, 1610–1671: Guildhall MS. 1124/I.
Minutes, 1659–1727: Guildhall MS. 1123/I.
ST. MARGARET, LOTHBURY:
Minutes, 1571–1677. Edited by Edwin Freshfield, 1887.

St. Mary-at-Hill:
Accounts, 1422–1559: Guildhall MS. 1239/I. Edited by H. Littlehales: *The Mediæval Records of a London City Church*, 1905.
Minutes, 1609–1752: Guildhall MS. 1240/I.
St. Mary Woolchurch-Haw:
Accounts, 1560–1672: Guildhall MS. 1013/I.
Minutes, 1647–1727: Guildhall MS. 1012/I.
Joseph Saxe: Bernard Shaw's Phonetics, 1936.
F. E. Schelling: *Elizabethan Drama 1558–1642*, 1908.
Granville Sharp: *A Short Treatise on the English Tongue*, 1767.
Thomas Sheridan: *Elements of English*, 1786.
B. Smart: *Walker Remodelled*, 1836.
G. Stoffel: *Studies in English*, "'Arryese", 1894.
Strafford Papers:
Letters from Anne, Countess of Strafford, to her husband, 1711–36: B.M. Add. MS. 22226.
Letters from Isabella, Lady Wentworth, 1707–29: B.M. Add. MS. 22225.
C. D. Stuart and A. J. Park: *The Variety Stage*, 1895.
A. W. Tuer:
The Kaukneigh Awlminek, edited by "'Enery 'Arris", 1883.
Old London Street Cries, 1885.
Lady Twysden: Diaries, 1645–51: B.M. Add. MSS. 34169–72.
Memoirs of the Verney Family during the Civil War. Edited by Lady Frances Verney, 1892.
Verney Letters of the Eighteenth Century. Edited by Lady Margaret Verney, 1930.
Vulgarities of English Speech Corrected, 1826.
Charles Vyse: *The New London Spelling Book*, 1791.
John Walker: *A Critical Pronouncing Dictionary*, 1791.
J. Wallis: *Grammatica Linguæ Anglicanæ*, 1653.
I. C. Ward: *Phonetics of English*, 1929.
J. Redding Ware: *Passing English of the Victorian Era*, 1909.
Ernest Weekley: *Adjectives and Other Words*, 1930. Chapter IX, "Mrs. Gamp and the King's English".
Axel Wijk: *The Orthography and Pronunciation of Henry Machyn, the London Diarist*. Uppsala, 1937.
The Writing Scholar's Companion, 1695. Edited by E. Ekwall, 1911.
H. C. Wyld: *A History of Modern Colloquial English*, 1925.
John Yeomans: *The Abecedarian*, 1759.
R. E. Zachrisson: *Northern or London English as the Standard Pronunciation*. Anglia, 1914.

INDEX